THE MIND'S EYE

THE MIND'S EYE

A Guide to Poetry Writing

Kevin Clark

New York Boston San Francisco
London Toronto Sydney Tokyo Singapore Madrid
Mexico City Munich Paris Cape Town Hong Kong Montreal

Acquisitions Editor: Matthew Wright
Development Editor: Kristen Mellitt
Executive Marketing Manager: Joyce Nilsen
Production Manager: Denise Phillip
Project Coordination, Text Design, and Electronic Page Makeup:
     Electronic Publishing Services Inc., NYC
Senior Cover Design Manager: Nancy Danahy
Cover Designer: Nancy Sacks
Cover Photo: ©Images.com/Corbis
Manufacturing Buyer: Lucy Hebard
Printer and Binder: R. R. Donnelley & Sons / Harrisonburg
Cover Printer: Phoenix Color Corporation

For permission to use copyrighted material, grateful acknowledgment is made to
the copyright holders on pp. 239–244, which are hereby made part of this
copyright page.

Library of Congress Cataloging-in-Publication Data

Clark, Kevin.
  The mind's eye : a guide to writing poetry / Kevin Clark.
     p. cm.
  Includes bibliographical references and index.
  ISBN-13: 978-0-205-49823-9 (paperbound)
  ISBN-10:   0-205-49823-X (paperbound)
  1. Poetry—Authorship. 2. Poetry—History and criticism. I. Title.
PN1059.A9C53 2008
  808.1—dc22

2007024785

Please visit us at www.ablongman.com

ISBN 13: 978-0-205-49823-9
ISBN 10:   0-205-49823-X

12345678910–DOH–10 09 08 07

To all my students

CONTENTS

PREFACE

Like most beginning teaching assistants, when I stood before the students in my first college-level poetry workshop many years ago I was passionately committed to bringing the deep pleasures of poetry to these new writers. I was a poetry advocate. I was a believer in the power of the lyric. But I was also fantastically naïve about teaching the art. I knew the sustaining pleasure of a good poem, and I knew that reading good poems would make the student poets want to write their own poems. Yet the transportive swoon I carried around inside did not equate to a course outline. I'd never taken a course in the pedagogy of poetry writing. Such a course didn't exist. I was game, but I didn't have a clear plan for helping students turn their raw intentions into real art.

So like most teachers, I borrowed heavily from my own teachers. No matter what the subject, my best instructors led me and my peers out of an ordinary environment into imaginary, transformational rooms where we were fascinated by the myriad aspects of existence we'd only begun to contemplate. Because I had wanted to "be a writer" since I was a boy, I was most attentive to those teachers who were enthusiastic about my poems and stories. In college it became clear I could work interesting phrases into the concise shapes of poems more effectively than I could mold plot-laden prose into stories. By the time I arrived in graduate school, I was, of course, obsessing every day about my own poetry—but I was also intrigued by the way different professors proffered the art.

From the beginning I made use of many proverbs and tips from all my writing instructors. Eventually I channeled these ideas through nearly three decades of my own experience as a poetry writing teacher, developing the "course" represented in the fifteen chapters of *The Mind's Eye*. I'd always wanted to find a reasonably concise textbook that would quickly lead to good writing. And so I've written this one with the following goals in mind:

- to recognize the foundational importance of imagery as well as sound in contemporary poetry
- to coordinate the sequence of chapters with a typical fifteen-week college semester

- to provide a wide variety of model poems by a dramatically diverse group of contemporary poets
- to offer many writing exercises that proceed progressively toward greater complexity
- to promote usability by arranging the book in a compact, handy size
- and, finally, to offer the book at a lower cost than many other textbook options, thus allowing professors to assign additional volumes of poetry without fear of charging too much.

In doing all of this, I've tried to balance a clear plan for learning how to write poems on one hand with plenty of latitude to try out many different options on the other.

At the pedagogical heart of this book is the notion that no matter what kind of poetry anyone wishes to write (whether it's free verse, narrative, formal, spoken word, etc.), a poet must paint a picture in the mind's eye of the reader. After all, the great difference between poetry and philosophy is that poetry uses imagery to imply its meanings while philosophy uses abstract words to state its meanings. Readers of poetry want to be emotionally moved while they're discovering something new about the world—and an evocative, unusual image is the key to making them feel deeply as they think deeply. In fact, readers who are emotionally engaged will be carried further into understanding the human condition than those who are not. Needless to say, a good poem will employ effective sound in order to guide the reader's feelings, and that's why as early as Chapter Three I focus on manipulating sound to correspond with the poem's images and to create a powerful overall effect in the reader.

The Mind's Eye features a progressively difficult gradation of writing exercises. Each chapter corresponds to a week of class and each ends with exercises of similar complexity. As new poets concentrate on the progression of key devices and approaches to writing poetry, they will proceed through a variety of discussions and prompts designed to give them fluency in the major aspects of contemporary poetry writing: imagery, implication, conflict, the lyric (and lyricism), structure, portraiture, narrative, sequencing, surrealism, and other facets of the discipline, including revision. In The Mind's Eye, beginners are not locked into a single, programmatic way of writing a poem, but rather they are encouraged to proceed with flexibility so that they are always learning how to stretch their imaginations further and employ more techniques.

Though students will move steadily ahead in their writing, I realize from nearly three decades of my own experience as a creative writing professor that they appreciate reviewing key ideas, and in such a way that they are not bored or insulted but rather increasingly challenged and inspired. Each chapter builds carefully upon what's come before and each contains The Poet's Note Card, which concisely summarizes its key points. As the book progresses, beginning writers will read brief discussions about technique and contemplate a diverse array of sharply written published poems by contemporary poets. Some people might ask why I include contemporary poets primarily? Why not Shakespeare? Why not the Romantic Poets? The Victorian Poets? As much as I love the Bard, and Keats, and Arnold, I think it's best that starting poets write in the idiom of their own times to avoid using language that sounds stilted today.

In the course of my pedagogical approach, some steps, of course, are more critical than others. By Chapter Four, for instance, most new poets will make big breakthroughs with regard to imagery and conflict. From that point on, they will begin to feel much greater confidence and look forward to the more complicated exercises. I wait until Chapter Eight to discuss traditional form because it's best to have imagery, conflict, transformation, transitions, and time shifting under control before working on structures that may otherwise result in rhyme-led phrasing or other awkward syntactical and sonic convolutions. By the last third of the book students will be exploiting their imaginations with increasing autonomy while simultaneously encountering ways to keep inflated rhetoric in check (though the textbook recognizes that occasionally they may find that inflated rhetoric actually fits a narrator's personality).

In its sequence of chapters, *The Mind's Eye* is designed to adapt immediately to a single-semester course in poetry writing. Depending on the course description and the number of weeks in a term, however, this book can be organized to suit a variety of other syllabi. Instructors at schools that are on a quarter system should have no trouble combining, rearranging, or paring back key chapters. (I'm on a quarter system myself.) Furthermore, I've found that an advanced undergraduate course in poetry writing will benefit by starting with Chapter Four. While I ask that advanced classes read The Poet's Note Cards in the first three chapters, I still require approximately one poem each week from students—but I often make the specific writing exercises after Chapter Four optional. Some teachers may wish to extend focus on chapters that adapt well to their personal aesthetics or a particular class demographic while skipping other chapters (and may find that The Poet's Note Cards can direct students to other areas of inquiry later). Finally, some teachers may choose to assign subsections in a particular chapter rather than the entire chapter itself. Again, *The Mind's Eye* is designed to adapt to all of these needs and more.

One last note: I remain a poetry advocate. As I wrote this book, I continually asked myself, How can I help students experience the literary excitement of writing a good poem of their own? After all, the book may be assigned by teachers, but it's written first and foremost for students. All good poets know that writing poetry is an art, not a job. The delight in finding fresh language that surprises as it renders the specific circumstance of the human condition may be had by anyone willing to open the imagination. It's my hope that the suggestions, model poems, techniques, and exercises offered here will not only help to make students better poets but will encourage them to write and read poetry long after they've stopped using this text.

Acknowledgments

I'd like to thank my first acquisitions editor, Erika Berg, who saw the pedagogical advantage in my approach to teaching poetry writing. Thanks to my current acquisitions editor, Matt Wright, for his continuing encouragement and vision. Thanks also to my developmental editor, Kristen Mellitt, who read the book repeatedly and made numerous important suggestions while offering many subtle encouragements. I'm also indebted to all of the reviewers who gave so much of their time to examining early drafts. They were both positive and constructive, and they should know that I applied their invaluable suggestions throughout the book.

Additional thanks to Dean Linda Halisky of the Cal Poly College of Liberal Arts, who granted me a course relief at a critical juncture in my writing. Many thanks to my father-in-law, William "Bill" Hewes, Jr., who was a naval officer in the Pacific Theatre during World War II and who made key suggestions in the section on war and witness. Thanks as well to poet and essayist Brad Comann for his expert advice on traditional form. Likewise, thanks to my colleague, the novelist, poet, and fellow Longman author Todd James Pierce, who consistently gave me support and helpful tips while I was writing the book and who reviewed the section on religious poetry. I'm grateful to all of the poets who gave me permission to use their poems here, and especially to Wendy Barker, Ralph Black, Lisa Coffman, Jim Cushing, Denise Duhamel, Sandra Gilbert, Sarah Grieve, Barbara Hamby, C. G. Hanzlicek, Ginger Adcock Hendrix, Luann Keener, Jacqueline Marcus, Martha Serpas, and Hannah Stein for telling me about their writing methods.

I am indebted beyond thanks to my own teachers. These include Thom Gunn, Sandra McPherson, William Martel, Robert Scanlon, Karl Shapiro, Richard Shust, Ruth Stone, and Alan Williamson. I am particularly grateful to my two primary mentors, Brandy Kershner at the University of Florida, who gave me the kind of encouragement that inspires a lifetime of putting pen to paper, and Sandra Gilbert of the University of California at Davis, whose direction, motivation, and pedagogy helped to make me a poet, critic, and teacher. Both are lasting friends. I'm also grateful to my fellow instructors over the years, especially those here in San Luis Obispo, who have spoken ardently with me about teaching literature and creative writing. No one taught me more than my colleague, the fiction writer Al Landwehr, who is the most dedicated creative writing teacher I've ever met and who read and helped me revise a good deal of this manuscript.

Ultimately any teacher who enjoys the job is grateful for the students who take the classes. I've learned nearly as much from my students as I have from my own teachers and my own reading and writing. While I'm of course happy that many of my students have gone on to excellent graduate writing programs and then on to exemplary careers in creative writing and teaching themselves, I've learned from all of my students about what works and what doesn't in a poetry writing workshop.

Finally, I'm profoundly grateful for the relentless encouragement of my wife and editor, Amy Hewes, who has supported all my many writing projects. She is the poem who sustains me.

Kevin Clark
Cal Poly
San Luis Obispo

Introduction

THE MIND'S EYE

Imagery

Poetry is the art of surprising yourself with your own words. You may start scribbling words self-consciously, but soon enough—when you're *on*—the poem seems to lead you. When you're in that fluid, creative state the act of writing a poem transports you out of yourself into the imaginary world of the poem itself. You sense where the words are taking you before you get there. The experience can be as good as dancing at a club to a hot live band or hitting a jump shot from outside the arc. You're in the zone; time is meaningless. The trick is to make sure your reader is also transported by your words. Poems aren't secrets. They're intense, compacted moments of communication with a reader. And the best poems move people by animating the imagination. Readers want to be carried into a different reality. They want to feel, to react emotionally. Boredom is their enemy—and yours.

The first rule for giving readers deeply felt literary pleasure is to give them fresh **imagery**, that is, mental pictures. We're all moved by vivid images, rarely by abstract words. Readers like to picture whatever you're writing about. They don't want dull philosophizing. The moment readers engage a new word picture, they enter a life they haven't lived. And they enjoy surprise. If your images are genuinely new, then your reader's imagination takes off with you. That's why I call this book *The Mind's Eye*.

1

The poet paints pictures with concrete words, and another person sees those pictures in the mind and lives the life they depict. Which is to say, your imagination writes, and your reader's imagination reads. As this book proceeds, you'll be trying your hand at many different types of poems, from two-line poems to enumerated sequences to sestinas to surrealistic free verse, but you'll always be coming up with original, even startling images to spice up your reader's imagination.

Poetry is the inverse of philosophy. While philosophy uses abstract words to communicate ideas, poetry uses concrete words to suggest meaning. Poetry relies on **implication**. When nineteenth-century poet Emily Dickinson rendered deep personal anxiety, she didn't resort to abstractions and say, "I was feeling truly apprehensive." She knew she had to make her reader feel that anxiety. So she wrote, "My Life had stood—a Loaded Gun." That's the kind of line that catches your attention. And it manages to imply an idea at the same time. A good image will render both feeling *and* idea.

The best way to begin writing poetry is to let the word-image percolate up into your consciousness and then get it on the page. Some beginning writers think that poems come first from great ideas. In fact, most great poems are anchored in the stuff of the five senses. Pleasant or unpleasant, the real world is depicted through those senses: the whistle of a tea kettle, the scent of new asphalt, the brine of barbecued oysters, the ease of satin sheets, the sight of a loaded rifle. You begin by rendering these kinds of images, and you let *them* build tension in the poem. As you will see, meaning most often derives from imagery if there's a clear conflict. Dickinson's quick image burns into the screen of the mind because it's unusual. A person's life isn't often compared to a loaded gun.

Good poets meld sharp imagery with evocative sound and rhythm. The poet Brenda Hillman has said that beginning writers should exploit and enhance what is idiosyncratically best about their own writing. Famous poets are celebrated for their **idiosyncrasy** of image and sound. That means they find inventive ways of expressing themselves.

But good poets don't strain to be unique by creating unnecessarily odd-sounding or strange-looking poems. In each poem they discover the form that works best for that particular poem. For instance, they may settle on uniform stanzas, or they may choose a more open, **irregular lineation** (pattern of line length or arrangement). In order to ensure a pleasing aural tension in the line itself, most beginning poets try to keep their lines to twelve syllables or less. The shorter the line, the less prosaic the sound.

Sound and Idiom

No matter how original your word pictures might be, readers won't want to read your poetry if you sound like some kind of stuffy old codger spouting old-fashioned words from another century or a hip-hop artist without the benefit of music. People who read poetry want to read language that sounds reasonably close to the language they speak, which is to say, their own **idiom**. End-rhyme may lead to rhyme-led diction rather than good imagery. That's why beginning poets may want to avoid end-rhyming for a while. And obsolete diction makes the poet seem out of touch. *Thee* and *thou* were fine words for Shakespeare's time because folks in his day actually used them. Anyone who uses such language today is considered weird. If you use words like *doth* and *forsooth*, you'll probably be considered hopelessly archaic.

Artists must be of their own time. Even Beethoven's Fifth Symphony would probably sound pretty stiff if it were introduced to fans of new classical music who had never heard it before. Why? Because its style is already a dated part of the culture. Likewise, we all have to remember that poetry doesn't come with a separate rhythm section, or a horn section, or a backup chorus. While poetry is sometimes performed aloud, it is most often read in silence. So it's generally best if you find a language style that expresses your own personality while also finding common ground with today's diverse poetry audience.

If you create fresh imagery in a good-sounding contemporary idiom, you stand a great chance at providing your readers with literary **impact**, that is, a strong visceral and mental response to your poem. To a degree, all poems teach a lesson of some kind, but all good poems are made memorable not by the lesson but by the intensity of our response to the language. When we feel deeply at the same moment that we intuit the poem's meaning, the poem takes hold of us in a special way. It enters the reservoir of the subconscious life and its words continue to ripple, to affect us indefinitely.

Because we want our poems to register that distinct rippling effect, we need to remember that impact relies on conflict, which is the existence of opposing forces inside a human being. If the life of Emily Dickinson's narrator is as dangerous as a loaded gun, we know there's something wrong with that life. We understand that the narrator is "conflicted." Poetry thrives on tension, and tension arises from the problems of the human heart. As we'll see in Chapter Twelve, Norman Dubie's poem "Radio Sky" depicts a married couple troubled by their infertility. Unable to sleep, they turn on the television "to where a station had just signed off." The "snow" they see on the screen appears to be "the original light of Creation. Genesis popping like corn in a black room." Dubie renders the conflict the man and wife experience by creating that wondrously idiosyncratic image. Some poets may be tempted to prettify the situation, to sentimentalize the couple. But good honest feeling is usually gritty, not sweet and soft. We write poetry to communicate with adults, not children. As Frost suggested, we write to discover what we didn't know we knew. Good poetry is for adults. That's why serious poetry written in the voice of a child is frequently unsuccessful. It's not frank; it's been sanitized.

Inspiration

Writers who come up with true, effective images are said to have **inspiration,** the confident feeling you have at the very moment you're creating. In truth, good writers have unusual access to the unconscious mind in which the images are originally formed. Very few poets truly believe in the muse, an invisible being alleged to hover above them, at least on good days, shooting arrows of creativity into their souls. Oddly enough, inspiration results from a combination of discipline and relaxation. You maintain a schedule. If possible, you write at roughly the same time each day. Maybe you read a few poems by a poet you like. You don't strain in front of the blank page or monitor. Neither do you think "logically." After all, poetry is a form of play. Rather, you relax and let your mind drift inward. The room around you disappears. You might do some free writing. You draw out a few word pictures, and these call up others. A cliché slips in, but you'll get rid of it later. The poem's direction becomes a little clearer. The shape of the sound, the rhythm . . . it begins to come together. You know the direction you must follow. And at this point you are officially, completely inspired. There's no knowing for weeks or even months if the poem is going to succeed, but you are riding your own intuitive enthusiasm. With luck, perhaps some reader will find your poem out there in the future and become inspired by *your* words.

Remember: Inspiration needs focus. So as you enter into the following chapters and begin choosing from the exercises, make sure you give yourself time and space to write. Most practicing poets thrive on quiet; some write in a room with the door closed, preferably without anyone else in the house. But other poets prefer the bustle of a coffee shop or the society of a park bench. Try to find a way to schedule your writing time. Try to avoid the breathless situation in which you're always trying to find time to "fit writing in." You'd be amazed at how much you can produce if you schedule

THE POET'S NOTE CARD

Rules to Know Now and a Few to Break Later

1. Always try to create interesting images.

2. Use contemporary language.

3. Be sure there's a conflict in every poem.

4. Use concrete language. It is better than abstract language. Concrete language renders images in the mind's eye, while abstract language renders ideas.

5. Remember that readers of literature are most often moved by images and stories that render meaning, rather than abstract words that simply contain ideas.

6. Remember that sentiment is honest, sentimentality is false.

7. Because good poetry is for adults, try to write in the voice of an adult.

8. Avoid clichés; like white noise, they distract.

9. Since you're concentrating on imagery first, consider avoiding end rhyme until you've had greater practice at wedding images to sound.

10. At the outset, it might be helpful to keep your lines to a maximum of twelve syllables so as to avoid sounding prosaic.

11. Give yourself enough time and a good place to write.

even four separate hours per week for your art. The subconscious mind, the place where your best images lie, functions best when you leave the world and give yourself over to the creative act.

There are numerous ways to begin working on poetry. Some teachers tell you to begin with traditional forms such as sonnets and villanelles. Others stress the importance of polishing the sound of a single line, perhaps focusing on metrical verse with its predetermined rhythm. Many new "spoken word" poets prefer to begin with story poems that are primarily written to be performed rather than read on the page. But from Chaucer to Shakespeare to Sylvia Plath, there's been a single potent commonality—and that is the reliance on strong images rather than on abstractions. Poems in traditional forms and spoken word poems both exploit the senses. And that's where we'll start in this book: with sensory imagery. Ultimately, any poetic style you eventually come to prefer will benefit from your expertise in creating vivid pictures with intense language. Very soon you'll come to surprise yourself with your own words.

1

WORDS THAT PAINT, COLORS THAT SPEAK

Painting Pictures with Words

Imagine you're in an art gallery. Picture a large, framed, white canvas on a wall. On it, printed in block letters, is one sentence: WAR IS HORRIBLE. Nothing else appears on the canvas. What do you feel?

Now, move to the next room of the gallery where another large, framed canvas is on a wall. This one is Picasso's famous picture of the Spanish Civil War, *Guernica*, a frenzied montage of overlapping images. A horse arches up from the carnage, screaming. Below, a woman appears fragmented, her tongue sticking out as she, too, screams, the distorted form of a dead child in her arms. At bottom center, from a scramble of layered forms twisted together, juts out the head of a dying soldier, his mouth open in a scream, a jagged broken sword in his hand. What do you feel?

How does the abstract sentence, WAR IS HORRIBLE, move you? How does *Guernica* move you? Is there a difference? Of course there is.

Let's try it again. You're in the next room of the gallery. A large, framed, white canvas is on a wall. On it, printed in block letters, is the following sentence only: MEMORY ALTERS OUR SENSE OF TIME. What do you feel?

7

Now move once more to yet another room. Here is a small, framed, colorful painting by Salvador Dali entitled *The Persistence of Memory (Soft Watches)*. On the left side of the painting is the corner of a table, and a pocketwatch is melting off the edge. Hanging from the leafless branch of a desolate tree stump that's growing out of the table is another watch, draped like laundry. In the foreground of the table, a closed amber-colored pocket watch is covered with ants. In the middle of the painting, where the colors turn dark, yet another watch is draped across a white form that vaguely resembles a human organ, perhaps a closed eye. Or maybe it's some kind of sea mammal. In the distance, in the painting's upper right corner, beneath a blue sky, an arid, fogbound peninsula juts into the sea. What do you feel?

Same question: How does the abstract sentence, MEMORY ALTERS OUR SENSE OF TIME, move you? How does Dali's famous surrealistic painting move you? Is there a difference? Surely.

An abstraction is an idea, not an image. When we read abstract sentences (WAR IS HORRIBLE), even in block letters, the effect is typically sterile, more like philosophy than art. Even if the statement is urgent, its very abstraction makes it less interesting than a picture or a story that will deliver the same notion and much more. Most of us like to read poems because they are textured by imagery to give us a sensation. They offer feelings, not just ideas. It's as if they convert the ideas into tactile impressions. That's why for nearly a century writing teachers have uttered their famous phrase: "Show; don't tell." As a poet, your primary job is not to write ideas. It's to create vivid images that will make readers respond deeply.

The Power of a Single Image

At the turn of the twentieth century, most published poems were burdened by too many abstractions set in sweet, ethereal-sounding language. Most poetry had grown so soft that readers could not respond to it. After all, when a poem moves from concrete imagery to a lot of abstract language, it's as if a runner has shifted from smooth asphalt to deep sand. Everything slows down, becomes labored. That's why early twentieth-century poets such as Ezra Pound and Hilda Doolittle and Amy Lowell promoted themselves as Imagists. They were tired of flaccid language that triggered only a narrow range of human response. They knew then what you might keep in mind now: Meaning in poetry is typically best communicated via sharp imagery and a complementing sound.

The most famous work of the Imagists is a two-line poem by Pound:

❀In a Station of the Metro

The apparition of these faces in the crowd;
Petals on a wet, black bough.

Despite its brevity, "In a Station of the Metro" was a breakthrough in its time. Rather than employ flowery, abstract words, the poem focused on a single image that rendered an idea without stating it. While the sound of the poem seems secondary, the rhythm rises in the first line and falls in the second. Though as a beginning poet you may concentrate on imagery, you always want to be aware of the aural quality and cadence in your work.

Now compare Pound's poem to this sentence: "When human beings gather in a crowd, they often forfeit their individuality." This statement may be the poem's main idea, but the sentence is comparatively dull, while the poem is intriguing. Pound doesn't even bother with a verb. He maneuvers us in such a way that we'll make the connection between all "the faces" of the metro (an underground Paris subway station) and the "petals." We can quickly intuit that the crowd of faces is like the many leaves of a flowering tree. And the long dark greasy station is like the wet branch, or "bough."

Here's what you should try to remember: One specific image can often render a multitude of ideas, not just one general concept. Most of us prefer concrete picturing to abstract reflection. That's why literature relies on concrete language to imply meaning about human experience. Philosophy typically uses abstract language to state meaning explicitly. In the hands of a good imagemaker such as contemporary poet Beth Ann Fennelly, even two lines can convey a complex human experience:

❀Gong

From the kitchen, fixing her bottle, I hear it:
two milk teeth against my beer can.

At first reading, this poem may seem a little mysterious. Is there *any* meaning here? What does the title have to do with the poem itself? In fact, when we realize that a "gong" is one of those big metal discs that produce a "gong" sound, we remember that the sound itself is often used in radio and

TV to indicate a sudden realization. It's the equivalent of a lightbulb turning on. Imagery can be aural as well as visual. In fact, you can create poetic imagery that appeals to any of the five senses.

So what does the narrator realize? Obviously, she's the mother of a baby girl. The poem places the narrator in the kitchen, where we see her doing the archetypal motherly job of "fixing her bottle." But, just as with Pound's poem, the last line is the most important. The words "milk teeth" indicate that the baby's new teeth are coming in, so we can assume the little girl is teething. Trouble is, she's teething on the mother's "beer can." Perhaps the mother is beginning to grasp the fact that her life has changed dramatically, that she can't leave beer cans around. After all, the baby could cut herself on the sharp edges. Or maybe she's realizing that in her new role as mother she shouldn't be drinking beer in the middle of the day. I'm sure you can think of other sudden realizations she may be having. Fennelly evokes much with her single unusual detail—a baby teething on a beer can.

Part of your fun as a poet is doing what Fennelly does: finding a fresh image that intrigues a reader while rendering some kind of conflict.

Rendering Human Drama

So, imagery is our primary tool for exploring the problems of life. Readers crave human drama of all kinds. Poet Luann Keener paints word pictures so deftly that we want to keep reading even when we are nervous about what's going to happen next. Note the way the images in this one-sentence poem draw us further and further into danger and exertion, mortality and heroism:

❦ The Blood-Tie

> My grandfather lifted my grandmother up
> from where she clung to stones in the dank shaft
> of the well, he clinging to the rope, his small
> body fear-hardened, lifted with a furious grip
> up from the ice-black water her who held in one arm
> their son and only child yet, first-born with
> honey curls, toddler in a white dress, baby boy
> who had fallen there where the packed stones' moss

was barely green in filtered light, where
water-singing had drawn him, while above their heads
the sky was a blue, bitten wafer; lifted her up
arms welding the shrieking child to her breast,
his life theirs, and heaviest, yet light
as the caught stars in her Cherokee hair,
its stout trunk wound in his fist:
Lifted up by the thousand roots,
sinew, vessel, bone and gene, the million
filaments, the blood-tie.

Here's a poem about the great strength and courage people will find when their children are in danger. Before the poem starts, we can see that the woman, the narrator's grandmother, had gone down into the well with a rope tied about her and had grasped the little boy. The poem begins with the father exerting extraordinary, nearly superhuman force while pulling both his wife and son to safety. Because of the details, we can picture all that's gone wrong and could go wrong again: The frightening "dank shaft" is dark and wet. The water at the bottom is not only cold and hard to see; it's "ice-black." The toddler's "white dress" emphasizes his youth and vulnerability.

Because we associate mortal fear with dark depths, Keener's rendition of the small patch of sky above the mother and child in the well's uppermost opening increases our anxiety: "above their heads / the sky was a blue, bitten wafer." The word *blue* characterizes the sky and a safe life. Like so many concrete details, colors (in this case, blue) often speak more effectively than generalizations. But the safety implied by the color blue is immediately negated. The word *bitten* is a brilliant descriptive choice because it does two things simultaneously: Due to the irregular brick top of the well, it accurately characterizes the irregular shape of the well hole. The word also implies a kind of violence, as if the mouth of the well had "bitten" the child right off the earth. The parents are in effect battling the agents of death.

The last eight lines of "The Blood-Tie" depict not only the successful rescue but also the deepest implications of the poem. Since the child may be the narrator's father, we know how important the rescue is to the narrator. After all, if her father weren't pulled out of the well, the narrator wouldn't be alive. Can you sense how the power of "blood" relations is rendered by key words?

The Verb as Catalyst

As you could see, Keener uses the verbs *welding* and *wound* to infuse her poem with a kind of muscular power. In fact, verbs are probably the most important part of speech in poetry. A nonpoet might think adjectives would be of primary importance because they are descriptive. And, while a prudent use of adjectives can be helpful, adjectives can also slow things down. They're often static. On the other hand, you can use verbs to catalyze internal or exterior events, to add vital energy to the language. The strong visual verb compels the poem forward. That's why it's best to avoid verbs such as *move* when *hustle* or *shoot* or *limp* or *arch* work better. These words add imagistic zing to the poem, while verbs such as *move* or *exist* offer very little sensory vigor.

Yusef Komunyakaa is famous for his frank poems about war veterans. Here he employs strong visual verbs to render the interior life:

❈ To Have Danced with Death

The black sergeant first class
who stalled us on the ramp
didn't kiss the ground either.

When two hearses sheened up to the plane
& government silver-gray coffins
rolled out on silent chrome coasters,

did he feel better? The empty left leg
of his trousers shivered as another hearse
with shiny hubcaps inched from behind a building . . .

his three rows of ribbons rainbowed
over the forest of faces through
plate glass. Afternoon sunlight

made surgical knives out of chrome
& brass. He half smiled when
the double doors opened for him

like a wordless mouth taking back promises.
The room of blue eyes averted his.
He stood there, searching

his pockets for something:
maybe a woman's name & number
worn thin as a Chinese fortune.

I wanted him to walk ahead,
to disappear through glass,
to be consumed by music

that might move him like Sandman Sims,
but he merely rocked on his good leg
like a bleak & soundless bell.

Consider some of the verbs in the poem: *stalled, sheened, shivered, rain-bowed, half smiled, consumed,* and *rocked.* All of these invest the poem with a kind of traumatic psychological energy that renders the narrator and the wounded sergeant's ambivalence about the military rituals they were afforded upon returning from the Vietnam War. The primary action of Komunyakaa's poem is psychological, and these verbs demonstrate how dynamic the inner realm really is. They contribute directly to the visceral reaction we have when reading the poem. If *stalled* were "stopped," if *sheened* were "drove," and if rainbowed were "waved," the poem wouldn't induce such a strong gut-level reaction.

Exploring with Images

Perhaps Beth Ann Fennelly originally intended to write a standard-length poem about her baby teething on a beer can. After she began drafting the poem, maybe she realized that her sudden recognition about the way her life needed to change was the most important aspect of the experience. That may have been the point at which she decided that only two key lines were necessary. When Luann Keener began "The Blood-Tie," she didn't know that she would make all of those connections between the rescue and the power of ancestry. After all, poets often use only a small percentage of the images they conjure up when writing any given poem. Keener wanted to write a poem about the rescue. But as she "painted" her pictures, more and more images came to her—many of which were surely edited out of the poem too. No one told her about the moss on the well-side. She made it up. Robert Frost said that often we have to lie to get at the truth. He knew that the facts of an event or even a life may not be sufficiently dramatic, that a poem may change the actual facts in order to render human truth more effectively. Keener knew what she was going to write about, but she didn't know what she was going to say.

For decades writing teachers have told their students to "write what you know." To a degree those teachers are right. They believe that emerging writers are more likely to be concrete and evocative when drawing on their own experiences. But it would be a mistake to think that you need to write exclusively about what you know. Poets have the freedom to write about literally anything. The poet John Ciardi once asked his students to write a poem about the inside of a ping-pong ball. He wanted to stimulate their imaginations. Some poetry teachers like asking students to write about the story behind a photograph they've never seen before. Others like to give their students a one-sentence news report, about a car accident, say, or an unusual event in a small town. The idea is to create your own version of the story behind the event, much as writers of historical novels do. What details can you add to the photo or the news story that bring it alive? What's the central conflict? What images can you come up with to render that conflict? Some new writers feel that the poem must be based entirely on the actual events, even the specific conflicts of the people involved. But as poets, we all should remember that poems need only adhere to human truth, not mere facts. That's why Frost's idea about "lying to get at the truth" is key. Readers understand that poetry is not journalism. Poets are interested in the hard-to-pin-down world where sensation and thought meet, where atmosphere influences behavior, where both decision and indecision are the result of myriad forces. Poets abandon themselves to the events of the poem, including the interior action of the people involved. Poets open their imaginations, and worlds both small and large are created.

A friend once told the poet Hannah Stein a true story about a man who was out walking along the edge of a woods when he came upon a wounded, dying fox. The brief events of the story fascinated Stein. She quickly went home and began to write a poem about the man and the fox, adding many of her own details:

⊕ Winter in Fox-Light

Under the flat sky a fox drags herself
to the edge of a brushwood.
New snow etches the shape
of each brown leaf, each

naked spray of twigs. He sees she is
shot in the spine: flailing, half-

paralyzed, white rings around the stones
of her eyes. A red cloak lays itself down for her
on the snow. Each flake stands out an instant
before it touches the dye.

Beneath the skin of her belly
a delicate jostling, as she
loses life. Quickly he slivers his knife point in

below the ribs, peels the thin wall back
like a grapefruit rind. He slits the muscled sack,

releases two cubs head-to-tail,
their blunt, tender clay. With his scarf
he dries the lacquered fur, zips them warm and squeaking
inside his jacket. They squirm against his chest
the three miles to the house, through a sky
that is reassembling itself on the land, everything
enveloped in the rush to bury

stubble, bury remnants; to bury all the broken
seedlings, their shapes rounding into identical drifts;
all the nests of summer hurled to the ground.

Certainly we can see why a poet might be interested in this story. Animals typically connect us to our own human concerns. In this poem the mysteries of death and birth are entwined. That a man can cut open a dying fox and facilitate the birth of two cubs is extraordinary in itself. We might be reminded of women who have died in childbirth. Or the great advance made by the nearly quotidian option of caesarean birth. Stein didn't know what she would come to see in the story, but she was certainly moved by what she'd been told. In effect, writing the poem gave her an opportunity to investigate not only the event itself but also her own reactions to it. By the end of the poem we can see that, among other things, she's fatally resigned to the way nature buries its dead so readily—and we can feel her empathy for the fox as well as for the rest of us.

But in her journey to the end of the poem, she had many, many decisions to make. Who was the man? How much should we know about him? What time of day was it? What season? How far does he walk? Where are the hunters? Of course she had to answer the first question all poets must: How to start? She knew she could always change her opening words, that she could revise the opening if she didn't like it.

Stein started with the sky. At first, she didn't know that she would return to the sky near the end of the poem, but the image of a "flat sky" calls up low, perhaps darkening, winter clouds portending snow. It's an image that creates some anxiety. Soon human creatures must get home, must protect themselves from the elements. In fact, as the third line tells us, "new snow" has fallen. In a brilliant, subtle use of a visual verb, she tells us that "the new snow etches the shape / of each brown leaf." We know that snow can't etch, but we also know what she means: It looks as if the imprint of a leaf has been made in the snow, when actually the fine dusting of snow has taken on the specific veins of the fallen leaf itself. As readers, we know that such attention to detail guarantees that we can trust this poet's eye. Other details are equally effective: the eyes of the fox are clouding over like "stones"; her blood is first a "red cloak [laying] itself down for her" and then it's "the dye"; the knife point "slivers"; the pulled-back hide is "like a grapefruit rind"; the cubs are covered in a "lacquered fur"; and so on. All the colors coalesce to make the highly unusual scene dramatically realistic and to create start-to-finish anxiety.

By the fifth line of the poem, Stein suddenly introduces the man who finds the fox. In the existential context of this poem, she intuits that we need not know anything about his reasons for being out at the edge of the wood. Nor why he likes to walk in the cold winter. We don't need to know anything about his personal life either. He's a figure of rescue, that's all. He catalyzes the action, and everything he does is described in extraordinarily vivid detail. For instance, consider these five words: "He slits the muscled sack." We can see the knife enter and slice the swollen abdomen that contains the cubs. The word *slit* is both visual and aural. We can see it and, perhaps awe-fully, we can hear it. The term *muscled sack* illustrates not only the abdomen but the gristled wall he must cut through.

Remember: Stein only knew the outline of a story. A man out for a walk finds a dying fox and uses his knife to save her unborn cubs. One of Stein's gifts as a poet is her ability to texture scenes so believably. She didn't know that it had snowed. She didn't even know it was winter. She didn't know that the fox had been shot in the spine. She didn't know if the man had a scarf, or that his house was three miles away. As Stein explored the event, her imagination supplied all of these details.

Certainly, she didn't know that it would soon snow again, as it does at the poem's closing: "a sky / that is reassembling itself on the land." In other words, as the snow comes down and covers the many shapes of the earth, the land begins to resemble the shapeless, low, white sky. Everything below is as dully erased as everything above. The last line emphasizes the mortal facts all creatures are bound by: "all the nests of summer [are] hurled to the ground." Nests surely remind us of summer and the births of birds and squirrels. The elements knock the nests from their perches, and these, too, are covered by the effacing snow.

In its extraordinary rendering of a compelling scene and its frankness about its subject, "Winter in Fox-Light" proves that we can use our imaginations to write about virtually anything. Stein succeeds so well as a poet because she sees the amazing details of events she's not actually experienced, and she proceeds to convert them to provocative imagery. She goes where her imagination takes her. Like Stein, you, too, might give your imagination the freedom to create the persuasive details that make a poem startling and memorable.

The Quicksand of Abstraction

"Winter in Fox-Light" demonstrates that strong poems don't require abstract language. If you search each stanza of the poem for abstract expressions, you'll probably spend your time admiring the concrete details. Stein doesn't have to make the following kind of philosophical statement: "A human being might see him- or herself in a dying animal." Or this one: "A parent may be compelled to save a dying fox's cubs in a manner that projects saving one's own children from untimely death." Both are **discursive statements**—i.e., proselike generalizations—that are implied in the poem, but the language of the poem is far more alive than the language we might use to characterize the poem's meanings. Truth is, when she started writing, Stein likely didn't know she'd be implying any of these ideas. Robert Frost suggested that a good poem reminds us how we don't remember what we've always known. While Stein may have intuited all of the above concepts, most were undoubtedly ideas that she didn't know she already knew. There's something about a good poem that can't be captured in any statement. The experience is beyond summary, beyond message.

Some new writers are nevertheless predisposed to think that good poetry is, by definition, abstract. They often wish to start with profound ideas. In fact, these writers think that broad generalizations arranged in lines constitute good poetry. Usually such writing only constitutes flat, lineated prose. Here's the kind of poem that a new poet may be tempted to write:

Growing Up

From a bed
of impossibility
an appearance of innocence
is unveiled.
A motion
Of pink discovery
Begins, questing
For final liberty and
An understanding
Of the perfect, independent self.

Now compare that poem about growing up to this one by Rodney Jones about the same subject:

Going

From the bootlegger's shanty at Five Points
to the swing sets in the Falkville schoolyard,
the road went underwater, which made
our twice-a-day bus rides through the bottoms

dead ringers for those geography tests
when I'd wonder if I'd studied enough,
guessing the brain's good dog might send up
Utah when I'd sent down for Nevada.

This was also the biblical road,
flood-fleshed with bedwettings and cold-sweat.
It clarified distinctions between tests:
fake true-or-false was wilting mimeographs;

real true-or-false was marked on the rail
where a neighbor girl, returning from a dance,

had flunked the bridge and fueled a sermon.
Geography turned to philosophy if we stalled,

and while the engine turned, some prayed,
some leapt up jeering, and would be chastised
mildly and then forgiven. Most tolerant of men,
Fred Jenkins, the shell-shocked veteran, drove.

While both poems are about growing up, the difference between them is like the difference between seeing a framed abstract sentence on a wall and seeing a graphic painting. The first poem is so abstract as to be nearly meaningless. On the other hand, Jones' poem is deeply textured, filled with the kinds of details that give it an enticing realism. While the first poem contains only one concrete noun (*bed*) and one concrete adjective (*pink*), it contains five big abstract nouns (*impossibility, innocence, discovery, liberty, understanding*) and two big abstract adjectives (*perfect, independent*). On the other hand, Jones' poem has only a few abstractions (*distinctions, tolerant*). Virtually the entire poem is composed of concrete details, from place names ("Five Points," Falkville") to comic terms ("the brain's good dog") to strong verb constructions ("send up Utah," "flunked the bridge," "fueled a sermon," "leapt up jeering"). The first poem wants to say something big about growing up, but its imprecise generalizations and the lack of specific images make the poem blurry and indistinct; we can't feel anything. But Jones' poem takes us on a childhood bus ride, and we feel the road dipping and the bus going deep into the flood waters. We sense being inside the bus with all of the noisy kids, and we understand that for him—and, by extension, all of us—growing up involves coming to terms with the threat of death.

I think you'll agree that "Going" is a better poem than "Growing Up." While the writer of "Growing Up" mistakenly believes that a poem should be baldly philosophical in its language, Rodney Jones understands that a poem should appeal to the mind's eye.

A Note on Revision

Poets such as Stein and Jones practice a good deal of revision. Some poets will take a poem through ten, twenty, even thirty drafts before feeling it's adequately polished. (Stein's poem took twenty drafts.) Very few good poets, if any, are satisfied with a first draft, even though they may have been transported into an ecstatic state in which the imagination seems to take off on its own. The fiction writer Al Landwehr once said that when he is writing well it's as if he's reading the greatest novel he's ever read. He can't believe how well the words flow, how the characters act so true-to-life, how the dialog spins out so crisply. When he's finally finished writing for the day, he gets up from his desk energized and gratified. But when he returns to work on the story the next day, inevitably his writing no longer seems as exciting as reading that great novel. Instead, there are problems he hasn't recognized, sentences that are clumsy, characters who aren't fleshed out, and diction that needs changing.

Landwehr's observation recalls the French poet Paul Valéry's words about revision: "A work of art is never finished, merely abandoned." Like many writers, Valéry was an inveterate reviser; he had to train himself to stop tinkering with his poems and to accept the fact that no work of art is perfect. Like Valéry, beginning poets should try to find a balance between revising and letting go. It's best to enjoy the very act of writing while also recognizing that the mesmerizing state in which you write well is not perfect. Good poets need to accept the fact that the first draft is usually not representative of their best work. They come to find that there is pleasure in revision.

That said, beginners will get to know what to save and what to change by reading plenty of good poetry and helping other emerging poets to craft their poems.

Getting Started

True story: A middle-aged woman had started to write poems; she had an extraordinary facility for rendering piercing, sometimes emotionally violent imagery. When her teacher told her that her work showed remarkable promise, she looked at him with confusion. "Listen," she said, "I have no idea what I'm doing. I don't know the way to start a poem. I don't know how to use lines. I don't know what to say next or how to finish. I'm just writing, and this stuff comes out. You need to tell me exactly what am I supposed to do." While she didn't realize that she was innately talented, her confusion about how to start and what to do thereafter is typical for many beginning poets.

Each writer often has a special writing ritual—and there are many. While there is no one way to begin writing, there are a few things you might want to try. For instance, as Virginia Woolf said, it's usually best, to write in a silent place removed from distractions. Close the door; tell your friends and family not to bother you; like some writers, hang a sign outside your door explaining that you're working and asking not to be disturbed. Some poets, such as John Ashbery, like to have music playing in the background, but most of us prefer as much quiet as possible. As for tools, it doesn't matter if you prefer writing on a pad or in a journal or right onto the computer. No matter what its form, the blank page is always inviting. Its very blankness suggests promise and exploration.

But how do you decide what words to write first? Some new poets don't know how to begin. They wonder, "Do I write out an idea first? Do I start with a nonsense image? Do I write in prose and then convert to poetry?" Questions abound. And other beginners see the blank page as arctic tundra—just too challenging to cross, a fearful opportunity for failure. The key is to have fun when you're writing. That's why poet Marvin Bell's advice is important. At the famous Bread Loaf Writers Conference, started by Robert Frost and held annually in Bread Loaf, Vermont, he told his seminar that they should lighten up and relax when they write. "Remember," he said, "it's only a poem." One member of the seminar gasped when he said this; that's how seriously some emerging poets take the creative act. Bell wanted his students to remember that poetry writing isn't a matter of life or death (even though we may often write about mortality). And besides, he reminded us, we could always change anything we put on the page. He was right; revision is a safety net.

No matter the subject, poetry writing requires some sense of play. One of the reasons successful writers spend so much time writing is that they have so much fun while they're doing it. In fact, when commenting on his approach to making poems, the great British poet W. H. Auden once said simply, "I like to play with words." So here's something to think about: It doesn't matter how you start the poem. But if you want a few suggestions, try these:

You might settle into your quiet location and, before you start writing, imagine something that caught your eye recently. Say a bird smashed into the big window of your favorite coffee shop this morning, knocked itself silly for a few seconds, and then flew away in an erratic circle. Start describing the bird. See if the description leads you to picture other forms of erratic behavior, perhaps in your own life or those of a friend or a relative. You can begin your words in prose or lineated verse. If you start with prose, then, after a little while, come back around to arranging the opening few phrases or sentences into lines. Look: You're underway. Your poem has begun. Can you feel the tug of the imagery? Just keep following it.

Or you might start with freewriting, that is, just quickly writing out whatever comes into your head. Let yourself go. Don't worry about spelling or form. Write in lines if you like. Short or long. Make lists. Or, if you prefer, write in sentences. Try to write in images. Don't worry about punctuation. Just keep writing fluidly. Try not to edit yourself. Because the brain tends to associate in a semiorderly fashion it's highly likely that the words you write will soon take on a few recurring subjects or themes. Freewrite for about three minutes. You should have a page of materials. Now take a break. Stand up and walk around your room. Then go back to your page. What pictures or events seem compelling? What draws your attention most immediately? Try to isolate one or two of these items and rewrite them in lines on a clean page. Perhaps you can describe them more completely. Add new details. Find something unusual in the way they are depicted in your mind—and try to describe that as well. Before long you will have forgotten that you have started your new poem.

Freewriting is "free" because there is no penalty for writing wildly crazy stuff, even nonsense. You have a free pass. After a good deal of practice, many poets find that they have trained themselves to enter that semihypnotic zone in which they simply start writing a new poem as if they're freewriting. After all, if their writing is a matter of play, then they are freewriting. The best poems come when we let go of our conscious, overeditorializing habits and mine the reservoir of images we have down deep inside. We can be most honest. Risk is easier when we realize that we're playing with those images, that we can always change them. When we nurture the idiosyncratic in our imagery, we often depict events most evocatively.

As you write your way into the body of the poem, you may start to toy around with the lengths of the lines. As mentioned in the Introduction, it's best not to go beyond more than twelve syllables at first. That way you can avoid sounding prosaic. You might want to play with short lines and long. You might also want to try different kinds of uniform stanzas. At first, you might try **tercets** (three-line stanzas) or **quatrains** (four-line stanzas). If these prove unsatisfactory, try organizing the same lines in **couplets** (two-lines stanzas) or **cinquains** (five-line stanzas). See if you can sense which form best organizes the sounds and details of the poem. Sometimes you'll want to get up and stretch, take a break, drink some water or coffee, maybe even wine. When you return to the poem again, you might simply review

THE POET'S NOTE CARD

Getting to the Roots of the Imagination

1. Poets render; they don't tell.
2. Good poets paint pictures using words.
3. The word *image* is at the root of the word *imagination*.
4. Poets find themselves inspired when they create images that capture their own imaginations.
5. The more unusual the picture the more interested the reader.
6. Meaning in contemporary poetry is typically best communicated first via imagery and then via sound.
7. It is important to invest your poem with conflict, with tension.
8. When starting a new poem, it's often best to explore an image or a story line; try not to decide exactly what you want your poem to mean before you write it.
9. Most abstractions are poetic quicksand; they aren't registered in the gut.
10. Literature typically uses concrete language and is implicit; philosophy typically uses abstract language and is explicit.
11. Reading poetry should be, first, a visceral experience and, subsequently, an ideational experience.
12. It's a good idea to put your poem away for a day or two, then come back and revise it. As French poet Paul Valéry suggests, a work of art is never finished, merely abandoned.
13. Writing well is an elevated form of play.

what you've already written and continue. See if the poem's invested with a conflict of some kind, if there's tension of some sort. Now keep writing until you finish for the day. Some poets like to complete a first draft the first time they write a poem. Others like to polish line after line before going on. See what works best for you. The important thing is, you've started. Your poem is taking shape. Enjoy it all.

WRITING EXERCISES

1. *Prose description.* In paragraph form write a highly concrete description of an object or an event. Concentrate on seeing something not usually noticed or sensed in the object or event. Don't be afraid of the odd or weird image. Underline all the abstractions. Remove all but one abstract word. Convert the prose to **lineated verse** (poetry written in lines). Here are a few suggestions for subjects: a squirrel's tail, a ring, a baseball glove or bat, a single shoe, an amethyst, a rocking chair, a hubcap, a sneeze, a car accident, a kiss, taking a bath, sliding into second base, driving on ice, dancing, drinking red wine, killing a fly.

2. *Spectacle poem.* Write a poem about an astonishing spectacle, a scene so unusual and vivid that you'll never forget it. Load the poem with fresh, pictorial details. Take care not to use abstract words or phrases. In other words, don't tell the reader about the meaning of the event. Render the event, and allow the reader to deduce your meaning. Don't let the poem exceed twenty lines.

3. *Revision poem.* Write a poem about any subject. Do your best not to exceed twenty-five lines. When finished, put the poem away for at least a day. Now underline all abstract words and phrases. Try to transform all of the abstract moments in the poem to vivid, descriptive moments that give the reader a unique experience. Rewrite the poem without any abstractions.

4. *Two-line poem.* Using "In a Station of the Metro" or "Gong" as models, try to write three or four two-line poems that startle the reader by virtue of their unusual compact imagery.

5. *Fingers poem.* Describe your own fingers in a poem. Try to find images that make the fingers completely real and yet truly strange. What kind of strange? Your choice.

6. *TV poem.* Many people think that television is the enemy of poetry. Maybe not. Turn on the TV, but make sure the sound is off. Now switch the channel. What image do you see? Now turn off the TV. Use your imagination to make that image into a poem.

7. *Eyes-closed poem.* Imagine an exciting event you've attended recently. Now imagine the scene if you had kept your eyes closed for five minutes while no one else noticed you. What would you experience? Write a poem in which sound predominates. Focus on two or three odd sounds you've never quite heard before.

2

THE LIVELY IMAGE VS. THE DEADLY CLICHÉ

Observations That Surprise

While we know poetry writing should involve play, we also know that sometimes it takes courage to write honestly. Good poets observe the world carefully and then choose concrete details to evoke deep feeling. When we sense a poem viscerally, we're more likely to remember it. In the following poem, Norman Dubie uses very simple language, but the few events of the poem are described with such detail that we hold them in our minds long after we finish reading:

Poem

> A mule kicked out in the trees. An early
> Snow was falling,
> The girl walked across the field
> With a hairless doll—she dragged

It by the green corduroy of its sleeve
And with her hands
Buried it beside the firepond.

The doll was large enough to make a mound
Which she patted down a dozen times.
Then she walked back alone.
The weak winter sun
Sat on the horizon like a lacquered mustard seed.

She never noticed me
Beside the road drinking tea from a thermos.
The noisy engine cooling.
Did you ever want to give someone

All your money? We drove past midnight, ate,
And drove some more—unable to sleep in Missouri.

A traveler has pulled off the road to rest. Across the field from him, he witnesses a girl bury a "hairless doll." We know that cancer patients often lose their hair, and while we can't be sure that the girl has lost a relative, even a parent, to cancer, we can sense that the narrator suspects this likelihood. Ultimately, the narrator is so haunted by the scene, he and his companion can't sleep. They drive all night through the state of Missouri. Dubie does not comment directly about his subject; his language is both specific and economic. Here, the narrator maintains an objective, even careful distance in his description—but this distance betrays his inner disturbance.

While the poem is plainly told, two moments are unusual: We rarely think of a "firepond," the little man-made ponds that are used to secure water in case a structure on a farm catches fire. The word suggests danger, and enhances the tension building in the narrator as he witnesses the girl's actions. And, in the poem's only comparison, the sun is described as "a lacquered mustard seed." For the most part, Dubie uses ordinary words and phrases to make the scene realistic: "a mule kicking in the trees," "green corduroy," "snow," "a mound of dirt," "tea in a thermos," "an engine cooling." The point is, he keeps our attention by capturing the key details of an unusual scene.

Metaphors and Similes

When Dubie compares "the weak winter sun" to "a lacquered mustard seed," we can picture the sun quite clearly. Just as the mustard seed shines palely, the sun shines with a dull sheen. Memorable poems typically employ images to make surprising connections. When a poem finds a sudden likeness, we're taken aback, delighted. Because the likeness often enhances tension, the poem grows in urgency. As we said in Chapter One, however, most poets rarely know how or what they're going to say before they actually start writing. They don't start making connections until they are in the midst of creating the poem itself. It's when they're using the best language they can to describe something of interest that they are often struck by a likeness—and that likeness often leads to an unexpected realization.

In poetry, direct comparisons are called **metaphors,** while comparisons using *like* or *as* are called **similes. (Personification** is another kind of comparison in which a nonhuman entity is ascribed human qualities.) While both rely on dynamic imagery to make the reader's attention intensify, generally a metaphor has a more immediate impact than a simile. A simile, on the other hand, can often add a more reflective tone to the poem. In either case, the object is to find an unusual likeness, one that will make the reader see in a new way. We all have looked up at the night sky, for instance, and thought that the stars "twinkle," but the word *twinkle* comes to us so readily because it's used by everyone around us so often. Such everyday redundancy is boring in poetry. There is probably a better way to describe the view. Perhaps a fresh metaphor would help. In his poem "The Embankment," T. E. Hulme came up with just that: He once described the dark firmament as "the old star-eaten blanket of the sky." Whoever had thought that stars could eat? Hulme makes us view the common sky in an uncommon way. If Hulme had employed a simile, his perspective would have shifted a bit: "the night sky is like a blanket eaten by stars." While this construction is still an effective comparison that makes us see the world in a new way, it takes longer to develop. When making our comparisons we decide which is best for the poem we're writing—the more instantaneous metaphor or the more ruminating simile.

The key is to open our minds to all kinds of comparisons available to our imagination. Charles Wright catches our attention in his poem "Ars Poetica III" with a metaphor to describe how the winter sky seems " [c]old like a shot of Novocain." In the first line of her poem "Smoke" Susan Brown employs a simile to tell us a lot about her mother: "My mother held her cigarette like a scepter." Michael Ondaatje opens his poem "Sweet Like a Crow" with a simile that might make us cringe: "Your voice sounds like a scorpion being pushed / through a glass tube." Poems often call for wild, even outrageous comparisons. Once you get used to seeing the things of the world in terms of other things, you learn to relax and simply find such comparisons in your imagination.

The poet Luis Rodriguez knows how to let his imagination fire up wild likenesses. In a poem called "The Blast Furnace," about working in a mill, he begins by comparing the noise of a hydraulic tool to a musical composition: "A foundry's stench, the rolling mill's clamor, / the jackhammer's concerto leaving traces / Between worn ears."

Rodriguez once worked in a mill, and he draws details from that memory. A "jackhammer's concerto" is the metaphor he uses to describe the relentless noise. Rodriguez knows that working in a mill with a roaring blast furnace deeply influences your daily life in many different ways that may scar. Whether his fellow workers are wielding ear-drilling jackhammers or not, the mill is rarely ever quiet; it's almost always filled with a racket of many different loud sounds. Rodriguez knows that a concerto is a complex piece of classical music with many different sounds produced back and forth by one or two soloists alternating with an entire orchestra. If he had written that "the jackhammers make a deafening noise," he would have bored the reader. If he had said "the jackhammers set your teeth on edge," he would have indulged in a tedious cliché. If he had written that "the jackhammers' sound makes ugly music," he would have created a comparison—but it would have been vague. By comparing a jackhammer directly to a concerto, he drives his point home. Those jackhammers in the mill make their own wild concert—but we all know that it's not aesthetically pleasing as is a planned, well-rehearsed musical composition.

In fact, the concerto of the blast furnace can be ruinous. Here's the entire poem:

The Blast Furnace

A foundry's stench, the rolling mill's clamor,
the jackhammer's concerto leaving traces
between worn ears. Oh sing me a bucket shop blues
under an accordian's spell
with blood notes cutting through the black air
for the working life, for the rotating shifts
for the day's diminishment and rebirth.
The lead seeps into your skin like rainwater
along stucco walls; it bends into the fabric of cells,
the chemistry of bone, like a poisoned paintbrush
coloring skies of smoke, devouring like a worm
that never dies, a fire that's never quenched.
The blast furnace bellows out a merciless melody

Listing   29

as molten metal runs red down your back,
as assembly lines continue rumbling
into your brain, into forever,
while rolls of pipes crash onto brick floors.
The blast furnace spews a lava of insipid dreams,
a deathly swirl of screams; of late night wars
with a woman, a child's book of fear,
a hunger of touch, a hunger of poetry,
a daughter's hunger for laughter.
It is the sweat of running, of making love,
a penitence pouring into ladles of slag.
It is falling through the eyes of a whore,
a red-core bowel of rot,
a red-eyed train of refugees,
a red-scarred hand of unforgiveness,
a red-smeared face of spit.
It is blasting a bullet through your brain,
the last dying echo of one who enters
the volcano's mouth to melt.

Rodriguez wanted to describe the way life in the mill may violently wound a worker's spirit, and he's especially aware of the need for evocative sound here as well. The entire poem is intentionally cacophonous, containing more than a dozen sonically charged comparisons, none of them pretty. Where in "Poem" Norman Dubie carefully chooses key images and makes only one comparison, Rodriguez wants a more violent expression to elicit the aggressive, chaotic environment of the mill. He doesn't settle for a single well-formed metaphor. Rather, he takes a risk by piling one comparison upon another in a tumble of lines that produces the kinds of images and sounds that render a worker's aural and emotional life. You might want to go back through the poem and notice how the sounds of the mill quickly connect to the sounds of a traumatized personal life.

Listing

Many beginning poets find that list poems help them sharpen their eye for finding unlikely likeness. A **list poem** does what the title suggests: In one line after another it offers a new direct description, metaphor, or simile. Because the list poem is not proceeding conventionally through a typical plot or into the interior life of a protagonist, the challenge is to make each of the lines intriguing units of poetry. (Of course, in any poem, your goal should be to make each line of your poem captivating, independent components that function seamlessly with the rest of the poem.) As we saw above, "The Blast Furnace" ends like a list poem. While "a red-scarred hand of unforgiveness" includes an abstraction, most of these images are striking metaphors that render the soul-destroying life inside the mill.

Sometimes a list poem can tell us about human life by describing the body. Employing both metaphors and similes, Lisa Coffman, in her poem about the pelvis, is particularly good at finding new ways to describe the function of a body part we usually take for granted:

About the Pelvis

Pelvis, that furnace, is a self-fueler:
shoveler of energy into the body.

It is the chair that walks. Swing
that can fire off like a rocket.

It carries the torso, it sets the torso down.
It connects the brother legs, and lets them speak.

Trust the pelvis—it will get everything else there:
pull you onto a ledge, push you into a run.

It is the other spine, prone, like the fallow field.
Here are the constellations of the pelvis:

Drawn Bow, Flame-of-One-Branch,
Round Star, and Down-Hanging-Mountains.

Here is the dress of the pelvis: crescent belly,
and buttocks shaken like a dance of masks.

Forget the pelvis, and you're a stove good for parts:
motion gone, heat gone, and the soup pots empty.

Coffman has a sense of humor here. Not only does she present a whimsical list of pelvis comparisons; she even makes up names for the pelvis: "Drawn Bow, Flame-of-One-Branch, / Round Star, and Down-Hanging-Mountains." The likenesses packed into this relatively short poem persuade us that the pelvis is not only at the center of our bodies but also at the center of our physical lives.

As you can see, Coffman uses an irregular pattern of listing. The pronoun *it* is repeated often, but not in a uniform manner. The poem consistently shifts its structure. Most poets prefer that their list poems shift patterning in order to demonstrate some kind of change, though some list poems are more synchronized than others. Whatever type of listing you attempt, remember that imagery and patterning are your two primary methods of expression in this form. Try to create intriguing images that startle your reader. Don't settle for the ordinary. You might adjust the pattern of presentation in a way to indicate the transformation that is taking place.

The Interior World

Some of the metaphors in Rodriguez and Coffman's poems not only describe the physical environment but also suggest the interior life. Sometimes it's quite helpful to use metaphorical language to imply what's going on inside a person, as in this famous poem by Anne Sexton:

Mr. Mine

Notice how he has numbered the blue veins
in my breast. Moreover there are ten freckles.
Now he goes left. Now he goes right.
He is building a city, a city of flesh.
He's an industrialist. He has starved in cellars
and, ladies and gentlemen, he's been broken by iron,
by the blood, by the metal, by the triumphant
iron of his mother's death. But he begins again.
Now he constructs me. He is consumed by the city.
From the glory of boards he has built me up.
From the wonder of concrete he has molded me.
He has given me six hundred street signs.
The time I was dancing he built a museum.
He built ten blocks when I moved on the bed.
He constructed an overpass when I left.
I gave him flowers and he built an airport.
For traffic lights he handed out red and green
lollipops. Yet in my heart I am go children slow.

Sexton's narrator actually resorts to an **extended metaphor** in order to dramatize the relation between the female narrator and her male lover. That is, for the length of this darkly comic poem she employs plain words to render captivating images of an industrial engineer to render the dynamics of their relationship. Like Dubie's, Sexton's language is largely direct and simple. By depicting her lover's compulsion to make her over as if she were an engineering project, the narrator conveys her own sense that her lover is not happy with her either physically or emotionally. First he reengineers her as a physical body. Persevering, he starts, fails, begins over. Notice how he has "numbered the veins" on her breasts. An "industrialist," she is "a city" he's building. He uses "boards" and "concrete"; he adds "street signs" and "museums." As we can see, he's not simply interested in changing her physically; he wants to revise her as a person. He's so "consumed" by his project that he can't acknowledge what she's like. At one point, she's dancing, but he tries to make an airport of her, something upon which he can land.

The extended metaphor helps us to understand what *both* people are like. By the end we can be sure that he sees her as almost childlike: "For traffic lights he handed out red and green / lollipops." The image of the lollipops tells us he's so needy and so controlling that he wants her to be like a child. On the other hand, while the narrator is letting him go some way in his contracting, she not only recognizes his disturbing obsession but secretly, down deep, wishes he would restrain himself, and she devises her own civil engineering tool to tell us so, a warning sign one would see near a grade school: "Yet in my heart I am go children slow."

We can be confident that Sexton didn't begin her poem by knowing all of the engineering references she'd use. But as she wrote, we can assume the poem's central comparison came to her. She may not even have explicitly understood that she was rendering the man's unhealthy compulsion as well as the woman's eroding patience. But she surely realized she'd tapped into an intriguing metaphor to describe the troubled relationship. Ultimately, her comparisons help us to grasp the interior lives of the man and the woman.

The Other Senses

We know that an image can appeal to any of the five senses. Since literature appeals predominantly to the visual, we often forget that good poems can appeal to taste, smell, hearing, and touch. Well-rounded poets are able to call on any of the senses to render their points of view, not just sight.

Here's a poem by Brendan Galvin that makes use of virtually all of the senses, while being especially evocative about soup:

✵ Kale Soup

The Mayflower Café, the Vets' Club on
Shankpainter Road, or maybe Cookie's Tap
before the name and linoleum
vanished and pork chops *vinha d'ahlos*,
meaning "wine of garlic,"
and *ameijoas*, meaning littleneck quahogs,
got kicked off the menu. Or maybe
you tried it first from a
back-of-the-stove stockpot in some
grandmother's kitchen, a dark,
fertile root of a woman
who drove to the hill above
Race Point and sat till she sighted
the family boat hauling home
from Georges Bank. In all those places
it was the same and different, with
or without carrots, with or without
chicken or lamb left over
from Sunday, but always simmered a day
over heat so low it never
raised a bubble, and built
with plenty of this, a little
of that, some more or the other,
a text brought by heart
from the Azores, when names like
Codhina and Gaspar entered
the whalers' logbooks. Always
linguica in it, which put the oak
in the forearms of doryman,
vinegar for the vinegar of it,
chourico for setting the otter trawls,
garlic and cumin that thickened
the blood and sent trapboats
toward sunrise and the bluefins

thrashing and cruising
in a jerry-rig of nets and stakes.
You bought a store downtown
and painted it heliotrope
to catch summer people. You called it
garbage soup and denied you ever
ate it. But some nights in autumn,
coming home, you pass through a fog
so husky with smoked pork and spices
you're gaffed by the hook
of this whole peninsula.

Galvin understands that one of the best ways to evoke taste is listing all kinds of different food. Here he names nine kinds and, taken together, the names sing the way cooking food sizzles: "kale soup," "pork chops," "quahogs" (a type of clam), "carrots," "chicken," "lamb," "linguica" (spicy Portuguese garlic sausage), "chourico" (Portuguese pork sausage), "smoked pork." He seasons this mix with the mention of "spices" including "vinegar" and "garlic" and "cumin." And the settings, utensils, and sounds help to evoke taste: the "Mayflower Café," "the Vets' Club," "Cookie's Tap," even "the menu." There was "a back-of-the-stove stockpot," a mix of food that "simmered" but "never raised a bubble," seasonings that "thickened the blood," and "a fog . . . husky with smoked pork." When you saturate the poem with such suggestive names and sounds, you evoke in the reader much more than the sense of sight.

Dramatizing Everyday Subjects

Anne Sexton's poetry is famous for its powerful depictions of unhealthy human relationships. Other less obviously dramatic subjects can ride on the strength of good imagery and metaphor as well. For instance, as in this poem by April Lindner, a simple kiss can catalyze both:

❈ First Kiss

This collision of teeth, of tongues and lips,
is like feeling for the door
in a strange room, blindfolded.
He imagines he knows her

after four dates, both of them taking pains
to laugh correctly, to make eye contact.
She thinks at least this long first kiss
postpones the moment she'll have to face
four white walls, the kitchen table,
its bowl of dried petals and nutmeg husks,
the jaunty yellow vase with one jaunty bloom,
the answering machine's one bloodshot eye.

Clearly, Lindner knows that all parts of a poem are important, but she also knows that the two most critical sections are the opening and closing lines. She opens with a strong simile: a first kiss "is like feeling for the door / in a strange room, blindfolded." If Lindner had merely said that a first kiss can be disorienting, the poem wouldn't work so well. Because its specific

THE POET'S NOTE CARD

How to Make Imagery Register

1. It's a good idea to employ vivid metaphors and similes.
2. Metaphors render immediacy. Similes suggest reflection.
3. Metaphors and similes can be used to chronicle the interior life.
4. Extended metaphors can add imagistic drama to a situation.
5. It's always better to be surprising, even outrageous, and to avoid blandness.
6. Clichés dull the mind; ordinary expression fails to excite the reader.
7. It's often helpful to make your images both specific and economic.
8. Big words usually call too much attention to themselves.
9. List poems can encourage intriguing comparisons.
10. Everyday situations are ripe with potential; imaginative expression can make virtually any subject interesting.

comparison elicits an almost dizzying confusion, we experience some of the protagonist's perplexity.

Lindner goes on to suggest that any bewilderment the woman feels is better than going home, where she'll be alone in her arid apartment. The poem closes on an eerie last line, one that evokes the strain she suffers from her otherwise solitary existence: "the answering machine's one bloodshot eye." Answering machines may call up all kinds of feelings for us. For a person living alone, an answering machine is a link to the outside world. A bloodshot eye is red, of course—and, again, a color is often more suggestive than ideational language. If that red light isn't blinking, the solitary person can feel that much more solitary.

Lindner's poem exemplifies what all good poets know. All events, even the ordinary, can be transformed into intriguing subjects. As you can see, with the help of fresh imagistic metaphors, any action or state of being can be made dramatic and the ordinary can become special.

WRITING EXERCISES

1. *Imagistic poems.* Write four poems in a short period of time (one to two days). Make sure each poem depicts a single interesting image or action. Keep each poem to about four lines of approximately ten syllables each. Make sure no line is longer than ten syllables. Use exciting, highly visual language. Don't be afraid to make unusual, even weird images or comparisons. Often, the more unusual the image the better the poem. Try to refrain from using any abstract words or phrases. And be on guard against using too many adjectives. Choose your verbs with an eye toward sensory appeal. Generally, the more verbs render action, the more effective they are.

2. *"Metro" poem.* Using Ezra Pound's "In a Station of the Metro" from Chapter One as a model, write four poems, each describing a different scene. Here's the challenge: While you may not use an abstract word in the title or the second line of the poem, you may use one abstract word, if you wish, in the first line. Notice that the first line of Pound's poem sets the scene and the second line is a metaphor rendering that scene. Try to heighten the impact of the poem by coming up with a visually interesting scene and an unpredictable metaphor.

3. *List poem with similes.* List poems give you practice in creating strong imagery while you also become attuned to the demands of rhythm. Write a list poem that uses similes. You may want to begin with one of the following phrases: "My grandfather's face looks like...." Or "My mother's skins feels like...." Or "My twin sister sings like...." Or "The clock in my head rings like...." Keep repeating the phrase and altering the end of each line. After four or five lines, vary the rhythm and pattern slightly to avoid boring your reader. Try to build to some kind of unpredictable resolution.

4. *List poem with metaphors.* You can also write a list poem that uses metaphors rather than similes. Metaphors usually render a more immediate sensation than similes, and similes generally render a more reflective or considered sensation than metaphors. Both are extremely important tools in poetry. In order to try a list poem using metaphors, you might begin with something like this: "My grandfather's face is a side of cooked beef...." Or "My love is a four-headed rose...." Again, keep repeating the phrase that begins the line and then eventually vary the rhythm and structure slightly. If you can, try to change the nature or intensity of the comparisons as you move toward the end of the poem. Such change might correlate to a change in understanding.

5. *Walk poem.* Take a walk in a familiar area. Try to notice the things you often miss seeing. Try to notice what's unusual or intriguing about things you often see. Now return home and write a poem about your walk. Invest the poem with transforming details and metaphors that bring your ordinary world into extraordinary perspective. What brings tension to your observations? In order to concentrate the imagery, try not to let the lines extend beyond ten syllables, and keep the poem to fewer than fifteen lines.

6. *Everyday object poem.* Think of some item that seems especially common or ordinary, something that you often see. Common things you might see include a toothbrush, the stuff on top of your bedroom dresser, your everyday shoes, the bus you usually take to school or work, the TV remote control, an old lamp, an old doll, a dress hanging in your closet, a CD you rarely play, a wall calendar, or dust under the coffee table. Choose one such thing. Now before you start writing, ask yourself, "Is there a way I can convert this thing into a strange, evocatively described item that might be linked to some kind of human problem?" Perhaps your best friend

from high school bought you the lamp, but you never hear from her any more. Perhaps there is something on the dresser you don't want to look at. Perhaps there's a reason you haven't changed the month on the wall calendar. If there is a way to convert the item into an object of intrigue, good. Start writing. In order to keep the poem intensely imagistic, limit yourself to one abstraction and twelve lines.

7. *Everyday activity poem.* Think of common everyday activities that you might do. These might include making coffee, tying your shoes, scratching your head, putting things in your pocket in the morning, feeding the dog, yawning, paying the bills, logging onto your favorite website, petting your cat, staring into space, cooking toast, lying down on the couch, shaving, getting cash from the ATM, crossing the street, or brushing your hair. Choose one ordinary activity. Let your imagination go wild. How can you make this one common activity into something weird or wild or bizarre? Write a poem that does just that. Since you want to emphasize the physical as well as the strange, concentrate on good verbs. In order to make your imagery concise, consider limiting the poem to fifteen lines.

8. *Five-senses poem.* Imagine a situation in which all five senses are at work. Write a poem that describes how all five senses were inspired. How can you describe this onslaught of sensory stimuli?

3

THE SOUND OF
CONTEMPORARY
POETRY

Why Poems Don't Sing Like Songs

Far more than fiction, poetry appeals to the ear. Most children like rhyme because it's playful. As kids grow up, they become more serious and more discerning. Imagine a twelve-year-old boy who likes to read. Perhaps at first he loves the pounding rhymes of Tennyson's poem "The Charge of the Light Brigade." When he gets to high school, he can't get enough of the melancholic speech of "Stopping by Woods on a Snowy Evening" by Robert Frost. Later, in high school he may be inspired by Langston Hughes's lyrical "Night Funeral in Harlem." By the time he's a freshman in college, he's dazzled by the high-velocity, sharp-edged work of poets such as Sylvia Plath and Alan Ginsberg. A year later and he may have yet more eclectic taste; he might like a great variety of styles, including types of poetic sound.

While imagery is the place to start when learning to write poetry, we should remember that many readers are drawn to good poetry because they like meeting up with a poet's voice. In fact, the term **voice** is used in poetry to characterize the way poets sound, what their attitude is. As former poet laureate Robert Pinsky once said, "Perhaps the most profound pleasure by which a poem engages our interest is by revealing to us the inward motion of another mind and soul." Today, when a poem's sound matches well with the poem's imagery, it reveals that inward motion. Before the twentieth century, the vast majority of poets favored end-rhyming, and they wrote in predetermined rhythmic patterns, often called **metrics.** As poetry developed after World War I, a nonrhyming, less restricted style of poetry, **free verse,** became more and more popular among poets. In 1956, the Beat poet Alan Ginsberg's long, free verse poem *Howl* began to revolutionize American poetic taste, and most of the greatest poetry since then is also written in free verse. Today's contemporary expression has room for formal rhyming, of course, but most poets prefer the freedom to improvise their own sound and rhythm.

While individual poets often practice many different styles of expression, especially in the beginning of their careers, contemporary poets are generally divided into two camps: the talkers and the singers. The **talkers** prefer a realistic, conversational type of speech that approximates the way people communicate with one another on a daily basis. This conversational style can help the writer cozy up to a reader, as if the poet and reader were old friends. The diction, i.e., word choice, is fairly straightforward, nothing fancy. The phrasing is often subtle, but in order to create the illusion of intimacy or friendship the poet usually wants to deemphasize any sonic fireworks. When you try this style of expression, try to keep the lines relatively short in order to avoid sounding prosaic, i.e., like regular prose.

The **singers** prefer an intentionally melodious expression that calls attention to musical facets of language. Sometimes this type of writing uses conventional end-rhyme, which means placing words that rhyme at the end of lines. But more often, contemporary musical verse takes advantage of a variety of other aural devices, which include the following: **internal rhyme** (the irregular echoing of sounds inside one or more lines), **alliteration** (the repetition or echoing of the first sounds in two or more words), **slant rhyme** (words or syllables that share some but not all sonic qualities; i.e., *lull* and *all*), and **repetition** (the repeating of key words or phrases in order to amplify the emotion). Some poets increase musicality by writing in short choppy fragments or long winding clauses—or alternating between both. Some emphasize hard **consonants** (letters and sounds without vowels), usually to create dense rhythm. Some prefer to emphasize **assonance** (similar vowel sounds with different consonants) in order to create a more ethereal or reflective sense. Some poems actually have many or all of these devices. Likewise, many poets employ both conversational and musical techniques to create a kind of hybrid idiom.

New poets often ask how they should go about writing in these conversational or musical styles. Here's a suggestion: Take your time and consciously attend to only a few techniques at once. At first, you might focus on making intriguing, highly concrete images that are carried in a relatively smooth-sounding line. Beginning poets often find that shorter lines are easier to control; such lines are less likely to blur into dull, proselike sound. But as emerging poets get more practice writing, they often find that they can "hear" the words respond to the sounds of previous words. Without sacrificing imagistic sense, they can intuit what the next word or phrase should sound like and they "hear" that word accordingly.

Conversational Poetry

C. G. Hanzlicek is an especially good conversational poet because his narrators "talk" with an economy of language while simultaneously creating a kind of intimacy with the reader. Notice the relaxed speech mannerisms in the following poem about the importance of mercy:

Room for Doubt

Two boys, using fish heads for bait,
Landed a four-foot angel shark.
Laid out on the pier,
It seemed never to take the right pose
For a serious study of it.
Again and again the boys moved it,
Poking fingers into its eye sockets
To drag it across the planks.

It was a creature worth studying:
Broad, blunt snout like a catfish,
White lips and belly
Under a black-speckled gray back,
And wide wings like a ray or skate.
Dianne wanted to say many things,

But only looked out to see
And asked how long sharks live in air.
Oh, a long time, the boys said.

I've heard all the stories
About the sluggish nerves of fish.
But if those stories are true,
Why did the shark tremble,
Pound the pier planks with its tail,
Each time forefingers sank
Knuckle-deep into its brow?

To Dianne and me the slaps and shudders
Looked a lot like pain.
What the hell, I don't care
If they were the crudest reflexes,
With no more feeling behind them
Than ripples rolling out on water
After a dropped stone.
What matters is the room for doubt,
The kind of room we all ask for.

This poem's narrator relies on a common American style of speech. Hanzlicek wants to make sure that both the concrete depictions and the narrator's point of view are what come through first.

Note that no line exceeds ten syllables; most are shorter in length. In fact, Hanzlicek is a master of **line breaks,** the point at which the line ends and the eye moves to the next line. Notice how he doesn't end on articles or prepositions. He doesn't even end on adjectives. Hanzlicek knows that line breaks usually work best when the last word completes an image or a thought. The reader perceives the sense of the line and then proceeds to the next line, which, in turn, modifies the sense of the previous line. Each line is a discrete unit of poetry, but none calls attention to itself. Never clichéd, certain phrases are drawn from American conversational speech: "I've heard all the stories. . . ."; "What the hell, I don't care. . . ."; "What matters is. . . ." Because the poem's language is so transparent, we immediately experience the speaker's "inward motion."

It may sound strange to say so, but Hanzlicek is primarily a lyric poet. While the imagery graphically depicts the situation, a good deal of the poem is dedicated to the narrator's inner feelings. Many new poets understandably confuse the terms *lyric* and *lyrical*. In fact, *lyric* has two different meanings: In music the word *lyric* means the words of a song; yet in literature it refers to a poem that renders the interior life by depicting the intense personal emotions of the speaker. (As we will see in Chapter Five, most poetry is broken into lyric poems, narrative poems, or a combination of both.) The **lyric poem** may or may not be musical in style. In most contexts, the term *lyrical* simply refers to a quality of sound, one that's melodious or conventionally pleasing to the ear. While "Room for Doubt" quickly establishes a kind of plot, it is a lyric poem because the narrator makes a point of rendering his feelings. Lyric poems often embed discursive language ("What the hell, I don't care") in stanzas with considerable concrete imagery. Note how Hanzlicek's poem begins with such a visually vivid description of the way the boys abuse the fish. Only after establishing a strong imagistic base do most good poets risk abstract language.

Musical Poetry

In order to heighten a particular aspect of reality, sometimes the poet wants to make sound a more overt factor. Like many musically adroit contemporary poets, Robert Wrigley doesn't often resort to end-rhyme for effect. In the following poem, he repeats sounds, uses slant rhymes, provides subtle alliteration, and develops long, coiling clauses in order to describe an encounter with snakes:

Following Snakes

Esses, esses, a glassine imaginary axis
rigid from the utterly linear and straightforward head:
I follow the elegant and anachronistic rattlesnake carefully,
for he would rather not leave the warm path
willingly but, spring and all and him half-blind
from nothing, happily would coil and fight
whatever thumping thing comes blundering behind him.

I could wait him out, but I have my stick after all
and a few body lengths between us, and also a plentitude
of stones nearby. I have killed and skinned his kind
before, but mostly I love the way he moves

out front of me, an undulant ornament on the car of my going
toward the river, except now I see the other one
headed our way, or his way, a snake so identical

in cross-hatch scale and motion, I cannot believe
I myself do not walk out of a mirror and into this other scene.
Now they are chin to chin and rise and twine
like paper streamers, a bunting of meat and bone,
then a ball of bulges or a fist two long fingers thick.
Their rattles tick and chatter, they are belly to belly
when the dog trots past and over them

unawares and keeps on going, bound for the river.
That's when they coil then spin
and slant off the trail to the brush. Cheatgrass signals
their going, a thin green wedge nodding off
from where they met, and from me who mourns
a little, who loves all undulant things and things that mate,
though now they may wait near the path I walk.

Can you hear all the many diverse sounds in this poem? Wrigley highlights
sound everywhere, but no more than in the first line. Most poets believe
that the first and last lines of a poem are the most important, because the
first captures the reader's attention and the last underscores the poem's
ultimate attitude. In "Following Snakes," the first line lets us know right
away that this poem intends a strong sensory experience. Notice the way
the sibilance of the S sounds implies the slithering quality of snakes: "Esses,
esses, a glassine imaginary axis." Most people are at least a little jittery
around snakes, and this opening line certainly may jangle their nerves. Not
only can we infer the hissing of the snakes from the alliterative use of the S
sound, but in this one line we're also engaged by repetition ("Esses, esses")
and slant-rhyme ("esses" and "axis"). Can you find other instances of
alliteration, repetition, and slant rhyme throughout the poem? What about
interior rhyme?

Wrigley knows that poems don't sing like songs. For one thing, good
poems usually have a more subtle rhythm than most songs. And because
singers can inflect in whatever manner they choose, songs can sustain
rhyme without seeming rhyme-led—even when they are *clearly* rhyme-led.
Because "Following Snakes" makes use of winding, elongated sentences,
the rhythm pulls us sinuously through the poem in a way few songs
ever could.

Most of his lines employ **enjambment,** a technique in which the grammatical sense spills without pause down to the next line. And rather than progress on a strong, consistent series of beats, these lines move less regularly, more smoothly; they evoke the "undulant" motion of the snakes and the resultant movements of the man who is following them. You too might try to match the sound of your language to the actions it describes.

How We Talk Back Home

Speech that reflects a particular locale is called **colloquial** speech or **vernacular.** The following serio-comic poem by Ruth Stone uses vernacular to make us laugh uncomfortably about the way some folks interact with those who grieve right after their loved ones die:

❖ Bazook

My aunt from St. Louis
Lost her husband,
So yesterday I invited her
And Dorothy to lunch.
Over in Dorothy's neighborhood
There was this couple
She used to think so much of—
Fred and Ida.
They had a lovely little house.
For two years all that two talked
Was, wait till we get to Florida,
Wait till we get to Florida.
It's going to be this and that.
Then finally they sold
And moved to Clearwater, Fla.
And built this place.
And the next thing we hear,
The wife's went bazook!
There they were in Clearwater
With this nice little place.
It got so bad Fred finally
Had her committed.
She didn't know him.

He was like a stranger.
He'd go to see her now and again.
But she was like a stranger.
He'd say, "Ida,"
And she wouldn't acknowledge.
He'd say, "It's Fred, Ida."
And the other day
We hear she died.
Now they're coming up to Tuscola
Where she was raised
To have the funeral,
And we're all going over there
To see them.

Think of all the conversational devices Stone puts to use: The narrator's uncle hasn't died; rather her aunt "lost her husband." The narrator doesn't buy them lunch at a particular restaurant; she meets them "over in Dorothy's neighborhood." Notice, too, her use of verbs and repetition.

Born in Virginia, raised primarily in Indianapolis and a long-time resident of Vermont, Stone understands rural Anglo-American dialect. She also knows that no matter where we come from, most of us don't always speak in grammatically correct English. Here her narrator speaks just like friends Fred and Ida. While mimicking the way the couple discusses future plans, she switches tense quickly from past to present. The language is at once grammatically incorrect and colloquially correct.

The poem ultimately uses a type of vernacular to demonstrate how human beings use understated expression in order to control their emotions. Stone knows exactly how certain types of people talk—and she chooses her words very carefully, even though they may seem offhand on first reading. The poem is economical, too. In just a few words, Stone conveys familial empathy as well as an emotional distance many people maintain in such situations. Her ending is perfectly understated. As the poet Louise Glück is fond of saying, a poem's ending should be both inevitable and surprising. Stone intuits that her characters don't want to reveal too much. So the narrator says just enough to keep her deeper feelings to herself (or maybe *from* herself): "And we're all going over there / to see them."

Not only may vernacular depend on region; it may also depend on ethnicity. For instance, while most American speech—such as that used by television newscasters—is called Standard American English (SAE), African Americans often employ Black English, an English-based idiom that has its own unwritten rules of grammar and inflection. Poet Thylias Moss sometimes blends both SAE and Black English in the same poem. In this poem about the strangeness of childhood, she writes in a deliberately musical Black English:

🏵 Maudell's Moon

> Moon on your back, where you get
> That moon on your back?
>
> She stops. She just stands
> And don't pose. She don't know
> How she got that moon on her back.
> She did not know she got the moon
> On her back. She turn around,
> She don't see no moon on her back.
>   *You lyin'.*
>
> Moon back on your back how you get
> That moon back on your back?
>
> *You got a parsnip? I'll trade you*
>   *That moon for a parsnip.*
>
> Deal.
>
> She walks on. She ain't had no moon
> At all, but she got something now.

The poem demonstrates the way vernacular can help to render the experience of a particular group. The narrator mimics both an African American child asking Maudell about some kind of mark on her back and Maudell thinking about the situation. In the end, the language brings the reader closer to the psychological truth of the girl. Can you identify the idioms that may be examples of Black English? What aspects of the poem seem deliberately musical to you?

Poems That Go Fast

If you compare Hanzlicek's "Room for Doubt" with Moss' "Maudell's Moon," you might notice a difference in pacing. The first moves more casually, less urgently, than the second. The speed of a poem influences the way we "hear" and understand it. Generally, the faster the line, the more immediate it may seem. Certain mid-twentieth-century poets such as Alan Ginsberg and Sylvia Plath practiced "fast" poetry, and more recently poets such as Linda Hull, Dean Young, Bob Hicok, Barbara Hamby, and T. R. Hummer have increased the cadence of their poems. Enhanced by some combination of run-on sentences, the consistent use of the conjunction *and*, a relentlessly progressive cadence, liberal use of enjambment, rapid alliteration, various types of interior rhyming, quick associative referencing, and simple repetition, speedy verse carries the reader on a wave of sound.

Notice all the ways Barbara Hamby makes her poem go so quickly:

❈ Vex Me

> Vex me, O Night, your stars stuttering like a stuck jukebox,
> put a spell on me, my bones atremble at your tabernacle
>
> of rhythm and blues. Call out your archers, chain me
> to a wall, let the stone fortress of my body fall
>
> like a rabid fox before an army of dogs. Rebuke me,
> rip out my larynx like a lazy snake and feed it to the voiceless
>
> throng. For I am midnight's girl, scouring unlit streets
> like Persephone stalking her swarthy lord. Anoint me
>
> with oil, make me greasy as a fast-food fry. Deliver me
> like a pizza to the snapping crack-house hours between
>
> one and four. Build me an ark, fill it with prairie moths,
> split-winged fritillaries, blue-bottle flies. Stitch
>
> me a gown of taffeta and quinine, starlight and nightsoil,
> and when the clock tocks two, I'll be the belle of the malaria ball.

Apparently bored by everyday existence, Hamby's playful narrator imagines the invigorating effect of all kinds of experiences, including those that most people might consider distinctly unpleasant. The point is, she wants to feel something—and the poem's sound mimics all kinds of quick, direct feelings. From the first to the penultimate line, the poem is **enjambed;** her lines rush to spill over each other. Alliteration cuts a poetry rug: "stars stuttering like a stuck jukebox." Slant rhymes abound: "atremble" and "tabernacle"; "stalking" and "swarthy"; "starlight" and "nightsoil." Hamby repeats the word *me* and yet the repetitions never seem redundant. Neither does her use of the imperative; she commands an imaginary other to "vex" her. The poem seems to force us to read it quickly, and our quick reading helps to render the visceral feelings her narrator longs for. This speedy kind of writing appears as if it's dashed off; but it's not easy to do. Ironically, when you write fast, you have to take plenty of time to craft that ultraquick rhythmic language.

Revising for Sound

Hamby is a very careful poet who works to make her poems flow with quick fluidity. Like the vast majority of poets, she revises all the time. In fact, she says she "tortures" all her poems "until they sing the song." She goes over each line repeatedly, making sure that there are no word-sounds that interrupt the flow. "Vex me" originally had end rhymes, but she couldn't make them work, so she says she "ripped the poem up and made it a free verse poem" but kept some of the internal rhyming. Here's what she says about how she started the poem and then revised it entirely: "This poem and another . . . were the beginning of a series of sonnets that had their beginnings in the Psalms. I also remember torturing myself over that 'tocks' in the last line. It was 'strikes' for the longest time, but that was not really a good enough word, and I knew it, but it took me months to come up with 'tocks.'" Hamby says that she has used highly structured forms to get wild associations she is looking for—and then she "capsizes" the boat of the poem, returning to free verse but with remnants of the rigor of form. One of her methods of revision involves moving from a formal sound to less restrictive expression.

Another way to revise any poem for sound is to do what many poets do: write a few lines and then read them aloud. Such a practice gives them a more dramatic sense of the rhythm. If any particular passage seems hard to pronounce easily, then they polish it into smoother expression. One of the advantages of reading the poem aloud to yourself is that you may find that some sections of the poem may differ in sound from one another. Such change can be fine if the narrator's attitude has changed, but if the attitude should be consistent throughout the poem, then you can "hear" the changes more readily and revise for sonic continuity. When you're writing, there's no reason not to read the poem out loud—even if your friends or family think it's a little strange to hear your recitation throughout the house . . .

THE POET'S NOTE CARD

The Sound of Sense

1. The musicality of a poem enhances the impact it has on a reader.

2. Some poets are "talkers"; others are "singers."

3. Once poets find just the right sound or melody in the poem they're writing, they often become inspired to create more imaginatively.

4. It's a good idea to become attuned to the varied pacing of different but equally successful poems.

5. Most poems contain "lyric" moments, i.e., expressions about the interior life.

6. Be cognizant of line breaks, that point at which the line ends.

7. Modern English language is hard to end-rhyme. **Rhyme-led** is a term describing poems that suffer because the poet cares too much about achieving the end rhyme rather than the overall effect or meaning of the poem.

8. Slant rhyme and internal rhyme often offer a pleasing lyric density.

9. Lines have **velocity**; their speed is primarily influenced by alliteration, line length, repetition, punctuation, and meaning.

10. Repetition can be a good technique in a poem if the repetition doesn't seem redundant.

11. Sometimes it's best for beginning poets to keep their lines relatively short in order to prevent sounding prosaic.

12. Good poets end each line on strong words rather than on articles or prepositions.

13. As Louise Glück says, a poem's ending should be both inevitable and surprising.

14. It's not a bad idea to read aloud to revise for sound.

WRITING EXERCISES

1. *Alliterative poem.* Using the third person, write a vivid prose description of the best meal you've ever eaten. Try to get striking sight, taste, and smell images into the paragraph. Make your reader hungry. Now convert the paragraph to four-line stanzas. Try to make sure each stanza contains at least one example of alliteration.

2. *Internal rhyme poem.* It can be fun to try your hand at internal rhyme. Most of the time, poets learn internal rhyme from lots of practice at writing, becoming increasingly sensitive to the nuances of poetic expression. That said, you might try this: Write a poem of approximately twenty lines about a difficult moment that led to a change inside yourself. After you've written the first line or two, try to allow the sound of any one of the words to suggest a sound you will use somewhere else nearby in the poem. Try to prevent the sound of the new word from leading you away from an apt image. Repeat the process four or five times throughout the poem. Remember: Always make sure the sound of a poem serves its meaning.

3. *Vernacular-in-time-of-danger-poem.* Oddly, we all speak in a variety of vernaculars, depending on the people we're with. Imagine yourself in a dangerous situation with your own friends. Imagine how you would—or did—speak to one another. What kind of speech would you use? Is it different from the kind of speech you use at the dinner table at home? With your grandparents? Now, using the vernacular of your own friends, write a poem about that dangerous situation.

4. *Vernacular-about-family poem.* Using the vernacular that you and your close friends use, write a poem in which you tell your friends a story about how you spoke or acted inappropriately at Thanksgiving dinner or some other formal event. Perhaps you drank too much wine and said what you have always believed about Aunt Harriet, even though you shouldn't have said it. Dramatize your blunder. Remember, you don't have to tell a "true" story for your poem to depict something insightful about life. Likewise, don't worry if you need to change the facts for dramatic effect. You might make up part or even all of it.

5. *Punctuation-free poem.* When people think of the sound of poetry, they generally think of its potentially melodious quality. But the

sound of poetry is deeply influenced by its velocity. Typically, the slower a poem reads, the more reflective it's considered; the faster a poem reads, the more visceral it's considered. One way to increase the speed of the poem is to drop all of the punctuation in the poem. Try writing a poem of roughly twenty-five lines in which you use no punctuation at all.

6. *Change-of-pace poem.* While most poems seem to maintain roughly the same pace throughout, others change speed to reflect an adjustment in the narrator's attitude. Try writing a poem in which you're walking through town or campus or the park while reflecting on a good talk you had the previous evening with an old friend. Now something happens in your field of vision that suddenly changes the way you're feeling. Perhaps a car blows a tire, or a siren goes off, or a snake crosses your path. Render the new sensation by picking up the pace of the language. How does the new, speedier sensation affect what you were thinking about the evening before?

7. *Revise-for-sound poem.* Take any one of the poems you've written recently and read it aloud several times. Are there any passages that seem to catch in the mouth? Any that trip the tongue? If so, rework them for smoothness. Now try rereading it aloud a couple of times. How does it sound? Keep doing this until you feel the poem flows well throughout.

4

CONFLICT AND TRANSFORMATION

The Problem of the Human Heart

At the center of all good literature is some conflict in the human heart. As the great American novelist William Faulkner famously said, only "the problems of the human heart in conflict with itself . . . can make good writing." Poets use imagery and sound to explore and illuminate the problems that attend us. As writers, we may hope that people can change for the better, that they can eliminate personal conflict, that they can transform themselves into something emotionally richer and healthier. But we can't know what any protagonist will do until we start writing—and then we must be true to that character. Some protagonists will change for the better; others will fail; yet others will fight their demons to a draw. Beginning writers are often most honest in their exploration of interior conflict when they reflect on lives they know—their own and those closest to them. Faulkner learned early that his own family and friends were at the core of his imagination: "I discovered that my own little postage stamp of native soil was worth writing about and that I would never live long enough to exhaust it, and that by sublimating the actual into the apocryphal I would have complete liberty to use whatever talent I might have to its absolute top. It opened up a gold mine of other people, so I created a cosmos of my own." Where does your "little postage stamp" lie? What part of the imagination holds the deepest, most dramatic subjects?

Where can first-time poets turn confidently to find conflict and texture? Which segment of our lives hosts the richest personalities? Where else but the family? No matter what age you start writing poetry, whether you're eighteen or eighty-one, you'll have plenty of material to draw from relatives as well as from all those old, often-told family stories. We know no one as well as we know our relatives. We may love them or we may hate them. We may simultaneously hold both affection and resentment for them. We can feel anxious or ambivalent about family members, but we're rarely neutral about them. We may love Grandpa Jack because he once taught us how to draw the puppies on a liquor label, but we may dislike Uncle Bert because of that day he deliberately swerved to run over a squirrel on the highway.

At this point in your development as a poet, it's probably a good idea to focus on family and portraiture in order to enhance your ability to render conflict and transformation. After all, the details and texture of family are always right with you—and they can lead to fruitful investigation. Sometimes we start writing about a dead relative and we realize that we haven't thought about a particularly important family event in years. Suddenly it floods back. How many details we quickly remember! How we recall the rasp of an uncle's voice, the scent of a mother's newly washed hair, the sight of the cracked flower vase in a grandmother's dining room, the feel of a father's prickly crew cut, the taste of an aunt's homemade adobo. How quickly, too, we recall that old emotion: the excitement in seeing our younger sister score her first bucket in a varsity basketball team; or the anger in seeing a cousin hit his young child; or the sadness in learning that your closest aunt, the one who always helps you through the tough times, is being transferred across the country; or your fear in hearing voices in the middle of the night indicating that your sick, young father has only days to live.

Since the 1950s, poets such as Robert Lowell have shown us how to use an individual's specific habits and surroundings to imply much more about that person's character. You might check out some of his longer poems, such as "Commander Lowell." Lowell knew that well-chosen concrete details can give us a sense of a person's inner life. What's more, human flaws can add energizing tension to the poem, even if they are *our* flaws.

When writing a portrait poem, try to use language to paint key evocative details; these specifics will act as shorthand tools for rendering the most important aspects of the person. It's often enlivening to include one or more of the following: names of places, historical flashbacks, dialogue, speech patterns, mannerisms, names of buildings, names of companies, clothes styles, interior decorating, old photographs, family tales and unconfirmed legends, weddings, birthdays, deaths, and funerals. Be sure to focus as well on one or two events in that person's life; avoid trying to capture his or her entire history. Such a broad breadth of time often diminishes the poem's effect.

Familial Tension, Personal Conflict

Poems are fueled by tension. Because we have such easy access to memories of stressful family situations, a relative portrait may come to us with conflict intact. This next, decidedly concrete poem by B. H. Fairchild is narrated by an adult recalling a single moment in which as a child he innocently asked his father a question:

❀ Little Boy

> The sun lowers on our backyard in Kansas,
> and I am looking up through the circling spokes
> of a bicycle asking my father as mindlessly
> as I would ask if he ever saw Dimaggio or Mantle
> why we dropped the bomb on those two towns
> in Japan, and his face goes all wooden, the eyes
> freezing like rabbits in headlights, the palm
> of his hand slowly tapping the arm of a lawnchair
> that has appeared in family photographs
> since 1945, the shadow of my mother thrown
> across it, green Packard in the background
> which my father said he bought because after Saipan
> and Tinian and Okinawa, "I felt like they owed it to me."
> These were names I didn't know, islands distant
> As planets, anonymous. Where is Saipan?
> Where is Okinawa? Where is the Pacific?
> Could you see the cloud in the air like smoke
> from Eugene Messenbaum's semi, that huge cloud
> when he rolled it out on highway 54 last winter?
> The hand is hammering the chair arm, beating it,
> and I know it's all wrong as I move backward
> on the garage floor and watch his eyes watching
> the sun in its evening burial and the spreading
> silver light then darkness over the farms
> and vast, flat fields which I grow so tired of,

so weary of years later that I will leave, watching
then as I do now his eyes as they take in the falling rag
of the sun, a level stare, gaze that asks nothing
and gives nothing, the sun burning itself to ashes
constantly, the orange maize blackening in drought
and waste, and he can do nothing and neither can I.

The question appears in the fifth line of the poem, embedded in the closely observed scene. Notice all the texturizing details: an image extended through the poem ("the sun lowers," "the sun in its evening burial," "the falling rag of the sun," "the sun burning itself to ashes"), names of people ("Dimaggio," "Mantle," "Eugene Messenbaum"), names of places ("Kansas," "Saipan, "Tinian," Okinawa," "highway 54," the farm), a key date ("1945"), the name of a car ("Packard"), mannerisms (his father "tapping," then "hammering" the lawn chair), a flashback (the semi leaving "that huge cloud . . . last winter"), a flashforward (how later he'll leave the area), and a key moment of dialog ("I felt like they owed it to me").

Fairchild provides all of these particulars in order to dramatize one telling moment in a time and place we come to inhabit in our mind's eye, even if we've never been to Kansas or thought much about Hiroshima or Nagasaki. The first unusually important detail lies in the poem's name, which is deeply ironic: "Little Boy" was the name of the bomb dropped on Hiroshima. Ultimately this and other details help the adult narrator to convey the deep tension between the father and young son that day, when the father's anger about the Japanese was countered by his imagining the destructive sunlike power of the atomic bomb. By titling the poem "Little Boy," Fairchild helps to render two things: the way a single memory can throw us back into a moment of early youth that will affect our development well into adulthood, and the way a name can illuminate the ironies of our human existence. In the face of such incomprehensible destructive power, we're all little boys.

As in many relative portrait poems, tension is doubled in the poem because there are, in effect, two points of conflict, one in the relative and one in the narrator. The father is emotionally torn by two realities: On one hand, there's his ongoing anger at the Japanese who started the war and who killed so many of his fellow soldiers in the islands of the South Pacific; on the other, there's his knowledge of the grotesque annihilation of human life caused by the two American atomic bombs. We can see his "eyes watching the sun in its evening burial," and we understand that he's not simply seeing the sunset. He's imagining the bloody battles and the gigantic explosions.

We know he's having great difficulty staying calm, because his hand is "beating" the chair arm. More critical, however, is the son's inner conflict. After all, the son is the speaker, and the speaker is usually the main character in a poem, sometimes called *the protagonist*. While as a child he had become fearful of his father's darkening change of mood, he had also felt guilt for having asked the question that precipitated that mood swing.

Because all good literary poems intend adult-level insight, it's difficult to write a poem about a childhood experience entirely in the present tense. By reminding us of past and future events, Fairchild clearly locates the poem in the past. Not only did he watch his father's troubled eyes that day, he watches them again now in his memory. The "little boy" may have been afraid of his father years ago, but the adult the boy has grown to understand what he couldn't understand then: that because his father had faced the virtually indescribable chaos and terror of war, the man couldn't escape the feelings of horror that came from such an experience. Ultimately, the speaker knows that there's nothing he could have done to eradicate his father's suffering.

A new writer may think, No way can I do all of this in a single poem! It's too complicated! And yet it's not as if Fairchild understood all of these ideas ahead of time. Actually, he probably didn't understand them all, even as he was writing the poem. Many of the events in the poem may not have taken place. (As we know from Frost, there's nothing wrong with making things up in any poem in order to dramatize the meaning.) Not always explicitly conscious of the implications in a poem, poets subconsciously intuit all kinds of insights as they paint their word pictures. Even after they finish, they usually don't understand everything the poem has implied. Often readers tell poets about issues they see in their poems that the poets hadn't realized were there at all—though, because the poets trusted specific imagery and a consistent tone, they knew the poem was succeeding as a slice of human drama. In poetry, relative portraits are fruitful because you have such access to the exact details of a real life. You can immerse yourself in the particulars of a single event involving one relative, and, before you know it, all kinds of subsurface relations are implied.

The Transformative Moment

Most relative poems employ a first-person singular speaker, or what's sometimes called an **"I" narrator.** That speaker is almost always the protagonist, the person in whom the central conflict takes place and with whom we're most likely to identify. The protagonist faces some kind of impediment to happiness. Virtually all protagonists are flawed—as are all human beings. The point at which the protagonist begins to change is **the transformative moment.** It's best, of course, to render that new understanding with imagery. Protagonists usually change because they have come to understand something new about themselves or the way they engaged that impediment. Sometimes called **epiphany,** such a realization often precipitates the change that occurs within the main character. (Change can also occur in other characters in the poem as well, but those changes are not the central moments of the poem.) In Fairchild's poem, the family tension is reexperienced and reconsidered by the adult son. Transformative moments typically take place near the end of the poem. By the end of this poem, the grown-up speaker has certainly undergone a poignant change: He's realized that he couldn't have saved his father from those dreadful memories.

Can you determine the transformative moment in the following poem by Sharon Olds?

The Moment

When I saw the dark Egyptian stain,
I went down into the house to find you, Mother—
past the grandfather clock, with its huge
ochre moon, past the burnt
sienna woodwork, rubbed and glazed.
I went deeper and deeper down into the
body of the house, down below the
level of the earth. It must have been
the maid's day off, for I found you there
where I had never found you, by the wash tubs,
your hands thrust deep in soapy water,
and above your head, the blazing windows
at the surface of the ground.
You looked up from the iron sink,
a small haggard pretty woman
of 40, one week divorced.
"I've got my period, Mom," I said,
and saw your face abruptly break open and
glow with joy. "Baby," you said,
coming toward me, hands out and
covered with tiny delicate bubbles like seeds.

The last few lines render the transformative moment, but long before that, Olds' deceptively simple writing draws us deeply into the situation. Of all the devices that engross us in this poem—use of past tense ("I went down into the house . . ."), habits of speech ("'Baby,' you said . . ."), bits of dialog ("I've got my period, Mom"), a key imagistic metaphor (descent into the lower regions of a home, which may also suggest the female reproductive system)—the most effective is Olds' fresh and concise imagery. The opening lines engage us with their implications of danger: After the speaker sees the ominously described "Egyptian stain," she descends the stairs "past the grandfather clock, with its huge / ochre moon, past the burnt / sienna woodwork, rubbed and glazed." It's almost as if we're in a scene from a suspense movie. Of course, as in some scary movies, this narrator is disoriented.

The poem is about a potentially embarrassing, even fearful moment for many girls. The speaker recalls how her parents have just divorced, and how she's just experienced her first period and wants to tell her mother. The description of the descent into the cellar charts her fear. How will her mother, made "haggard" by the divorce, react to the news? The language is decidedly eerie, even suffocating: "I went deeper and deeper down into the / body of the house, down below the / level of the earth." But by the end, the language shifts in tone, becomes lighter, buoyant: Rather than the frightening descriptives, the poem shows her mother using the endearment "Baby" while approaching the girl with love. The last image of the mother's outstretched hands renders the transformative moment: "covered with tiny delicate bubbles like seeds." What does such a picture tell you about the adult narrator now? What does she realize about her mother's action that she may not have first understood? Did the speaker have anything to fear? What change has taken place in her?

Again, you don't need to think everything through before you begin writing. When you try to predict all of the events in a poem, as if you were outlining an essay or an itinerary, you are likely to produce a poem that's mechanical and boring. Start by listing the key details. Let the sights and sounds carry you. Make sure there's some tension. Follow your intuitions. Seize the image. Render the change.

Portraying Stasis

A portrait poem, even about a family member, may focus on one person only. Sometimes that person fails to change. You might ask, "What about the transformative moment? Is it missing?" No. In any good poem it's there. Change must take place—but sometimes the poet demonstrates the personal tragedy of a person who cannot recognize anything about the key impediment to his or her happiness in life. *In poems such as this, the transformative moment actually takes place in the reader.* The poet indicates to the reader what, sadly, the protagonist cannot understand. Here's such a poem by Lorna Dee Cervantes about the psychological effects of trauma:

❊ Uncle's First Rabbit

He was a good boy
making his way through
the Santa Barbara pines,
sighting the blast of fluff
as he leveled the rifle,
and the terrible singing began.
He was ten years old,
hunting my grandpa's supper.
He had dreamed of running,
shouldering the rifle to town,
selling it, and taking the next
train out.
   Fifty years
have passed and he still hears
that rabbit "just like a baby."
He remembers how the rabbit
stopped keening under the butt
of his rifle, how he brought
it home with tears streaming
down his blood soaked jacket.
"That bastard. That bastard."
He cried all night and the week
after, remembering that voice
like his dead baby sister's,
remembering his father's drunken
kicking that had pushed her
into birth. She had a voice
like that, growing faint
at its end; his mother rocking,

softly, keening. He dreamed
of running, running
the bastard out of his life.
He would forget them, run down
the hill, leave his mother's
silent waters, and the sounds
of beating night after night.
            When war came,
he took the man's vow. He was
finally leaving and taking
the bastard's last bloodline
with him. At war's end, he could
still hear her, her soft
body stiffening under water
like a shark's. The color
of the water, darkening, soaking
as he clung to what was left
of a ship's gun. Ten long hours
off the coast of Okinawa, he sang
so he wouldn't hear them.
He pounded their voices out
of his head, and awakened
to find himself slugging the bloodied
face of his wife.
            Fifty years
have passed and he has not run
the way he dreamed. The Paradise
pines shadow the bleak hills
to his home. His hunting hounds,
dead now. His father, long dead.
His wife, dying, hacking in the bed
she has not let him enter for the last
thirty years. He stands looking,
he mouths the words, "Die you bitch.
I'll live to watch you die." He turns,
entering their moss-soft livingroom.
He watches out the picture window
and remembers running: how he'll
take the new pick-up to town, sell it,
and get the next train out.

One of the first things we may notice is that the narrator never enters the poem. The title is our only clue indicating the poem is about a relative; the poem is entirely focused on one man who never recognizes that the hatred he has for his father makes him a dangerous, unlikable person. When he's ten he's traumatized by the sound of the rabbit he's shot, and, as he grows older and more emotionally ill, he never figures out the problem. All he does is blame the people around him for his suffering, especially his father and his wife. Although we can sympathize with his plight, Cervantes shows us how "Uncle" never tries to counter the hatred he carries around in himself. We know what he should have done but never does—that is, confront and reverse his own self-loathing.

Employing many of the devices we saw in the early poems in scene after scene (mesmerizing imagery, names of places, mannerisms, bits of dialog, an extended metaphor), Cervantes pulls us into the action. We want to tell the uncle that his father should have told him about the potential pain of killing another creature. That it was his father who physically abused his mother, who precipitated the death of his baby sister. We want to tell him that a traumatized ten-year-old can confuse a killed rabbit with a dead sister—and feel guilty about both deaths. We're the ones who recognize how he must change; the transformative moment takes place in us, the readers. By the end of the poem, we watch helplessly as he destroys his life. We recognize that he cannot and will not change.

Sentiment vs. Sentimentality

Cervantes is especially good at uncovering the truth about relatives. For many beginning poets, however, family members—especially, it seems, grandparents—call up such warm, affectionate feelings that the poems can become a bit too sweet. It's as if our love for certain grandparents makes us enshrine them in an unlikely, saintly glow. As we know, there's no such thing as a good poem purely about happiness. Some emerging writers want to make all things "nice," not just people. We can get excessively sentimental about any kind of subject: our best Chanukah gift, the baseball glove our father played with, our first kiss, the lullaby our grandmother sang, our first car, the dog that just died. That's why it's important to remember that in poetry honest feeling, i.e., **sentiment,** always trumps syrupy feeling, i.e., **sentimentality.** Sentiment is true; sentimentality is false.

On this issue, the great British novelist Iris Murdoch differentiates between two types of art. She says that the first provides us with "a consoling fantasy," something that unrealistically relieves our insecurities, that makes us feel good inside without adequate reason. According to Murdoch, the second type of art is grittier, more willing to face the issues of life realistically, truthfully, without flinching. Sentiment is true because it reflects strong, adult sensibility. From the Greeks forward, literature teaches us that mature people are not seduced by a "consoling fantasy." They prefer to be frank. They know when they are being manipulated to identify with art that bathes their egos in a soothing, even magical golden light. They find such art boring.

An excessively sentimental poem usually asks us to believe that life should be approached with childlike emotions. Children, after all, are naturally given to fantasy; they want to believe in the improbable, if not the impossible. Mature adults have learned the value of candid assessment. And, at its core, good art manifests honesty and complexity. While often deeply emotional, all of the previous poems in this chapter depict difficult personal issues in a sincere, unsentimental way. New poets may sometimes confuse intense emotion with syrupy feeling. During the first couple of weeks of a poetry workshop, a few beginners may be tempted to write poems such as this one:

❀ His Last Christmas

> When my Grandpa came to live with us
> that last Christmas, his hands were shaking
> every day. Ten, embarrassed, I thought
> those trembling hands seemed like windblown
> branches. The shaking made me nervous
> about something in me I couldn't figure out.
> At the dinner table, I worried he'd knock
> mother's favorite china platter into
> smithereens on the floor. Once Grandpa
> saw me staring at his trembling, and I felt
> awful, as if I'd hurt his feelings. Grandpa
> just held up his blurry right hand, smiled,
> and winked at me. On Christmas Eve
> we had a big ham with pineapple rings.
> As I was passing the meat platter
> to Daddy, the sauce made my fingers slip,
> and, when I gripped harder, the platter
> flew onto the floor, where it broke
> into a hundred pieces. When I looked up
> my father had a terrible look of anger
> and the eyes of my Mom were real watery.
> Soon little salty tracks flooded down my cheeks.

> For a second, nobody knew what to say.
> The dinner seemed ruined. Then Grandpa
> got up real slow and went into the big old
> utility closet as if he were going to get
> cleaning utensils. You know, he said
> from the depths of the closet, at first
> I didn't know why Santa asked me to hide
> this present before he got here, but now
> I guess I figured it out. Before I knew it,
> Grandpa was wobbling by my side and
> a little golden retriever puppy
> was licking the tears from my face.

This writer may become a very fine poet. She's found some good imagery ("hands . . . like windblown branches"). Tension arises from a conflict, the poem moves quickly enough, and the lines don't break on articles or prepositions. She knows down deep that the poem is about coming to grips with mortality: "The shaking made me nervous / about something in me I couldn't figure out." These lines may be too abstract, but they indicate a psychological awareness that is helpful in a poet.

That said, the poem surely needs to be elevated to a more adult perspective. To appeal to adult readers, its diction could be less childlike in places. For instance, the poet could replace "Daddy" with "my father," and "Mom" could be changed to "mother." It's almost always better to avoid using terms like "Daddy" or "Dad" because such words make the narrator seem too young, thereby reducing credibility. Because images of crying can seem clichéd, it's likewise best to avoid those at first as well. Most importantly, this poem will gain greater credibility if its approach to mortality were more serious, less sentimental. The poem defers to the easier and sloppier image of the puppy. It's sometimes appealing, but "cute" writing is the equivalent of sentimental writing and, therefore, the equivalent of bad writing. Why? Primarily because it appeals to the insecurities in us, to the need for happy endings, not for honest understanding. The writer wants to make sure we know just how great a guy her grandfather was. But the last lines are designed for a child, not for an adult. The story of the puppy may appeal to ten year olds, but not only does it diminish the intensity of the fact that the grandfather will be dead within a year—it distracts from our understanding of how the child (and perhaps, by extension, most children) learn to confront death.

In a few places in the poem, the writer also struggles too hard to make absolutely sure that we "get" her meaning. Such a problem is called **overdetermining** and usually means that a writer uses abstract language to control the reader rather then let imagery and other poetic devices do their work. Rather than *show* us how she's self-conscious and discomfited by her grandfather's shaking hands, she *tells* us by using the word "embarrassed." Soon after, she has to tell us that "I felt / awful, as if I'd hurt his feelings." Again, she avoids showing; she's controlling her readers. They may know exactly how she feels, but they'll feel manipulated and probably bored, too. Later, instead of showing us her father's anger when the speaker drops the platter, she tells us: "my father had a terrible look of anger." Here, too, she's not indulging in the fun of writing; she's not exploring her own infinite reservoir of images.

The best way to avoid sentimentality is to ask yourself, Am I being honest about this depiction? Or am I aiming for an easy, prettified way of resolving a conflict? The best way to avoid overdetermining is to ask yourself, Am I rendering to imply? Or am I using abstract language to explain? All of us fall into unfortunate little habits, especially as beginning writers. But we need to remember that a poem is never finished. We always have a chance to revise.

Revising for Clarity

If you're like many emerging poets, you may be so excited about writing a new poem that you'll show it to your friends right away. And yet if you remember that most poems take time to come clearly into focus, you'll be more likely to set your poem aside for a while and return with a revisionist's eye toward polishing it. (Surprisingly, most established poets have as much fun revising a poem as they do beginning it.) While there are many ways to go about revising a poem, you're often well-served to keep in mind two keys: First, as we discussed in Chapter Three, the poem's sound and rhythm should correlate to its meaning. Second, as we'll see now, a good poem should be rendered with reasonable transparency. After all, since poets write to communicate, you surely want your reader to understand what's going on. While some writers may think that the best and only way to revise a poem is to examine its language (does it flow smoothly? are the metaphors making sense?), there are, in fact, three structural issues that also can be reviewed: the surface relations of the poem, the conflict in the protagonist, and the transformative moment.

Accessibility, conflict, transformation . . . These are factors you might consider when you're revising your poems for clarity. Whether practiced or new, all poets benefit from this revisionary process. Let's take a look, then, at a first draft of a student poem, followed by the finished version of the same poem. Before going on to the final draft, try asking yourself what aspects of the poem do you think the author, Sarah Grieve, revised.

keep narration — give her more to do
identify w/father as somebody at one time semi heroic
narrator recognizes it ———>
report it

Jesus Christ and Holy Shit in the Church Softball League

Stronger up the ante

The Holy Brothers of Mount Carmel Seminary
called them ringers. I suppose the accusation
may hold some water—although not of the baptismal,
holy kind. Mostly their wives, mothers, sisters
were the ones who slide gracefully into the pews,
popped out to the annual woman's league pot luck—
the men donning their suits twice yearly when
the alter arrangement contained poinsettias or lilies.   *too many syllables*   *laiden in*
The other squads bore conspicuous signs of affiliation,   *"obvious"?*
white collars peeking above their two toned t-shirts,   *Spelling*
Yamicas revealed when batting helmets came loose
rounding first. Mint green shirts, a mix of tattered caps,
our bunch prayed from the beginning of April
to late July at the mandatory prayer circle held   *rep.*
each Saturday morning before the first pitch. They'd all quit
the men's league, job or kids keeping them home weeknights,
arthritis, bad knees starting to slow their runs to first. But, the sprint to   *slowing*
Jay could still catch a fly ball hit to deep left after starting   *shag*
in short center. He'd show up ten minutes late with a pack
of Marlboro Lights, smoke between innings, permanent
grease beneath his nails from his mechanic job on upper   *actual action*
State Street. Rob played short or right, grew up in the church
but hadn't been back since, well, the unfortunate incident
with the sacrament wine. Phil played second mainly;   *— she makes him*
newly married, his wife took him to church, he brought
her to the field—a strictly co-ed league. I kept score,
too young to count for one of the women. My father
played first, batted clean up. He'd curse, *Holy shit, ump.*
Sorry, Reverend. But, Goddamnit, ump, call it even, wouldya?
The reverend, going three for four on the day, would bow his head,
scuff his cleats in the dirt, and try to hide his toothy grin.   *language,*
more interesting

I drive by that field on my way to my parents' house sometimes,
out behind the old junior high. The league was cancelled

about the time I turned fourteen—didn't foster the kind
of community the deacons had hoped. But somehow,
looking over the diamond dotted with weeds, I can still see
my father walking away from the field with ~~his hand on my head~~
his cleats clinking against the parking lot asphalt, his glove—
cracked leather, dirt—~~warm against my chest~~. Shirt still sweaty
from his two-run drive, he'd say, *Jesus Christ, that was fun.*

sentimental

league cancelled his response

early in poem
consciousness of language   Jesus Christ ... more!   too easy

If you were revising this draft, what questions might you ask yourself?
Keeping in mind the three keys often used to revise for clarity, perhaps
you'd find it helpful to start with these: Are the imagery and events of
the poem reasonably accessible? Is the protagonist's conflict rendered
clearly enough? What is the transformative moment? When revising, you
can ask these questions of *any* poem. Now here's the finished version:

Jesus Christ and Holy Shit in the Church Softball League

My father smoked a shot over the priest's head
in right, a walk-off in the seventh. I scurried down
the line, picked through the bushes, brushed off
the burrs, and saved it. The Holy Brothers of Mount

Carmel Seminary hissed *Ringer!* as he crossed
the plate. I suppose the charge may have held some
water—though not of the baptismal sort. Those days
it was mostly the wives, the mothers and sisters who

slid gracefully into pews, popped out to the annual
woman's league potluck. The men donned ties twice
yearly as the altar's surface hid beneath potted
poinsettias or lilies. The other squads bore obvious

signs of devotion, white collars peeking above
their two toned t-shirts, yarmulkes still fastened as
batting helmets slipped off rounding first. In mint
green shirts, a mix of tattered caps, our bunch only

prayed from April to late July at the mandatory
meditation held each Saturday morning before first
pitch. Only thing religious was our Sunday morning
perusal of the weekly stats. Sprawled in my church

dress, I'd sit on the floor as he read the sports page.
He'd say, The catch is hitting the crap outta the ball.
Sure is, my finger tracing the ribbie column. I'd
heard they'd all quit the men's league, the job or kids

keeping them home weeknights, arthritis, bad knees
slowing their sprints to first, Ben-Gay in their bags.
But Jay could still snag a drive hit to deep left after
starting in short center. He'd show up ten minutes

late, smoke a pack of Marlboro Lights between
innings. Rob played short, grew up in the church
but hadn't been back since, well, the unfortunate
incident with the sacramental wine. My father

batted clean up. He'd curse, *Holy shit, Ump. Sorry,
Reverend. But, Goddamnit, Ump. Call it even,
wouldya?* The reverend, a hit short of the cycle,
would bow his head, put a hand in my father's back,

guide him to the bench, chuckling. Next inning,
playing first, he'd tighten the mitt's laces, holler
Better pray! to the batter. They called off the league
about the time I turned fourteen—didn't foster

the spirit the deacons had hoped. My mother lay
the church bulletin before him. The text simply read
Softball League Cancelled. For a moment he stared
—Jesus fucking Christ, you've gotta be kidding me.

He never apologized, didn't try to catch himself.
I watched as he strode from the room, closed the door
with one smooth swing, the lock clicked gently. I sat
alone in the cold streaks of late winter light, shut out.

As you can see from Sarah's notes, not only did she attend to matters of
sound but she also looked into issues of accessibility, conflict, and transformation. While reducing the "prosey" feel of the language by shortening her

lines and employing four-line stanzas, she quickly recognized that the narrator should be the center of the poem, not her father.

She came to realize that the early version of the poem was not adequately focused on the narrator. At that point, she had a choice: One, she could remove the narrator and focus exclusively on the father. Admittedly, the father's behavior on and off the ball field could be a rich subject in itself, and such a decision would allow her to explore the relationship between men and amateur athletics. Or two, she could render the girl's response to her father's playing in the church league (which she ultimately did), because she was interested in exploring the psychological relationship between father and daughter. As a daughter, the narrator knew that baseball and softball were not simply games she enjoyed watching; they also formed a common area of interest that enhanced her relationship with her father. She knew more about a father's love for the game than "the wives, mothers and sisters who / slid gracefully into pews, popped out to the annual / woman's league potluck." Ultimately, however, her special relationship with her father would lead to a unique kind of conflict.

And so Sarah made key changes in subsequent drafts: we realize that by learning the arcane language of baseball from the father the narrator develops a special vocabulary that links her to him. (Almost every stanza contains at least two baseball terms, many used as metaphors for action outside the game, i.e., "smoked a shot," "walk-off," "Ringer!" "ribbie column," "a hit short of the cycle," and "cold streak.") By watching his teammates, the girl learns the ways of adults, especially men who play a weekend game because it gives them a respite from the pressures of their daily lives. Told in the past tense, the poem uses language that suggests not only an intimate knowledge of baseball but also an adult understanding of the past. In the first version, the ending focuses sentimentally and almost exclusively on the father, but tells us virtually nothing about the girl's interior life.

The final version, however, is far more trenchant: Because she was revising for truth about human behavior rather than reporting actual events, a few details veer from the original actions upon which Sarah based the poem. When the father reacts despondently to the games' being canceled, the daughter becomes despondent, "shut out" of this aspect of his life. In the first draft, the identity of the protagonist is not clear; likewise, the conflict and transformative moment are quite blurred. In the final draft, all these components are clarified. We know the narrator is an adult woman looking back at her girlhood. We know the conflict concerns her relationship with her father, and we know the transformative moment comes when she recognizes the inevitable distance between them. Looking back, she realizes—among other things—that children can't always be as close to a parent as they'd like, especially when that parent experiences deep disappointment. She never states this idea directly; rather, she renders it with sound and imagery. As we know from the first draft, she didn't start out to write about this

THE POET'S NOTE CARD

Painting Portraits

1. Good poems are registered first viscerally and then intellectually.

2. In the early stages of a poet's work, inspiration is often found in writing about what he or she knows well, and most of us have strong feelings about relatives.

3. When writing portrait poems, concentrate on a few events, not an entire life.

4. Human flaws add energizing tension to a poem.

5. It may seem strange to consider, but in fact all good poems render a conflict.

6. Memories of relatives are often loaded with conflict.

7. All good poems contain a "transformative moment" that indicates some kind of change.

8. Sentiment is true; sentimentality is false.

9. Provide enough material to suggest meaning (but not too much). Beware of overcontrolling the reader. Avoid "overdetermining" the poem.

10. Poets are not imprisoned by the factual events of real life. Don't be afraid to make things up.

11. When revising for clarity, it can be helpful to ask three questions: Are the imagery and events of the poem reasonably accessible? Is the protagonist's conflict rendered clearly enough? What is the transformative moment?

personal "change" or realization; she just wanted to write about the way her father used to swear in the church league. While once it was wordy and without adequate tension, now the poem reads with a persuasive structural integrity.

Though the title of the poem came to Sarah just as she began writing, she actually went through quite a few drafts before getting to the "final" version. But who knows if it's truly finished, ready to be abandoned? That's up to her. Setting the poem aside again, Sarah may refine the poem even further. Many poets refine their poems after they've been published. But it's clear that by asking herself those three questions about structure, she discovered ways to bring the poem into sharp focus. When you revise your poems, you'll no doubt find it helpful to go through a similar process.

WRITING EXERCISES

1. *Description-of-a-relative poem*. Write a poem that is a portrait of a relative, preferably a grandparent or parent. Don't be afraid to render conflict. Concentrate on some of the following devices and techniques, e.g., names of places, historical flashbacks, speech patterns, mannerisms, names of buildings, names of companies, clothes styles, interior decorating, old photographs, family tales and unconfirmed legends, weddings, birthdays, deaths, and funerals. Try to portray both positive and negative aspects of the relative's personality. Remember, nobody is perfect. Nobody is completely evil. By rendering a personality flaw or even a vice, you will add an energizing tension to the poem. Avoid writing about long spans of a person's life. Portray a few key moments.

2. *Change-of-mind poem*. Write a poem about a relative, but this time demonstrate how you originally misunderstood the relative. Try to portray both positive and negative aspects of your own personality. Using the first person singular, take the point of view of a family member who has only recently realized that he or she was wrong about their perceptions of the adult relative. That relative may have been deceptively good or deceptively bad.

3. *Change poem*. Write a poem portraying an adult you know. Using fresh, concrete images throughout, demonstrate a key change that a person goes through.

4. *Covert change poem*. Try the above assignment, but use the third person; find specific metaphors and visual images to render the process you actually went through yourself. In other words, write a poem in the third person about a key transformation you once experienced.

5. *Self-portrait poem*. Here's a way for writers to get a new view of their lives. Find a photo of yourself from not too long ago. Now give the person in that picture an entirely new first and last name and place him or her in another city or town. Both of you have the same consciousness, but the facts of each life are completely different. Imagine the new life, and look at the face in the picture. Try to find out what is bothering him or her. Write about that.

6. *Revising-for-clarity poem*. Choose any poem you've written as an exercise from the first three chapters of this book. Ask yourself the three questions that help to clarify structural relations in any poem: Are the imagery and events of the poem reasonably accessible? Is the protagonist's conflict rendered clearly enough? What is the transformative moment? Try to revise the poem so that the answers to these questions are satisfactory.

5

DO POEMS HAVE PLOT?

Keeping Your Reader on Edge

When you could hear the high-velocity pitch of a car from blocks away, you knew trouble was coming—and I'd heard just that sound. A couple of times every winter certain streets of my hometown became so icy that it was often impossible to steer a car in a straight line. I was outside with some local guys when I heard the loud engine grow closer. At night sometimes you can't even see the ice on the black asphalt. It's that polished. Not only was the street I grew up on one of the slickest that night, but right in front of my house it began a steep three-block drop before curving hard-right at the woods and heading east out of town. That oncoming sound promised something. If you were a driver from another city, you might make the mistake of thinking the street was safe.

If you're like most people, you're asking yourself, "What happens next?"

Everybody likes a good story. Idiosyncratic situations intrigue readers. Dramatic events make readers anxious to know more. **Narrative poems** tell stories, usually in much shorter time than your average short story. As we know, all poems have *some* degree of plot; after all, plot is the internal or external shape of the forces of conflict. Many narrative poems piece out the action of the plot more obviously and quickly than stories. The poet Ted Berrigan is rumored to have said that "poems are stories with the boring parts left out." We may love good novels, but poems certainly have an immediacy that few novels can match. Often more visual and action-oriented, narrative poems can have twice the immediacy of **lyric poems,** which predominantly render the interior life. While lyric poems typically trump story poems in rendering reflection or deep consideration, story poems often use quick pacing and a hint of peril to keep the reader asking, "What happens next?"

In order to heighten the tension, good narrative poems simultaneously compress events and delay the moment of most intense conflict. This poem by William Matthews also heightens tension by keeping its lines far more taut than any story could:

Bystanders

When it snowed hard, cars failed
at the hairpin turn above the house.
They'd slur off line and drift
to a ditch—or creep back down
the driver squinting out from a half-
open door, his hindsight glazed
by snow on the rear window
and cold breath on the mirrors.
Soon he'd be at the house to use
the phone and peer a few feet out
the kitchen window at the black
night and insulating snow.
Those were the uphill cars. One night
a clump of them had gathered
at the turn and I'd gone out
to make my usual remark—
something smug about pride disguised
as something about machines and snow—
and to be in a clump myself. Then
over the hillbrow one mile up the road

came two pale headlights and the whine
of a car doing fifty downhill through
four tufted inches of snow atop a thin
sheet of new ice. That shut us up,
and we turned in thrall, like grass
in wind, to watch the car and all
its people die. Their only chance
would be never to brake, but to let
the force of their folly carry them, as if
it were a law of physics, where it would,
and since the hill was straight until
the hairpin turn, they might make it
that far, and so we unclumped fast
from the turn and its scatter of abandoned cars;
and down the hill it came, the accident.
How beautifully shaped it was, like an arrow,
this violent privation and story
I would have, and it was only beginning.
It must have been going seventy when it
somehow insinuated through the cars
we'd got as far away from as we could,
and it left the road where the road left
a straight downhill line. Halfway
down the Morgans' boulder- and stump-
strewn meadow it clanged and yawed,
one door flew open like a wing, and then
it rolled and tossed in the surf of its last
momentum, and there was no noise from it.
The many I'd imagined in the car were only one.
A woman wiped blood from his crushed
face with a Tampax, though he was dead,
and we stood in the field and stuttered.
Back at the turn two collies barked
at the snowplow with its blue light
turning mildly, at the wrecker, at the police
to whom we told our names and what we saw.
So we began to ravel from the stunned
calm single thing we had become
by not dying, and the county cleared
the turn and everyone went home, and, while

the plow dragged up the slick hill the staunch
clank of its chains, the county cleared the field.

Matthews sets us up with two intriguing opening lines that suggest danger: "When it snowed hard, cars failed / at the hairpin turn above the house." In fact, the last two words of the first line—"cars failed"—immediately provide a little jolt of intrigue.

Now, once we're hooked, he can build tension by taking a little time to tell us about the perilous road and how some uphill drivers tried to navigate it. We breathe slightly easier. After all, even though we know the oncoming driver is in danger, the other uphill drivers are uninjured. Then in the nineteenth line apprehension elevates again.

The language is much sharper, moving faster than the prose that begins this chapter. From here on, the poem pulls us further and further into the danger that the narrator foretold, even though he wasn't exactly right at first. He thinks the car is loaded with passengers, but later he realizes there was only a single driver. He tells us how the passengers could survive ("Their only chance would be never to brake. . . .") But soon we know nothing will stop the deadly accident. We're hooked. We read on.

Lyric Interludes

"Bystanders" doesn't simply succeed because of its harrowing car accident. Matthews knows that all good poems need to have a conflict and a transformative moment. While much of the action of the poem involves the doomed car, there is a yet more important kind of psychological action that the opening prose section of this chapter doesn't anticipate. In a few key spots in the poem, the narrator tells us something about himself. Before reading on, you might try to find them. What does he realize about himself?

Ultimately, the narrator recognizes his own insecurity: "and I'd gone out / to make my usual remark— / something smug about pride disguised / as something about machines and snow— / and to be in a clump myself." Soon after, he says that "we turned in thrall," suggesting an interior shift toward excitement. About ten lines later, his excitement is made even clearer: "How beautifully shaped it was, like an arrow, / this violent privation and story / I would have. . . ."

Not only do we see that his enthusiasm for the accident has made it potentially "beautiful" but—because the word *privation* suggests being in a state of deprivation—we know the oncoming crash is something he has felt deprived of, something he's never really seen before, and he wants it to happen. Of course the accident is fatal. Reality sets hard. The narrator and the onlookers "stood in the field and stuttered." We might assume that they'd all wanted the accident to happen and that they all wanted to be together, as if to own a special group identity. But ultimately that collective unity feels empty, false. They "ravel from the stunned / calm single thing" and go home, the mechanical noise of the county workers marking the night.

Of the poem's sixty-two lines, only twelve tell us much about the narrator's inner life, but they're key because they help Matthews render the conflict. These types of lines are sometimes called **lyric interludes,** brief expressions depicting the inner conflict. While not always necessary, they offer clues that quickly depict the protagonist's central concern, even as the exterior action swirls about. New poets often improve when they practice transitioning in and out of lyric interludes without awkwardly staggering the flow of the narrative. One key is to present the interludes in the same rhythm as the rest of the poem. Another is to keep them short. Most important, the best of these interludes are virtually never ordinary phrases; they are usually metaphorical; if they're abstract at all, the language is fresh in expression: "So we began to ravel from the stunned / calm single thing we had become / by not dying. . . ."

Braiding

Narrative poems don't always focus on a single story. In fact, many poets like to combine two or more stories in one poem. Usually the poem holds one main account and other subordinate, typically shorter accounts. Often termed **braiding,** this multistory technique does *not* simply present one story and then another and another in the same poem. Rather, the stories are woven together. Rendering the vagaries of memory and the way language functions in times of stress as well as recollection, the following poem by Philip Levine concerns a narrator and his brother, who was a veteran of World War II. The poem starts by describing a photo taken during the middle of the war in London, then shifts into a scene in the mid-1990s in East Anglia (a region in eastern Britain), then into another scene a few hours later, and finishes with an exchange between the narrator and his brother.

Innocence

Smiling, my brother straddles a beer keg
outside a pub. 1944, a year
of buzz bombs. He's in the Air Corps,
on a mission to London to refill
oxygen tanks for B24s, the flying coffins
as they were dubbed by those who flew
them night after night. Fifty years later
a German writer on a walking trip
through East Anglia meets a gardener
who recalls as a boy of twelve hearing
the planes taking off at dusk to level
the industrial cities of the Ruhr
and later when the Luftwaffe was
destroyed whatever they could reach.
"50,000 American lads died." The gardener
recalls waking near dawn, the planes
stuttering back in ones and twos.
How many Germans died he may
never know. "Must have been women,
children, and the very old what with
all the eligible men gone to war."
The German novelist writes it down
word for word in his mind and goes
on to an appointment with an English
writer born in Germany, a Jew
who got out in time. My brother
recalls a young woman who lived above
the pub, a blond, snapping the picture
outside the pub with his own Argus
C3, and points out a horse & wagon
around the corner loaded with kegs
but without a driver. The pub is closed
for it's just after dawn and the city
is rising for work and war. We call the time
innocent for lack of a better word, we call
all the Germans "the Nazis" because it suits
the vengeance we exact. Some hours later

the two writers born in Germany sit
out in a summer garden and converse
in their adopted tongue and say nothing
about what they can't forget as children,
for these two remain children until they die.
My brother, blind now, tells me he is glad
to be alive, he calls every painful day
a gift he's not sure he earned but accepts
with joy. He lives in a Neutra house
with entire walls of glass and a view
of the Pacific, a house he bought
for a song twenty years ago in disrepair.
He accepts the fact each year squadrons
of architectural students from Europe and Asia
drop in to view the place, and though
he cannot see he shows them around
graciously and lets them take
their photographs. When I tell him
of the 50,000 airmen his blind eyes
tear up, for above all my older brother
is a man of feeling, and his memory is precise—
like a diamond—and he says, "Not that many."

The poem's first account gives way in line seven to a second more contemporary story, which bears directly on how the past is viewed. It's not until line twenty-eight that we realize the opening scene was captured in a photo taken by a young woman who lived above the pub in 1944. The narrator, the blind old veteran's brother, has gone to England to visit the scene of the photograph, and there he has encountered the German, the German Jew, and the gardener. While listening to these men, the brother encounters the claim that "50,000 American aviators died." He returns to California (the Neutra house is an architectural style of home famous in Southern California) and reports to his brother, who reacts with poignant doubt to the gardener's statistic.

In order to demonstrate the way trauma is recollected and retold, Levine uses the writer and the gardener in a kind of parallel subplot that is braided into the story. He begins with the war and shifts fifty years ahead where two older men, a German writer and a local gardener, reminisce about the war. Eventually the poem returns to the narrator's brother who looks back to the time he was in London. Thus, Levine interweaves narrative threads to tell stories about the past while also telling stories about the present. At the end of the poem, when the narrator's brother is tearing up, we realize that not only are numbers inaccurately recalled but that numbers themselves can't capture the horror of war and the poignancy of its recollection. Just as important, we also may realize that many of us use words such as *innocent* to explain the way we are compelled to reduce the complexity of past events to justify how we function in times of danger. You might ask yourself, "What is the chief point of conflict in the poem?" Keep in mind that the poem's title is, in fact, ironic.

The complexity of all of these events is demonstrated in part by the multiple settings and times. Notice how the events shift from one to the next. Levine understands that if the transitions are apparent, readers enjoy the quick shifting and interweaving of narrative threads. The second little story is signaled with the simple phrase "Fifty years later. . . ." The next begins with the short clause "My brother / recalls. . . ." A few lines later the poem indicates its shift forward with the plain but effective term "A few hours later. . . ." While there's no one rule about how to facilitate these transitions, doing so can be inspiring fun. Sometimes a single seamless word will do. Other times a phrase, other times a sudden shift in place. Sometimes the very sound of the poem will tell you when shifts are needed. One key is simply to be aware of the need for them. While the poem doesn't have to proceed chronologically, the reader should be able to reconstruct the order of events. Without overdetermining, try to make sure the reader can navigate all that shifting.

Poems of Childhood

Most poems about childhood involve vivid narrative passages. It's important to remember that a child usually perceives important events without grasping their full implication. We saw this limited awareness in Rodney Jones' poem "Gong" in Chapter One, in which the children in the school bus are only beginning to understand the implications of mortality. Like Jones' poem, childhood poems are usually best when told in the past tense by an adult narrator remembering the key actions with a mature level of understanding that, by definition, a young person could not have had.

In the following poem by Jim Barnes, an adult remembers being a ten-year-old boy reenacting war battles on a pile of sawdust in his yard:

❈ The Sawdust War

On the early summer days I lay with back
against the sawdust pile and felt the heat
of a thousand pines, oaks, elms, sycamores
flowing into my flesh, my nose alive
with that peculiar smell of death the trees
became. Odd to me then how the summer rain
made the heat even more intense. Digging
down the dust, I began to reshape a world
I hardly knew: the crumbly terrain became
theaters of the war. I was barely ten.

What I knew of the wide world and real war
came down the valley's road or flew over
the mountains I was caught between. Remote
I was nightly glued to the radio,
wondering at reports of a North African
campaign and Europe falling into chaos.
All daylight long I imitated what I
thought I heard, molding sawdust into hills,
roads, rivers, displacing troops of toys,
claiming ground by avalanche and mortar

fire, advancing bravely into black cities,
shrouding the fallen heroes with white bark.
I gained good ground against the Axis through
long summer days. Then one morning, dressed in
drab for hard work of war, I saw real smoke
rising from the battlefield. Crawling from
beneath the sawdust like vague spiderwebs,
claiming first the underground, then foxholes,
it spread like a wave of poison gas across
the woody hills I shaped with a mason's trowel.

I could not see the fire: it climbed from deep
within. No matter how I dug or shifted dust,

I could not find the source. My captured ground
nightly sank into itself. The gray smoke
hovered like owls under the slow stillness
of stars, until one night I woke to see,
at the center, a circle of smoldering sparks
turning to flame, ash spreading outward and down.
All night the pile glowed red, and I grew ashamed
for some fierce reason I could not then name.

Barnes realizes that in a good poem about childhood the adult speaker typically recognizes the young person's naiveté (or ignorance), thus granting the poem its energizing tension. After all, the narrator can't do anything to change the past. Here, just as the ten-year-old boy can't figure out how fire is slowly consuming his sawdust battlefield, he also cannot grasp the severity of war. The deep smoldering fire is a dramatic image that also serves as a metaphor for the spread of war and for the way young boys can misperceive war as simply a romantic quest. The boy senses that he's at fault, but he's not sure why. Only now does the narrator, all these years later, understand how he had reduced the horror of war to the pleasures of a game while he played upon the sawdust pile.

In Chapter Nine we'll see how different stanza patterns can influence the atmosphere of a poem. Notice for now how all of the many small details of this narrative are arranged in four ten-line stanzas. Because **uniform stanzas** contain the same number of lines organized in the same visual pattern, Barnes and many other poets use them to assert a kind of order on the chaotic series of events and images that may appear in a poem. If uniform stanzas prove unsatisfactory, you might try organizing the same lines in less uniform stanzas, as Cervantes did.

In rare cases a poem about childhood will use sophisticated, adult expression and insight while also mimicking the consciousness of a child. In the following poem by Denise Levertov the narrator is a very young child who has become fascinated with the details of the new world around her:

Earliest Spring

Iron scallops border the path, barely
above the earth; a purplish starling lustre.

Earth a different dark, scumbled, bare
between clumps of wintered-over stems.

Slowly, from French windows opened
to first, mild, pale, after-winter morning,

we inch forward, looking: pausing, examining
each plant. It's boring. The dry stalks
are tall as I, up to her thigh. But then—
"Ah! Look! A snowdrop!" she cries,
satisfied, and I see

thin sharp green darning-needles
stitch through the sticky gleam of dirt,

belled with white!
                              "And another!
And here, look, and here."
                              A white carillon.
Then she stoops to show me precise
bright green check marks

vivid on inner petals,
each outer petal
filing down to a point.

                              And more:
"Crocuses—yes, here they are . . ."

and these point upward, closed
tight as eyelids waiting a surprise,

egg-yoke gold or mauve;
and she brings my gaze

to filigree veins of violet
traced upon white, that make

the mauve seem. This is the earliest
spring of my life. Last year

I was a baby, and what I saw then
is forgotten. Now I'm a child. Now I'm bored

at moving step by step,
slow, down the path. Each pause

brings us to bells or flames.

Oddly, Levertov's highly concrete poem knows more than its speaker. The exceptionally precise language details the story of a child and mother taking a little walk among flowers. The child records each little sight, and—at first—the child is bored. Soon enough, though, there's a transformation; everything becomes interesting: "But then— / "Ah! Look! A snowdrop!" she cries. . . ." Now we realize that the child has been replaying many of the mother's words, and that the mother's excitement catalyzes the child's new fascination.

The narrative of "Earliest Spring" serves to render the cognitive processes of learning. Very few young children would have the language facility of this speaker. The vocabulary and exactitude are clearly adult. Likewise, few precociously brilliant two-year-olds would be self-conscious enough to explain that they are bored. The poem functions not only as a short narrative about a walk but also as a metaphor for the way human beings, young and old, process information. The child's view is enhanced both by the mother's language and an appreciation of the incremental processes of cognition. In fact, the narrative demonstrates those processes. In a way, the steps the child takes mark the steps of learning. Note, too, that the poem understands its subject, that it never stoops to cheap emotion. Levertov doesn't opt for saccharine references to the mother.

Just as good poets usually refrain from the sometimes seductive allure of sentimentality in poems about childhood, they also refrain from self-consciously writing toward large metaphors. Though the two poems by Barnes and Levertov ultimately employ metaphors about larger issues, poets are assured of becoming arch or precious when—right from the beginning—they aspire to being metaphorically profound. One sure way to write the childhood poem is to tell a good story. I doubt either Barnes or Levertov started out intent on big metaphors. A conflict rendered by a set of unusual images unfolding throughout a compelling narrative is good enough. Readers will enjoy the poem. If a metaphor should happen to emerge organically from the poem, fine. But remember: It shouldn't be willed or forced.

Poems of Adolescence

Psychologists tell us that adolescence is an inherently dramatic period because it's a time of individuation. The child advances away from the parents' influence, vigorously testing new borders. Because conflict is unavoidable, these years are emotionally frenetic. While we transition .from childhood to adulthood, we undergo curious, even frightening physical changes, and we experiment with new behavior. Some experiments result in danger, others in comedy. Some result in happy or painful discovery—sometimes both. Memories of adolescence are therefore rife with evocative details and forceful stories.

In Chapter Four we noticed how Sharon Olds' poem "The Moment" told the story of a girl getting her first period—certainly a hallmark event in a girl's life. On one hand the poem renders the psychology of growing into womanhood. On the other, the poem is about the larger issues of a girl beginning to cycle into adulthood as her mother cycles out of childbearing years. So the guidelines concerning poems about childhood also apply to poems about adolescence. Poets have to remember that serious poetry intends an adult perspective. The best poems are informed by a mature perspective on life that most young people don't yet own. By the time our college years are here, almost all of us quickly and irrevocably cross the border into newfound maturity.

Vern Rutsala, who grew up in the 1950s, sometimes writes poems about young men coming of age in suburbia. This poem "chronicles" the rituals common to many American teenage boys:

The Super 99 Drive-In Chronicle

We cut the lights before sneaking
through the low gate in the back—
Carl slipping the latch, Jim giggling
dangerously, the rest of us hissing,
pipe down! The small danger
thrilled us, tickling our neck hairs—
that huge sound of the tires munching
across gravel over those endless
back rows, expecting a cop's
snooper, maybe even a siren.
We crawled like a mole to one
of the crowded lines and hooked up
a speaker, careful as safecrackers.
Mostly we didn't care for the movie,
all anti-climax after that drumming
of sneaking-in fear made the skin

tight on our faces, and, bored, we left
at intermission looking for action
dragging Broadway's crowded
desolation past midnight's curfew.
The next year we parked on the road
behind the gate. The distant silent
faces on the screen meant nothing—
each of us was alone with a date,
trying like surgeons to learn how
to unhook a bra with two fingers,
aching to release those lovely
moons in the steely moonlight
while in the distance a mute Doris
Day flailed crazily as if protesting
what we tried to do, her honor at stake.
Nothing much happened though
until we bragged by the lockers
Monday mornings. Later, it got
serious. Going steady, we paid our way in,
raising everything to a higher level—
the speaker mumbling in our left ears
all through the movie we never watched.

Can you detect the points at which the first and second narratives transition to the next? And can you isolate the lyric interludes? Rutsala chooses the word *chronicle* for his title because, while a synonym might be the noun *narrative*, *chronicle* suggests a report of events arranged in the order they took place. While the poem gains mature perspective from the past tense and the personal statements, it doesn't flash back or forward. As the poem arcs from the first time the boys snuck into the drive-in to the time they each were alone with a girl to the more committed, sexual goings-on, it tells the story of the narrator's increasingly eroticized experience.

Rutsala succeeds despite the risk of relying on **the royal We,** the first-person plural pronoun, which could defuse the tension by diverting our attention away from a single protagonist. Though the poem opens out to include all the narrator's friends, thereby suggesting a nearly universal series of occurrences, the details are vividly reported. (Note how the tires were "munching across gravel"; how each boy "crawled like a mole"; how they eventually learned "to unhook a bra with two fingers"; how they "bragged by the lockers / Monday morning"; etc.) The poem stretches over two or three years. Each section raises the tension, just as each stage of adolescent development seems elevated to greater levels of responsibility.

No matter what type of poem you write, it's best to simply describe what's going on. Rutsala wanted to tell a few good stories. Upon beginning, he probably didn't say to himself that he was about to convey the texture of an important developmental experience. And he surely didn't begin with the idea that he'd write a poem about the archetypal late boyhood experience involving cars and girls. He based his poem at least partly on his own memories. Just as Barnes and Levertov eventually discovered larger metaphors in their poems, Rutsala eventually intuited that the royal *We* worked well for his poem. Still, writing in the first-person singular (*I*) or in the third-person singular (*he* or *she*) is generally the best way to ensure focus, especially when you're starting out.

Closure

In poetry the term **closure** indicates the way the poem concludes. Whether a poem is lyric or narrative, it will almost certainly have a closed ending or an open ending. The **closed ending** is more definitive; it may indicate the final stage of the external and internal action. Or, it may indicate to the reader specifically how the poet wishes the action to be perceived: Positively? Negatively? Neutrally? Matthews' poem "Bystanders" employs a fairly conventional, closed ending. We know that those echoing sounds of the county's clean-up crew mimic the way the narrator's desire to be part of a special group turned out so badly, even shamefully, for him.

As with some stories, most famously Stephen Crane's "The Open Boat," you may end your poem without definitive finality; this type of ending is typically called **open closure,**which refers to an ending that is less conclusive or summative. The poet usually wants to provide the reader with the same sense of uncertainty that the protagonist experiences. Sometimes what we sense is a wrenching **ambivalence,** i.e., strong but simultaneous opposite feelings about a subject. In the following poem Suzanne Lummis uses vernacular to tell her story in the voice of a woman out of a 1930s detective novel. We know that she's both caustic and fraught, desiring a connection with a man, and we suspect that a one-night-stand will not solve her problem. Her ending takes a surprising turn:

Gin Alley

> The women who enter there find nothing
> but desperation and lust to drink.
>
> —*cover blurb from old pulp novel*

It's 1939, a Monday, and a Depression.
So me I fasten one tall heel the color
of heart's blood on each foot
and go to Gin Alley.
I'm not thirsty tonight,
desperation and lust will do fine.

Inside another tall heel catches my eye.
His silk shirt looks like it's been
hand-washed by some
dye-job blonde. It's got three
open buttons, three closed, and the last
tucked away in the realm of the imagination.
Something about him makes me
slip a thin cigarette in my mouth
and start tapping my bullet shaped nails.
When he catches my drift he walks
his arms and legs over my way
and says something witty like, "Hi."

I take a smooth sip from a lousy year.
I say, "Not yet but I'm getting there."

He says, "You look lonely. I can fix that."

I say, "I'm short a buck for a fifth.
Can you fix that too?"

He says, "Oh, hard luck case, huh?"

I give him the kind of look
that makes a man feel needed.

"Yeah, so let's hope you're good for
a half night of hard luck."

Then, in the middle of page 24 three big things
happen at the same time: 1) the bar man smacks
down a glass of bad tap water and bad gin;
2) the dreamboat locks onto me like heavy machinery;
and 3) you, the page turner, decide I'm a tramp.

Yeah? Listen, Joe, the only one around here worse
off than me is you, the loser who's reading this book.
At least I get to jump this hayride on page 236,
but you'll sail right past it and keep on going
—probably to the corner diner where you'll perch
round-shouldered—Mr. Small Change and Big Dreams,
with a fry stain on his lapel. It's the real world
you're in, kid, where no one's quite good enough
to wisecrack their way through.

This particular example of open closure is more dramatic than most. Not only does the poem leave us contemplating the speaker's ongoing anxieties—it tries to distract us from them by accusing a would-be reader (*all of us?*) of being deluded.

Whether open or closed, good poems provide both surprising and inevitable closure. Lummis' ending is both unexpected yet perfectly well-suited to the genre of the tough-gal story. Detective novels typically feature surprising reversals—and the end of "Gin Alley" is certainly in that tradition of the neck-snapping plot turn. Your own endings don't have to be as startling, of course, but they'll be most effective if they find a way to dramatize the poem's conflict.

The narrative poems we've just discussed are not unlike the portrait poems in Chapter Four. Textured by strong imagery, narrated in undeniably real voices, designed to surprise the reader, both types of poems capture the reader's attention. While the portrait poem may employ carefully drawn observations to intrigue the reader, the narrative poem usually relies more on external action. Both render the conflict of the human heart, and, like most good poems, they are best written when you open your imagination to unforeseen possibilities. When you ask the key question, "What happens next?", surprise yourself. After all, you're in charge.

THE POET'S NOTE CARD

The Surprise of Story, The Story of Surprise

1. Though we don't often think of poems as stories, virtually all poems have plots.

2. Good narrative poems compress events for immediate impact.

3. Even narrative poems typically have "lyric" moments.

4. It's often more dramatic to weave two (or more) stories into one.

5. Transitions between plot lines should be as seamless as possible.

6. It's a good idea to privilege dramatic situations and make your reader eager to know about the situation.

7. It's important to remember that idiosyncratic situations intrigue readers. Often, the weirder, the better.

8. Childhood stories are best told by adult narrators looking back on their pasts.

9. Good poets tell a good story in verse; they don't worry about profound metaphors.

10. Open closure often renders uncertainty or ambivalence. Closed endings usually suggest finality.

WRITING EXERCISES

1. *Best story poem.* Think about the best story you were ever told, not one that you lived through. Now tell that story as if you were the protagonist. Use the first person.

2. *Danger poem.* Think about the last time you were in any kind of danger. Tell that story either in one, long, fast-moving column or in tight, uniform stanzas. Feel free to use first, second, or third person.

3. *Narrative poem about childhood.* Write a narrative poem about yourself as a child. Using many of the methods of the relative poem, concentrate on one story from your youth. Carefully plot

transitions. Make confrontations clear. Bring the end of the poem into the present so that the reader may sense how the story came to influence your adult life. Note: It is typically best to speak in the voice of an adult. Remember, the poems you are writing are for adult readers. In the course of the poem, it's good to concentrate on looking back on your childhood, not becoming a child.

4. *Earliest-memory poem.* Write a poem describing your earliest memory, using sensory, concrete language only. Provide specific details such as odors, sights, and all the colors you can remember. After getting the imagery of the earliest memory down, ask yourself how the poem fits into your life. Instead of using multiple abstractions to clarify the relationship between the earliest memory and your present life, write the second part of the poem using contemporary parallel details. Go back and forth, relating two brief narratives. You may use one abstract word anywhere in the poem, but try to keep both sections to fifteen lines. Remember, even as you describe an early memory, it's usually best to write in the voice of an adult.

5. *Narrative poem in stanzas.* Write a narrative poem on any subject. You may want to model the poem after the style of a narrative poem above. Set the poem in uniform stanzas.

6. *Journey poem.* Write a poem in which you take a trip and end up in a place totally unexpected, perhaps a foreign countryside or alien town or in the throes of an exciting and/or suspenseful discovery. Tell the story while focusing on graphic action verbs.

7. *The story of an object.* Like dollar bills, all objects have a story—or you can make one up. Seize upon any object and imagine the object owns a consciousness. Just as a dollar bill passes through many hands (and, thus, lives), an object may also pass through other lives. After all, we human beings do the same. Now tell the story of its life, or the story of its most unforgettable moment. Personify the object. Make it no more than one page.

8. *End-of-adolescence poem.* Write a poem about a moment in which someone has an experience that signals the end of an adolescence that had been characterized by a relatively carefree existence and the beginning of adulthood that is now marked by a sudden recognition of mortality or serious responsibility. Be sure to paint a clear picture of events leading up to the moment of new understanding and maturity.

6

EMPATHY AND CREATIVITY

Becoming the Other

Once poets become adept at letting their imaginations range deep within and far outside themselves, they can take us inside events that they have not experienced. After all, fiction writers do this all the time. They write about historical events with uncanny authority. When in *Beloved* Toni Morrison writes about the slaves who lived a century before, there's no doubt about the verisimilitude of her characterizations. We're also familiar with fiction writers who use their imaginations to write of many other seemingly alien experiences, especially those of the opposite sex. When in *Sense and Sensibility* Jane Austen enters the hearts of male characters in her remarkable evocations of love and jealousy, we are perfectly persuaded. We don't have to be alive during a social cataclysm to render its effect on people. And we don't need to be male to depict men—or female to depict women. We need two things: to be imaginative and to be practiced in empathy. **Empathy** is the act of projecting yourself into the life and mind of others. Sensitive to the feelings and even the imaginative lives of other people, empathetic poets write convincingly about other people by projecting the inner and outer lives of their characters. Because they don't include too many of their own biases, such poets don't distort the rendition. They develop ways to avoid the strain they might otherwise feel in trying to "be" someone else.

If, at this point in the act of writing poems, you have regularly allowed your mind to break from its comfort zone of ordinary language so that unusual, evocative images percolate on the pages of your poems, you're probably ready to try stepping away from your own personal subjects and writing poems in the voice of others. At first it may be best to do so by writing in the third person. The following poem by Archibald MacLeish uses the third person to render the inner life of a mute eleven-year-old boy:

❋ Eleven

And summer mornings the mute child, rebellious,
Stupid, hating the words, the meanings, hating
The Think now, Think, the Oh but Think! would leave
On tiptoe the three chairs on the verandah
And crossing tree by tree the empty lawn
Push back the shed door and upon the sill
Stand pressing out the sunlight from his eyes
And enter and with outstretched fingers feel
The grindstone and behind it the bare wall
And turn and in the corner on the cool
Hard earth sit listening. And one by one,
Out of the dazzled shadow in the room,
The shapes would gather, the brown plowshare, spades,
Mattocks, the polished helves of picks, a scythe
Hung from the rafters, shovels, slender tines
Glinting across the curves of sickles—shapes
Older than men were, the wise tools, the iron
Friendly with earth. And sit there, quiet, breathing
The harsh dry smell of withered bulbs, the faint
Odor of dung, the silence. And outside
Beyond the half-shut door the blind leaves
And the corn moving. And at noon would come,
Up from the garden, his hard crooked hands
Gentle with earth, his knees still earth-stained, smelling
Of sun, of summer, the old gardener, like
A priest, like an interpreter, and bend

Over his baskets.
                    And they would not speak:
They would say nothing. And the child would sit there
Happy as though he had no name, as though
He had been no one: like a leaf, a stem,
Like a root growing—

MacLeish uses common vernacular to render the inner and outer life of the boy who can't speak. The poem renders the boy's frustration with the echo of accusatory adult words: "hating / The Think now, Think, the Oh but Think!" Most impressive is the way MacLeish makes the transition from the boy's frustration to his respite, the cool dark shed, where the understanding gardener gives the boy a place to relax, to feel at home. The poem's signature insight is to understand that when each of us is alone and comfortable, we might feel as if we're "no one" in particular. We just exist. In the shed, with the gardener's silent encouragement, the boy begins to develop, "like a root growing—"

MacLeish, who died in 1982, was not mute. In fact, he was a fine public speaker and a speechwriter for President Franklin D. Roosevelt, who appointed him assistant secretary of state for cultural and public affairs. A rhetorician, policy maker, and Washington insider, this worldly man also had such an empathetic imagination that he could release all the trappings of his political concerns and enter into the mind of a rural boy who could not speak. There is a lesson in his approach to art: For MacLeish, poetry writing was like the boy's time in the shed. He could relax and give up his public personality. He could be no one and give himself over to being another. We can all do the same.

The Historical Persona

Placing yourself in the shoes of someone who lived in a historical era can be an exciting, creative challenge. Just as MacLeish entered into the consciousness of a mute eleven-year-old boy, Norman Dubie, in the following poem, enters into the consciousness of a young German woman just before World War II started. Here, the first-person-singular narrator affects an eerie immediacy. Notice how the sad, elegant soliloquy of the highly observant speaker draws us into her life.

❈ Monologue of Two Moons, Nudes with Crests: 1938

Once, Lily and I fell from a ladder
And startled the white geese that were
Concealed in the shadows of the house, and
I wrote much later that the geese
Broke from the shadows like handkerchiefs
Out of the sleeves of black dresses

At a burial. When the matron was sick
It was work to carry the powders
On blue paper and the clear water
With a spoon into her large, cold room.

In the evenings we would look out
At the spruce trees. It was wrong to have
Visitors. It was wrong those clear nights
To remember that boys were out on the hills
Falling onto sleds or into their gray baskets.

We were two young girls with black hair
And the white cones
Of our breasts. Lily said, "I will put
My hand, here, on you and follow the rib, and
You can put your hand, here, on me,
Up the inside of my leg."
We spent that Christmas morning pressing
Satin skirts for the boys' choir. We take
Butter away from the closet.
We take the lamp away from the green
Cadaverous child who is not ours.
I have a little violin pupil who eats
Bread in cream.

We love the details mice leave in flour.
The way the clouds
Are low before a storm in early summer.

Lily slept with a Jew once in Vienna.
I opened my hand that morning
On a milk jug that had frozen and cracked

On the doorstep.
Yesterday, I saw the perfect impression
Of a bee in asphalt. It was under a shade tree.
Lily said, "I will kiss in the morning
Your mouth which will be red and thick
After sleep." She has left me
For a banker she met in the gardens.
The gas jets are on: they are
Like fountains of the best water. I am

Remembering the vertical action of two birds
Buidling a nest. It's in Munich and
Both birds are dark and crested,
But the female, I think, is the one whose
Nesting materials are wet things:

Twigs, leaves, and an infinite black string.

Common to theatre but very often found in modern poetry as well, a
soliloquy is a dramatic monologue rendering the thoughts of a character. By
getting deep into the girl's thoughts, Dubie recreates prewar consciousness.
He recreates the voice of a young woman who is still in love with a girl
with whom she worked as a maid. The formality of her speech, especially
the dialog ("I will kiss in the morning / Your mouth which will be red and
thick / After sleep"), mimics the way European relationships were highly
formalized during that time. Likewise, her employer is not called by name
but is termed "the matron."

More important, Dubie captures the sorrow of the speaker who is about to
die. The title tells us that the poem takes place in 1938, five years after the
Germans had begun the concentration camps. Since homosexuals were committed to the camps along with millions of Jews, we can assume that the gas
jets near the end of the poem signal her extermination by the Nazis. Taking
the safer option, her lover, Lily, has married a banker, thereby sparing herself.

Dubie's poem renders a different time, a different country, a different gender. Without straining, he opens his imagination to all of these things. By
doing some research on the period and by attending to key details (in this
case regarding speech and domestic work), the poet persuades us that the
situation is real, eventually making us feel the unspeakable injustices of
German society at the time. This mode of poem is the kind of project that
many emerging poets enjoy because it gives them a chance to enter a world
other than their own. Before you begin, ask yourself, "Who is the character?

What do I need to know about her historical period, if anything?" After you begin, let her personality determine the direction of the poem. Discover for yourself what she likes, what bothers her, what happens to her.

Dramatizing Current Events

How often have you pretended you were someone else? Dubie's poem is a **persona poem,** meaning the first-person narrator is a person distinctly other than the poet. Like most people, writers like to imagine being another person—and they can make art of this little mind game by writing persona poems. Intended to explore a different consciousness, persona poems can be especially good tools for dramatizing contemporary news events by rendering what the human situation is like behind the "facts" of the story. How are real people behaving? What are they thinking? How are they affected?

This persona poem by Julianna Baggot was written after President Clinton left office:

Monica Lewinsky Thinks of Bill Clinton While Standing Naked in Front of a Hotel Mirror

We will watch each other age
in front of cameras, in newsprint,

a public decay. It's already started.
Look at my new sway;

my body seems more ample
among the miniature shampoos,

the thin rectangles of wrapped soaps.
Look at the pale shifting of my skin

under the red eye of the ticking heat lamp.
And I've noticed your hair's gone white,

your face loosening.
              I'm shocked

how you can still appear—
not televised, not some public memory

of the two of us swimming valiantly—
but the intimacy of teeth,

>   breath and breathing.
And I carry you sometimes

>   for a day or two,
like a bird hidden in a pocket

>   and I imagine
that you know how I live.

>   And while the bird shifts
and rustles and keeps one wet eye

on my life, I am more purposeful.
I stride.

>   But today you see me here, naked,
standing in front of this hotel mirror.

You are someone who knew me before
I was the world's collective joke

about cigars, thongs, stained dresses,
when I was a girl named Monica.

I miss her much more than I miss you.

Unlike Dubie's unnamed persona, Baggot's persona is Monica Lewinsky, who is still mentioned from time to time because of her infamous liaisons with the president. Baggot's poem reminds us that public events often lead to private trauma for the people involved in those events—even long after the news is no longer "new."

Like most good writers of persona poems, Baggott is finely attuned to the habits of speech that reveal genuine personality. When writing about contemporary events, beginning poets should try to create speech that echoes the verbal traits of the people in those events. Using the ordinary vernacular of a young, professional woman, Baggot renders Monica Lewinsky's inner struggle. The poem's language is authentically reflective. The narrator doesn't speak with urgency; rather, she's saddened, not because she longs for the president but because she no longer feels her authentic self. She sounds as if she's writing an elegy to herself. And by placing her naked in front of a mirror, Baggot renders the vulnerability—and irony—of a woman known for her sexual behavior.

Baggot tells us about "Monica's" inner life by having the narrator provide both descriptions ("Look at the pale shifting of my skin / / under the red eye of the ticking heat lamp") and commentary ("I miss her much more than I miss you.") As here, contemporary event poems will be further enhanced when they provide readers with details that will signify the event in its own time. For example, Baggott's Lewinsky goes so far as to mention "cigars, thongs, stained dresses." We may cringe at these images, but they legitimize the reality and atmosphere of the times. Such texturizing imagery reminds readers what they may have forgotten, and thus returns them to their own memory of the subject. It's the poem's job to go further, to show readers the hidden story.

Myth

The persona poem is an excellent vehicle for reinterpreting myths. In order to explore changes in human behavior, some poets enjoy writing poems about mythic characters. The speakers are usually famous figures from classic mythologies who reveal something about their inner lives that leads us to question the traditional lessons derived from the myths. Wendy Barker is interested in the way Persephone, the figure from Greek mythology, is misunderstood. Stolen from a divine meadow, she's taken off to the underworld by the god Hades. Ultimately, her mother, Demeter, cuts a deal in which Persephone can live on earth during spring, summer, and fall but must spend winter down below with Hades. Persephone is typically perceived as a victim deserving great sympathy. Both a persona poem and a myth poem, Barker's rendition of the story reveals how Persephone is not the usual victim:

❀ Persephone's Version

My mother never
understood how, after that first time
(when the earth cracked and the blackness,
like a magnet,

dragged my feet down to the ore)
how after that, I went by myself, how
every October the pears rotting on the ground
blocked the way down, how

I burrowed under the brown fruit,
found my way, tunneling through loam
past bedrock, drawing nearer and nearer
to the fire. In the light of flame

veins of silver, clots of gold
fed my eyes,
my hands glowed scarlet
as I held them toward the hearth.

I never could explain him to my mother,
how I set up my own forge,
had my own hammer, tongs, built
circlets of rubies, diamonds, topaz.

He didn't nag like Apollo,
always saying "Look at me, look
up, look into my eyes when you
speak." I could carve all day.

Neither my mother nor her
brother ever understood
I went because I wanted to,
year after year. They never knew

that was how I was able
to return each April
to find Narcissus, and to feed
my brilliance to the breeze.

In one version of the myth, Demeter remains angered by the fact that her daughter must spend a full season each year in the underworld. Persephone returns after the winter and gives the roots and crops the power to grow again. Barker's poem reinterprets the myth. Rather than simply see Persephone as a victim of godly patriarchy, she recognizes that the annual winter interlude gives her a new freedom from the influence of her family and the world at large. What can be seen as a prison is now a kind of retreat in which Persephone individuates by making art.

Like poems based on historical or current events, myth poems give new poets a chance to expand their imaginations. Barker changes our perception of the myth by reimagining the conflict. The argument is no longer between Demeter and Hades with Persephone as the impotent adolescent child. Rather, the conflict here is about the mother's control of the daughter. By the end of the poem, Persephone is telling us of her own desires. Based on a myth that usually renders excess victimization, "Persephone's Version" suggests that sometimes dire circumstances can lead to unpredicted liberation. Barker's single change in perspective opens the classic myth to a new interpretation. Sometimes that's all it takes—a new angle of inquiry—and your poem begins to write itself.

The Psyche Under Pressure

In novels, in movies, in plays, in real life, we're all intrigued by situations in which human beings undergo severe emotional responses. In fact, narrators experiencing mental distress are often good for poems: the greater the urgency in the voice, the greater the tension in the poem. Poems about the psyche under pressure can make readers simultaneously anxious and fascinated. Like the protagonist in the next poem, many of the characters in T. R. Hummer's poems experience severe emotional turmoil when their native anxieties are exacerbated by traumatic external events. Notice how at first this speaker seems separated from normal existence, only to grow more paranoid:

St. Augustine

I was looking for the return of the body's story, a radical sunrise,
Starbursts over the estuary where fishing boats chafed the yachts—
But I only saw the city's brilliant towers, refinery lights wasting
Silver in the predawn essences. None of us had understood.
In the brain, there is a sensitive blister of images we call the lesion
    of light.
If I close my eyes on a morning in Florida, I can focus the bed
With its abstract tracery of sheets, the fanatical hotel paintings, the lovers
Still in coitus, the woman superior, both of them magisterially lonely.
What I remember is memory itself, breath, the tongue on the skin
Of the thigh, a shadow surrounding the furniture, something that is not
Precisely darkness, but an absence more pure, colorless,

The echo of the blind spot. Confession never happens in the dark.
There is always the naked blinding bulb dangled from the black cliché
Of the cord, the fist and its afterglow. I was talking about my life
In the metropolis of assassins, I was tied to the bed with golden ropes,
And the questions never stopped, the tying and untying of knots.
In the parking lot 27 floors below my hotel balcony, in the middle of the
  night,
A man beat a woman senseless and stole her empty purse.
When morning finally blew in, there were primitive herons mixed up
  in it,
Astonishing birds the stormy color of ocean, with wingspans wide
As a nine-year-old is tall: real birds, but the sort of image I could believe
Rises out of the deepest caves of memory when a blackjack cracks the
  skull.
Who knows what happens after the brain shuts down?
If you're lucky a thumbprint will glow on the plate glass door
In sunlight, the color of ectoplasm. If you aren't, that song you danced to
In the bar last night will turn up on the elevator's tape loop.
Over the water now, in a sky like the side of a mackerel,
A quarter-moon offers one of its half-lives to the bodiless sunrise,
A celestial residue smeared on the city morning. Seven Stars of David
Painted graffiti yellow on the firmament of asphalt liquify
In the criminal atmospherics of sidewalks' corruption and acidic dew.
A cruiser circles the pavement, its blue strobe corrosive and clean.
But what did the saints have left when their eyes dissolved in holy light?
Nobody's left to testify. The evidence washes away.
Take everything, somebody whispers. *I'll give you anything.*

The opening line, "I was looking for the return of the body's story, a radical
sunrise," is immediately disorienting. We're not sure where we are or what
the speaker means, though we know by the end of the first sentence that
he's in or near a city, that the urban landscape has a nearly hallucinogenic
affect, that the scene can spill into terror.

"St. Augustine" is a lyric in which high-velocity thoughts of a man are
depicted in a fragmented style; we understand he's on the verge of losing
control—though he hasn't quite yet. The man free-associates quickly
through a series of increasingly terrifying images. The speed implies that the
speaker needs to keep moving, to maintain an ongoing kinetic state, in order

to sustain his barely unified self. In short, the guy is scared. The ferocity of events outside the room parallels the horror he's feeling. The poem, then, is a fracturing portrait of fear.

In many poems rendering the psyche under pressure, logical sense often gives way to a fearful scramble of thoughts, one rushing to replace the other. While Hummer's poem may be slightly more scrambled than some, it models the mind of a human being near panic. New poets should remember that the poem has to make sense, that there must be conflict centered in a protagonist. Speed helps. The lines should move quickly; the images should change quickly. Most important, the reader needs to be able to order the details in a way the panicked narrator probably cannot.

The goal of this chapter is to begin to practice poems that take you out of your own comfort zone, maybe even out of your own life. In fact, the five types of poems here bring us a kind of news about a variety of human experiences. But it's not the usual news. When writing these types of poems, it may be helpful to remember what William Carlos Williams said: "It is difficult to get the news from poems, but every day, men die for lack of what is found there." As a poet, you need not worry first about reporting the kinds of news we might see on TV or read in the paper. Rather, you should create the human experience that is often lost in the telling. To create that experience, don't obsess about ideas. Relax. Block out that newsy world. Look into yourself. Call up intriguing images. Now, no matter what the situation of the poem, render the sense of being alive and in trouble.

"But," you might ask, "where do such critical situations come from?" Well, for some people, they just have to look out their window, like the narrator of this poem. Other poets look back on a time of crisis. Perhaps you almost drowned. Perhaps you were robbed or mugged. Perhaps you witnessed a terrible car crash. Some people like rewriting bible stories. Others like to reconsider fairy tales. Of course it may be just as effective for you to write a persona poem by listening to the words around you, the stories, the little vignettes, even the brief, sharp expressions of fear. Like you, your friends, family, total strangers, they, too, are fascinated by drama. You overhear them on the bus or in a coffee shop or before class or at work. Don't overlook the worried stare, the nervous tick, the fright in the eyes. Start with one of those; feel the fear . . . . Now, go with it.

THE POET'S NOTE CARD

The World Without, The World Within

1. Regional or world events can provide excellent subjects for poems.

2. One of the poet's jobs is to imagine what the experience felt like and to render that experience for the reader.

3. Repeat: It's okay to lie to get at the truth; don't be hostage to actual facts.

4. Myths and legends are good starting points for poems.

5. By changing traditional perspective, myths, legends and historical figures can be transformed as subjects into fresh new poems.

6. Narrators under psychological distress are often good "voices" for poems.

7. Readers are usually intrigued by situations in which human beings undergo severe emotional responses.

8. The place where key change takes place is always in the interior.

9. That interior must be rendered with urgency.

10. Anger and/or desperation are often the hallmarks of distress poems.

11. A good poet needs to listen to people express anxiety and mimic it.

WRITING EXERCISES

1. *News-event poem.* Pay attention to news events, preferably local events as they are described in your newspaper. Write a poem based on a particular news item. Place a summary quote in an epigraph after the title and before the first line of the poem. Use your imagination to fill in the untold details of the event, particularly the more subjective human responses. Be concrete. You may want

to write it as a narration of events leading up to the main news event, or a narration of events during or after the main news event.

2. *Newspaper-epigraph poem I.* Write a poem based on the following actual UPI news paragraph: "Justice Marshall McComb, 82, did not contest his wife's petition to be named conservator of his estate after she told the court her husband is 'obsessed with the moon. He gets quite excited about it . . . . He enjoys it but it's not a normal enjoyment of the moon.' " Place the passage between the title and the first line of the poem.

3. *Newspaper-epigraph poem II.* Choose a particularly strange or engaging passage from any newspaper, magazine, or literary work you've read. Use it as an epigraph and write a poem based on that passage. Make the poem even more intriguing than the passage.

4. *Quotation-epigraph poem.* Read through a book of quotations and select a quotation that is about anything except poetry. Employing strong concrete imagery, write a poem based on the quotation. What altogether new story does that quotation lead you to imagine? Try to view the quotation from your own perspective as a person living in this present moment. Try to forget why the original speaker said what he or she said. Don't be afraid to veer far from the impulse originally catalyzed by the quotation.

5. *Historical-figure poem.* Write a poem based on a famous or little-known event in the life of a famous person. Write the poem in the first person, if you wish. You may want to research the concrete specifics you'll need.

6. *Myth poem.* Write a poem that modernizes a classical myth. Rewrite the old myth in modern terms. For instance, Sisyphus is doomed to push a car up the hill forever. You may make yourself the classical figure if you wish.

7. *Fairy tale poem.* Write a poem that modernizes a fairy tale. Be sure to add a new twist to the story. You might want to blend the old tale with modern language or references. Most important, make sure your "revision" of the fairy tale has adult application.

8. *Letter poem.* Write a poem in the form of a letter. Tell two interrelated stories in the one poem. Make sure each story has a problem and that each problem enhances the understanding of the other. Be sure to make the events of the poem accessible to any reader.

9. *Letter-to-an-enemy poem.* Write a poem to an enemy explaining in concrete language how you are just like him or her and how this realization is the reason that you (1) hate the person, (2) fear the person, (3) have suddenly come to reconcile with or even forgive the person, or (4) all of the above. Use uniform stanzas.

10. *Overheard-story poem.* Go to a busy coffee shop alone. Bring a notebook. Buy a large cup of coffee and drink it slowly. Listen to the conversations of the people nearby. When you hear all or part of a good story, write it down. Take notes. Then go home and use the intriguing story you've just heard as a basis for a poem. Feel free to make up whatever details you wish.

11. *Imaginary distress poem.* Write a poem that renders the consciousness of a human being who is under extreme duress and who is either (1) about to act or fail to act in a critical, horrifying and/or tragic circumstance or (2) speaking after having acted in such a circumstance. You should make everything up. This exercise is something like the "change" poem in Chapter Four. While this type of poem is usually written in the first-person singular, you may write in the second- or third-person singular as well. Here, the narrator (your "persona") has been driven to a psychological extreme where "normal" perceptions of reality and morality don't necessarily adhere. When writing the poem, try to use sound and diction to capture the edginess in the persona's state of mind.

12. *True distress poem.* Write about something that happened in your life that was extremely difficult to bear. But write it in the third person. This way you may find yourself able to gain some perspective on the event and therefore create even more vivid language.

13. *Fear poem.* Write a poem that is intended to scare your reader. While the ending may be left unresolved (see the discussion of open closure in Chapter Five), make sure the poem has a transformative moment. Something is changed.

14. *Crime poem.* Write a poem about a crime. It can be about friends proposing a crime to each other and never executing it. Or it can be about an actual or imaginary crime itself. Find a way to emphasize the danger involved.

7

LEAPING THROUGH TIME AND SPACE

The Poetic Sequence

When music videos became the rage in the 1980s many adult viewers were confused. The videos were hard to understand because they virtually never offered a continuous story line. Watching videos by the Eurythmics, RATT, Culture Club, Def Leppard, Duran Duran, and even Bon Jovi could be a mystifying experience if you had trouble tracking quick shifts in visual stimuli. By the 1990s bands such as Public Enemy and U2 produced avant-garde cut-and-paste music videos that differed in speed and style but achieved similarly high levels of artistry amid the usual mediocre commercial offerings. For many, no matter what the style of music, the video images jumped around too quickly and often without apparent logic.

But there were many others who enjoyed authentic originality and took delight in the new art form, especially if the music was aesthetically rich. Audiences who were devotees of modern art and cinema were excited by the immediacy of discontinuity. Certainly, avid readers of modern poetry were just as well prepared for "reading" MTV. After all, they were deeply familiar with the poetic jump cuts of poets such as T. S. Eliot in "The Waste Land" or Gwendolyn Brooks in "The Blackstone Rangers," both of whom wrote poetic sequences.

Unlike music videos, poetry must rely entirely on the arrangement of words. There are no actual music or light images—only words on a page. The poetic sequence can quickly facilitate shifts in time and space. Put simply, a sequential poem is divided into distinct sections. It's the poetic version of a collage or a montage. Overt transitions between segments are unnecessary because the reader understands that each new section may jump to a new time or place or attitude—or new versions of all three at once. Eventually, the main theme of the poem emerges. Just as the next chapter in a novel may signify a change in occasion or outlook, the next sequence can do the same. Because the form can accommodate the many splintering aspects of life, the sequence helps us deal with great internal disorder brought on by modern life. Life can be overwhelming, and the poetic sequence can render many different aspects of the pressurized, fracturing mind. (The poet Howard Nemerov said that a poem is more like a mind than a thought.) As we'll see, not all good sequential poems are about uncontrollable personal chaos—but, like all successful poems, they are about conflicts of the human heart.

Multiple Pictures

When writing sequential poems you have a few options. Most poets choose numbers to indicate the breaks, but you may choose simple visual signifiers such as asterisks or even lines. There are no absolute rules about the type of break you choose. If you want to force the reader into a reasonably long stop, Arabic numbers work well. Capitalized roman numerals make the divide between each segment even stauncher. On the other hand, lowercase, italicized roman numerals are softer, implying a less decisive stop. Other marks—e.g., three asterisks or a short line—may imply a yet softer, more permeable pause between sections. More important, you might want to use the sequential form itself to enhance the tension in a narrative—or you can maneuver the form to demonstrate the myriad ways a single circumstance or idea can be perceived.

In the following poem, Madeline DeFrees considers the different way her narrator, a nun, will be perceived upon leaving the convent.

With a Bottle of Blue Nun to All of My Friends

1
Sisters,
The Blue Nun has eloped with one
of the Christian Brothers. They are living
in a B&B Motel just out of
Sacramento.

2
The Blue Nun works the late shift
in Denver. Her pierced ears
drip rubies
like the Sixth Wound.

3
This is to inform you
that the Blue Nun
will become Mayor of Missoula
in the new dispensation.
At fifty-eight she threw her starched coif
into the ring and was off to a late win
over Stetson and deerstalker,
homburg and humbug,
Church and State.

4
When you receive this you will know
that the Blue Nun
has blacked out
in a sleazy dive
outside San Francisco.
They remember her in Harlem.
She still carried her needle case
according to the ancient custom.

5
You may have noticed
how the walls lean toward the river
where a veil of fog hides a sky diver's
pale descent. The parachute

surrounds her like a wimple.
That's what happens when Blue Nuns
bail out.
It's that simple.

The sequential form allows DeFrees to demonstrate the pressures she experiences upon leaving her vocation as a nun. It helps to know that "Blue Nun" is the brand name of a wine. And that many Catholic nuns also dress in blue habits (long robes) and wear wimples (cloth wrappers placed around their heads, neck and chin). And that, upon becoming nuns, they enter the convent and take vows of chastity. Nuns are typically held in high esteem; they're ideals of virtue, discipline, and charity. As the poem indicates, however, when a nun gives up her "calling," her family and friends can be threatened in a variety of ways.

Each of the sections here is a small vignette that plays against type. We expect nuns to be pious and irrevocably modest. But under the capricious wit of this poem, a woman is breaking free from cultural expectations. Not only is she announcing her own declaration of independence, but she's forecasting the kinds of extreme reactions that her leaving the convent will inevitably produce. The poem is, in effect, an exercise in surprise and hyperbole, and sequencing gives DeFrees a way to render the variety of strange critiques.

DeFrees uses five sequences to provide five different views of the narrator's life. We see how she sees herself in the act of being seen by others. Each sequence relies on exaggeration, and each manages to depict a truth: Despite the fact that she has never rejected her faith, she knows others will act as if she had. As the last section illustrates, not only will her new life result in the usual hardships one encounters when making a dramatic vocational switch, but she will also be more isolated than before. This realization is the transformative moment. She understands that those who once revered her may abandon her and that her life will be freer and more difficult. The sequential form provides DeFrees with a way to depict the effect of this isolation. While she doesn't need to worry about transitions, she keeps the poem unified, primarily by building the poem around the central act of leaving the sisterhood, by rendering the exaggerated anticipations of those who know the nun, and by punning on the term *Blue Nun* in each of the sequences.

Multiple Stories

Each numbered sequence can serve as a hard break in a poem, much as a numbered chapter can serve as a clear break in a novel. By staggering the elements of the story, you can raise its tension. Enumerated sequences, therefore, enable you to divide a large story into ministories. The effect is to raise the dramatic pressure. In the following poem by Wanda Coleman the numbers dramatize the anxiety in the relationship between the narrator and her romantic partner:

❀ You Judge a Man by the Silence He Keeps

1

he calls to tell me something. the something
gets caught and can't make it out
he struggles with it over the wire
my eyes straining to sniff the slightest touch

2

biting snarling snapping words come out dum-dum bullets
into my chest and blood jumps out on me
and a little gets on him
he goes into the bathroom for a towel
hands it to me, mutely

3

dialing the phone number
click—he's there on the receiving end
I hear him waiting for my voice
hang up hastily, flushing
he knows it's me

4

my eyes are trapped in his fists
his mouth shapes the syllable that translates bitch
the scream hides between cold sheets
it snuggles against my thigh

5

his smile enters the room cautiously
finds its way to my face
stays until I wash.

Here Coleman uses the sequential form to depict a cycle of intimacy and withdrawal in a relationship. While each section details part of the cycle, the chapterlike numbers force the reader to pause before anticipating the next stage. The first section is predicated on a phone call that the troubled, often silent man makes to the narrator. Something is bothering him, and it's intimidating the relationship. Whatever's bothering him seems like a trapped animal. In section 2, the couple is together. The man spits out "dum-dum bullets" (soft-edged bullets designed to explode on impact), and the woman is "wounded" by his remarks. In fact, each sequence is a different stage in the cycle, and key metaphors dominate all but the middle section: The man is a trapped animal; his words are bullets; his anger is a scream; his entrance is a smile. Throughout the poem, the narrator varies her response to his volume or his silence.

Notice that between sections 1 and 2 there is no transition announcing that both people are in each other's presence. In each sequence, Coleman simply jumps to the next scene, which is, almost inevitably, a surprise. For instance, in section 3 they're apart again; this time the woman calls the man, only to hang up on him before he speaks. In section 4, the scene shifts once more and they're together in bed, where his anger has wed itself to their intimacy. Between sections 4 and 5, we can assume they part physically, perhaps into separate rooms. Now he returns, smiling temporarily. Coleman uses the poetic sequence to demonstrate the way a relationship can quickly shift in and out of familiarity and confidence.

Neither this poem nor the DeFrees poem is especially long, but the form enables both poets to depict a good deal. As these models demonstrate, when writing in the sequential mode you are freed from transitions. You can shift quickly, much as the mind shifts rapidly from one subject to another. On one hand, you can use enumerated sequences to show simultaneity of perspectives or attitudes. On the other, you can use the form to render a series of external events.

Flashbacks, Narratives, and the Lyric

There are, of course, other options. In many poems, you might find it liberating to try combining both narrative and reflection in a sequential poem. After all, since the sequential form is well-suited to facilitate backward or forward shifts in time, you could potentially describe an intriguing scene, then tell a story set in that scene, then use highly imagistic metaphors to reflect on the story, and then go on to provide different but thematically related stories and reflections—or some variation on this method. If your poem spills past a page or so, you should remember that like all poems, longer poems must find ways of keeping the reader intrigued. Generally, you want to invest a longer poem with three things: an arresting narrative that echoes throughout the poem, some kind of intriguing language that keeps readers involved, and a compelling theme that warrants the complexity of the form.

In this evocative six-part poem, Martha Serpas weaves together past events about growing up female in Louisiana. The first girl in her family, she's trying to pin down her adult identity, which is still evolving.

First

1.
    the oyster grass gathers
around the bow, then the white housefronts,
a saving wash across the shore.
Porches where grandmothers
shell pecans and watch children
ferry the bayou to school. *Au revoir*,
but they do not answer, their language
beaten out of them.

History thickens like warm
air on a June night. At sixteen

We sat on Claude LeBlanc's
dead uncle's front porch and drank to our selves.
    I drove my Buick right up the lawn,
as if I could will myself into that grave beginning,
or smash it, like a lovebug, against the grill.

2.
I was born, late one season,
in a blue tin clinic, Our Lady
of the Sea. My mother slept—
or tried to. A jaundiced barmaid
played chank-a-chank music on the ward,
while her boyfriend chain-smoked.
I was somewhere, quiet.

During Betsy I was in the womb.
By Camille, just out. By Carmen
I knew what *native* meant
and that my father was not.

3.
The boys' side, the south side, at Holy Rosary—
damp and mysterious—had the ball field
and most of the swings.
Sometimes I walked to the end
of the north's covered sidewalk and watched
their khaki figures flung across the grass.

Under the silktrees I told myself
I was a character in a bedtime story.
I'd forget my name, then remember,
the field blurring into pink mimosa
blossoms and flat bean pods.

After morning rain the road
steamed like dark roast coffee.

4.
At Mardi Gras he wore a large
translucent mask, black eyeglasses
strapped across the nose, and rode
with all the other fathers,
Krewe of Neptune, Float 28.
I stood on the car hood and waved.

Beads by the gross
rained all over me.

5.
One night I was driven out of a pool hall
two-hundred yards
from the house that I grew up in,
tossed out like an outsider—a *Texian*.
Exile at least claims a severed belonging.

In my mind he leaves
quietly, stops among the oyster-shells
to wipe dust from his soles—
he is the eye of my storm—
as I brandish my cue, a crusader
just landed on the white coast
of a fearful new world.

6.
Since I was born I have felt the earth
pulling away toward
a white coast of brilliant foam
and sand, gleaming not with some
great absence, but with the fusion
of all possibilities, radiant without color:
wild marsh and oyster grass on a trackless
path for a roustabout God.

Serpas uses numbered sections to present an account of growing up in bayou country. Each segment of the poem tells a little story from the narrator's life. The segments also hold lyric passages that render something about her interior life as well.

The opening section begins in the present tense, but then switches to an incident from the past. The narrator is well aware of the thick "history," not only of this locale but also of that which is "fearful" for girls and women everywhere. The grandmothers don't speak much because their language has been "beaten out of them." In this stifling context, as a teenager she once drove her car "right up the lawn"—an act of independence. The second section is a flashback to the narrator's birth between two hurricanes; figuratively, we can see she's as wild or unpredictable as big storms, though she also acknowledges her native roots. The next enumerated break gives Serpas an opportunity to move without transition to a scene from the narrator's grammar school age, in which the girl imagines herself as different, a fictional character. Due to her sex, the narrator doesn't have access to the ball field. The fantasy here gives her a way to transcend the disadvantages experienced by girls. We can presume that section 4—about her father's role in a Mardi Gras krewe—takes place at roughly the same age. During the parade his beads "rained all over" her, a sign of his love. By section 5, she's considerably older, a young woman kicked out of a pool hall.

As we've seen throughout the poem, girls and assertive women were kept out of certain venues and experiences traditionally meant for males only. Like her father, the narrator is not native to the pool hall, especially since she wants to play pool rather than passively watch the men. Though he apparently leaves her family ("In my mind he leaves / quietly"), her father is strong and loving, a man who has always seen something special in her, perhaps a strength of character, something he himself needed because he was not a "native." The transformative moment occurs in the sixth and last sequence, which shifts into a far more reflective voice. Here, the narrator links the vision of the "white coast" with that of a more accommodating, liberating God, one who loves strong-willed, similarly "roustabout" women. The poem ends on an exquisite lyric (and lyrical) moment: She shows us how the coastal topography represents that ecstatic potential.

The poem's structure grants Serpas the freedom to do many things. She shifts back and forth in time. She extends the imagery of the local environment throughout the poem. She offers revealing stories as well as two key, empowering fantasies. And she reflects on the "path" her unconventional life has taken. Because she relies on sequencing, she can include all of these devices without worrying about transitions. Given the quick shifting that a sequence can provide, "First" mimics the way the human mind works as it maneuvers in an indirect, associative manner toward some kind of cumulative sense, even when that sense is more provisional, less conclusive.

Nonnumerical Sequences

Some poets employ nonnumerical breaks in poems to facilitate a reflective consciousness rather than a series of related episodes. Sometimes nonnumerical sequences can simply imply a less intentionally logical relation between sections, even when the sections are narrative in style. In the following, almost prayerful poem by Charles Wright simple lines are used as breaking devices to suggest a mind considering the mysteries of human identity. Wright ponders the words he kept in a journal while in Europe years ago:

Light Journal

To speak the prime word and vanish
                              into the aneurysm
Unhealed and holding the walls open,
Trip and thump of light
                              up from the fingernails and through
The slack locks and stripped vessels

At last to the inarticulation of desire . . .

———

What did I think I meant then, Greece, 1959:
                              Beauty is in the looking for it,

The light here filtered through silk,
The water moving like breathing,
Moving in turn to the tide's turn,
                    black thread through the water weave.
Whatever it was, I still mean it.

Everyone stands by himself
                    on the heart of the earth,
Pierced through by a ray of sunlight:
And suddenly it's evening.

It's odd what persists
                    slip-grained in the memory,
Candescent and held fast,
Odd how for twenty-six years the someone I was once has stayed
Stopped in the columns of light
Through S. Zeno's doors,
                    trying to take the next step and break clear. . . .

Notice how the lines Wright uses to separate the sections suggest far less linearity than numbers might. The narrator is mystified by both the words he wrote long ago and the strangeness of existence itself. While all the sections relate to the other sections, each section is also self-contained. By the end of the poem the narrator happens upon the fact that his past self seems distinctly separate from his present self, even though that old self is still doing what he's trying to do now: find a way to understand the universe and break clear of unknowingness. Because the lines imply no order or hierarchy, the poem is a kind of circular, free-associating meditation.

While there's no reason to feel you must be as philosophical as Wright is here, you, too, might try employing nonnumerical breaks (lines, asterisks, ellipses, etc.) to foster a reflective atmosphere in a sequential poem. Perhaps you've been pondering a quiet series of images that intrigue you, that you've been thinking about for a while. These might lend themselves to the nonnumerical sequence. After all, even if you aren't yet sure what they mean, your poem might be about the way you ponder them rather than their ultimate meaning.

THE POET'S NOTE CARD

Breaking Poems into Wholes

1. Enumerated sequences can facilitate shifts in time and space.
2. In sequential poems overt transitions are often unnecessary.
3. Poems benefit from surprise, and sequencing generates surprise.
4. The sequence provides an excellent opportunity for flashbacks.
5. Sequences are often good for telling more than one story at a time.
6. In order to maintain the reader's interest, longer works especially benefit from three things: a captivating narrative, intriguing language, and a compelling theme.
7. Sequences can help to unbottle associative themes and multiple narratives.

Revising Toward the Sequence

Just as music video directors improvise on the spot, writers such as DeFrees, Coleman, Serpas, and Wright improvise structure as they're writing. Poets rarely plan out each section of a poem. The sequence allows the writer to cope with chaotic concerns. It helps to unbottle associative themes and multiple narratives. Since poets don't always plan a poem's structure ahead of time, sequential poems often start more conventionally.

For instance, you may begin writing a poem you believe will be of average length. Rather than funnel into a singular lyric or a descriptive moment, the original image may lead you to wider, more diverse scenes or themes. You can sense some creative potential exploring these concerns, so you might choose not to force the poem into that tighter structure. Instead, you investigate various imagistic tributaries that don't seem obviously connected—and yet you can sense that they are. Perhaps it's sheer associative linking. Or perhaps you "hear" a tone connecting everything. As that tone becomes clearer to you, you can revise each section with more certainty. Such a method is called **recursive writing.** As you proceed, you realize how previous sections may be altered. You may see that you have too many bulky transitions. Perhaps you're spending too much time and space on wasted words. That's when the option of the sequence emerges. So you go back and begin to divide the poem into sections. You write and revise and delete, always returning to that nearly magical, hidden, poetic tissue that connects everything you've written. Ultimately, you find all the images, metaphors, sections, and themes of the poem meshing into an intricate whole.

The sequential form becomes an option when—in the process of creating the poem—the poet eventually senses that a variety of small, differing narratives and metaphors might be best-suited to explore some complicated aspect of life. They can be brought into an organic relationship to one another under the larger umbrella device of sequencing. Whether you're writing about the way others view you, or about a love relationship that never finds comfort, or about coming to terms with your own uniqueness in a close-minded culture—or about any intricate, multifaceted aspect of life, the poetic sequence may be the form that helps you bring the many related factors into aesthetic balance.

WRITING EXERCISES

1. *Sequential poem.* Write a poem using enumerated sequences. Note the jumps in time and space a poem can take simply by starting a new section.

2. *Multiple pictures poem I.* Write a poem that describes multiple ways of observing any single object. Enumerate each section. While writing your first draft try to be as idiosyncratically imaginative as you can. Then, while revising, see if you've created an unstated connection between the ways you are seeing the object. If you have created that connection, let it guide you into imagining a helpful title.

3. *Multiple pictures poem II.* Write a poem that describes multiple ways of rendering radically different perspectives on a highly emotional issue. Try to invest the poem with several different and unexpected metaphors.

4. *Multiple story poem.* Using sequences, write a poem that tells a story. Adding key details to the "plot," use each section to raise the drama in the narrative. Let it build, holding off the transformative moment for as long as possible while also keeping your reader with you.

5. *Two-narrative-sequence poem*. Using enumerated sections, write a poem that alternates between two dramatic narratives. In the beginning, don't show the reader how both are ultimately linked. By the end of the poem, of course, you want to bring both stories together. You may want to concentrate on tight, sharp lines.

6. *Reflective poem*. Write a sequential poem that combines narrative and reflection. Be sure that each section relates thematically to every other section. The challenge here is to keep the reflective sections short and highly metaphoric. Be sure not to indulge in overt philosophizing.

7. *Nonenumerated-sequence poem*. Write a poem that uses nonenumerated breaks to indicate changes in subject, time, or space. For instance, you may wish to break the individual sections up with three or four asterisks or with a thin, dark line. Discover which suits you best.

8. *Old-poem-sequential-revision*. Take an old poem that just hasn't come together for you. Does it describe more than one event? If so, break the multiple events into sequences (with or without numbers). Try rearranging the chronology in order to give yourself a new perspective on the conflict.

8

FRAMES AND FORMS

Free Verse and the Question of Form

Robert Frost famously said that writing free verse is like playing tennis without a net. While most American poets would disagree with Frost today, he believed that formal structures—predetermined rhythm, rhyme, and repitition—encourage poets to find alternative ways of expressing themselves. If, for example, you decided each line should be eight syllables and every other line was to rhyme (*ababcdcd*), then you would be compelled to invent intriguing language to suit these particular conditions. Since poetry relies so much on surprise, a formal poem challenges the writer to satisfy the sound patterns while also making sense. In effect, because form leverages invention, it catalyzes creativity.

While some contemporary poets who write in free verse also dabble in traditional forms, these same poets do not believe that free verse is without formal requirements. As the poet T. S. Eliot once said, "no vers [verse] is libre [free]". Writers of free verse—i.e., the large majority of American poets—almost always apply formal measures to their poems, though these conditions are usually more irregular or inconsistent than those found in traditional poems. Most poets believe that the imagination can catalyze magically surprising language without the presence of

121

predetermined structures. These writers are certain that the form of the poem should emerge as the poet is writing the poem. This kind of emergent shape is sometimes called **organic form**. For instance, if you begin writing about a snake that you suddenly come upon during a hike in the woods, you might begin to intuit that undulant sentences and *s* sounds are alliterative devices that will make the poem livelier. Visually speaking, the *s* even resembles a snake. You may not want to convert the *s* poem to a fourteen-line sonnet, but you will find ways to render the snake and your own reaction to it. Perhaps you'll find sibilant sounds while enjambing your lines, thereby imitating a snake's movements. Many American poets suspect that, too often, poems with traditional formal requirements inhibit imagination, leading to work that suffocates itself or sounds stilted. So who's right?

In effect, both groups are correct. Skilled formal poets can use the demands of form to innovate. Skilled free-verse poets can discover effective formal devices while writing the poem. But why do comparatively few American poets write in traditional form? There are a number of reasons. For one thing, formal poets usually favor rhyme, and, unlike the romance languages (Italian, Spanish), the English language is difficult to rhyme. Most word endings don't sound the same. Given the sonic variations of the language, poems that rhyme risk sounding rhyme-led, as if the word choice satisfies sound rather than sense. Frost began writing at a time when readers of verse expected and liked the sound of rhyme. He was brilliantly adept at rhyming because he had an ear for bringing common words together so that both sound and sense were satisfied. Even so, while some of Frost's greatest poems—"Mending Wall," "Home Burial," and "The Witch of Coos"—do not rhyme, others—"A Winter Eden" and "My November Guest"—don't sound quite as natural as many contemporary readers might prefer. Their rhyme and rhythm effect an unpleasing, sing-song quality. The trick is to use form to create dynamic ways to express yourself in a present-day vernacular.

Syllabics

While contemporary poets write primarily in free verse, many have written at least a few poems in some kind of traditional, predetermined line length or rhythmic arrangement. By restricting yourself to an exact number of syllables per line, or to a regular beat in a line, you might find that the form makes you stretch your imagination in order to find just the right words. But first, a few definitions: The term **syllabics** is used to indicate lines requiring a certain number of syllables, though not a certain rhythm. Today, some poets write in syllabics, thereby eschewing a predetermined rhythm. In these poems, though, one can often hear the "ghost" of iambic pentameter. Here's a disquieting poem by Samuel Maio that uses syllabics to render the consciousness of a man who visits a gathering in which another man displays an idiosyncratic collection of the personal items of anonymous dead people.

Reflections from a Pastel-Covered Box

Containing her life's most precious pictures,
All taken since their divorce some years ago,
How often she removed it from the shelf
Of the bedroom closet and reminisced
During the final months of her dying,
Or whether she wished it found afterward,
Or how it came to remain the possession
Of a stranger, he didn't care to know.

He thought of her delicate hands wrapping
The box with a decorous precision—
Her deliberate measuring of his worth
He saw reflected in everything she left.
She would have let the lid fall gently closed.
Now it's opened before him, in the hands
Of his host for the evening, an old man
Filled with embittered memories of women—

Who explained away the strange collection
Of dead people's private remnants, acquired
From dealers in the macabre on both coasts.
"Unknown to me, every one of these dead,"
Said his host. "Not even as acquaintances.
I show their things for my guests' amusement."
The enchanting box was the first brought out.

"Let's guess, shall we, who was behind the camera."
"A husband," someone shouted! "Maybe not—
She's too happy," said a drunken other.

"A lover, then—look at this one in black lace!"
Asked by his host to offer the last guess,
He declined, turning instead to items
Other dead had left, hoping to find there
Something more personal to the living.

As the poem goes on, we come to see that the items are keepsakes arranged by their original owners just before death. It turns out that the collection contains an item—a special box with photos of a woman who was dying—that belonged to the visitor's ex-wife. While the poem doesn't employ end-rhyme, the steadiness of the syllabic arrangement provides a measure of the man's growing imprisonment. He's captured by an astonishing realization. We read with an absorbing eerie attention to the morbid circumstances. The visitor realizes that another man had taken the pictures of his ex-wife in the period before she died, which is why he experiences such an unsettling regret. That the collector is "macabre" only enhances the ex-husband's silent lament. The poem's syllabics add a kind of polite, uncomfortable control to the visitor's thoughts—perhaps the kind of restraint that doomed his marriage.

You might try a poem in syllabics before going on to a poem in metrics, which is a bit more challenging because it requires that you write in a predetermined rhythmic cadence.

Metrics and Blank Verse

The term **meter** is used to indicate a predictable beat, usually two or three stresses composing a verse unit or, more commonly, a **metrical foot.** The beat of a line is measured by hard and soft stresses (sometimes called "long" and "short" stresses). A single syllable may be long (stressed) or short (unstressed) depending on the words surrounding it. Note that both long and short syllables are the result of context: What goes before or after a given syllable helps to create an emphasis or stress. No syllable by itself is inherently stressed.

When writing in metrics, English-language poets have most often written in an **iambic** rhythm, which is a two-beat foot comprised of a soft stress followed by a hard stress. There are four other primary metrical beats: The two-beat **trochee** reverses the iambic pattern, delivering a long beat, then a short beat. The three-beat **anapest** is short, short, long. The three-beat **dactyl** is long, short, short. And the **spondee** is long, long. When a line follows its metrical rhythm, it is said to **scan.**

Many years ago the critic Babette Deutsch listed fine examples of each:

iambic: ˘ ¯
Thĕ braīn ĭs wīdĕr thān thĕ skȳ.   (Emily Dickinson)

trochaic: ˘ ¯
Eārth, rĕceīve ăn hōnoŭred gūest. . . .   (W. H. Auden)

anapestic: ˘ ˘ ¯
Ănd thĕ pēak ŏf thĕ moūntaĭn wăs āpplĕs, thĕ hūgĕst thăt ēvĕr wĕre seēn. . . .   (Alfred Lord Tennyson)

dactylic: ¯ ˘ ˘
Ăh whāt ă pleāsŭre ĭt īs tŏ dĭscōvĕr. . . .   (John Dryden)

spondaic: ¯ ¯ these delicacies
Ī meān ŏf Tāste, Sīght, Smēll, Hērbs, Frŭits, ănd

Floŭrs. . . .   (John Milton)

Most commonly, poets use five feet in a line; thus a poet using iambic pentameter would employ ten beats. Since it would otherwise have the clap-CLOP-clap-CLOP rhythm of children's verse, poets will vary the pattern of stresses within their primary metrical cadence. Formal poets inevitably use metrical variation, i.e., a change in the metrical expectation for the sake of idiomatic emphasis. In other words, by occasionally breaking out of the predetermined metrical cadence, they can better approximate normal speech.

Notice how Jim Barnes uses iambic pentameter and metrical varia-tion in the following poem about a man and a boy, each bitten by rattlesnakes.

�֎ Touching the Rattlesnake

The neighbor's leg was black from toe to thigh,
with yellow pus oozing from cuts he'd made
trying to stop the poison from reaching
his heart. He showed the three of us stumbling
into his house, after Sunday school set
us free, what he said we would be afraid

to see. The swollen blackness made me shudder
with adolescent sins I knew we were doomed
to hell for. He dared us to touch the leg

Tight as the shell of a dried gourd, the skin
seemed to break with each slight movement he made.
I left with the smell of venom in my lungs,
my eye careful with every rock we passed
on the way to the swimming hole. I lay
on the shoal and felt the current crawl along
my body until all thoughts of fangs were washed
away and the rattle of leaves above my head
seemed only leaves. *Amazing grace, how sweet*

I sang straight up into the Sunday sky.
The others splashed my face, and we wallowed
like carp in the mud. We could not know that one
of us would die before the sun went down, fangs
buried in his neck as he reached over a boulder
to pull himself up the face of the cliff above
the swimming hole. Nor that he would live just
long enough to climb back down, boasting that
he touched the snake before it struck his neck.

The neighbor did not die but thrived on guts
he said it took to have a snaky leg.
I could not forget the oozing blackness
and never crossed his door again, nor how
white the naked body of my friend lay.
The wind rose that late day and made the limbs
crash above our heads. That night it rained.
The sound of thunder and shotguns carried us
through a domain of snakes we would annihilate.

Barnes knows that the most important thing is to adhere to the narrator's authentic speech inflections, not to the predetermined cadence. The goal is authenticity of voice. As we know from his poem "The Sawdust War" (Chapter Five), Barnes is excellent at remembering childhood. In this poem an adult narrator looks back at a time during which two people he knew were bitten by rattlesnakes, one fatally. The iambic cadence gives the poem a kind of reflective control that it may not have had otherwise.

Look, for instance, at the opening of the last stanza; you can see that the opening two lines scan in very smooth iambic pentameter:

The neighbor did not die but thrived on guts
he said it took to have a snaky leg.

Remember that each syllable is a stress. The degree of stress (hard or soft) depends on the surrounding syllables and words. Standing alone, the words *did* and *not* would have virtually the same stress. But given the kind of inflection one would apply to this clause, *did* is stressed more than *not* in the line's iambic cadence. But normal inflection makes for a change in the next line in which Barnes applies metrical variation:

I could not forget the oozing blackness. . . .

In iambic pentameter the first two stresses should be short/long. But here Barnes converts to trochees (long/short) in order to stay true to the speaker's normal inflection.

If you try metrics, you might first try to make the lines scan as perfectly as possible, and then during revisions alter some of the lines so that the rhythm is natural and matches the narrator's feelings.

Rhyming

The desire for natural sounding speech drives today's formal poets to write in ways that typically subvert old-fashioned rhyming. When today's poets rhyme, they often avoid **hard rhyme** (*boom* and *doom*) in favor of **slant rhyme** (*gong* and *spring*) or **eye rhyme** (*gone* and *alone*). Sometimes they blend both hard and slant rhyme in the same poem. Since they are interested in simultaneously rhyming and providing a more natural type of speech, they also tend to **enjamb** much more than poets in the past. By guiding the grammatical flow of the line past the line break and onto the next line, they avoid the sound of a nursery rhyme while also sustaining both conversational and evocative sound.

Poets who use contemporary rhyme challenge themselves to imagine gists of language that not only make sense but also own the pleasing density that comes from repeated sounds. In this poem by Bruce Smith, marked mainly by slant rhyme, the speaker remembers working on cars with his temperamental father.

❈ His Father in the Exhaust of Engines

All his life I used my father
to get somewhere

else—the game, the shore, the power,
the color, the middle class, the other

side. When he bent over
the maw of the Ford—the generator,

the alternator, the plugs he muttered
motherfucker into, the sputter

and choke and dying spark—a fender
in one hand, a frayed wire

in the other, bent like a wanderer
in the middle ages before

a statue of the virgin—I swore
I'd never bow and scrap before

the orders. He swore
softly and finally, the R's

caught somewhere in the rivet and bloom
of the engine. A coughed *harom*

while we idled on the spur
of Philadelphia, America, nowhere

fast. A small purchase, a seizure
like what a moan and shudder

is from a man tortured
or bored or dying *la petit mort*

and I'm the son ignorant of motor
but prodigal of fuel and air.

I'm the emir of the four cylinder,
the chopped and channeled lord

of Detroit and Japan. I floor
it, my foot on his back, or,

his on mine, his face in the mirror,
his death doubling me over.

Smith uses slant-rhymed couplets to generate an auditory concentration
that dramatizes the psychic pressure felt by the narrator. Nothing about
the poem sounds rhyme-led. All of the near sounds reinforce the intensity of the speaker's memories as well as his guilty recognition that he
treated his father more as a vehicle than as a parent. He recognizes now
what he was too self-involved to recognize then: that, when his father
coughed, it was an indication he would die. (Sometimes associated with
sex, *le petite mort* is a French term meaning "the little death.") Without
those reverberant sounds, the poem may feel more prosaic, more distant
from its subject. As the speaker looks back into the rearview mirror of
history, his father's death hurts deeply—and the echoing rhyme adds
intensity to his pain.

Smith doesn't worry about syllabics or metrics here. Though it
moves with great fluidity, the poem has no prescribed beat. He
combines the liberty of free verse with the demands of end rhyme. Such
a style can be a particularly good model for beginning poets. This
way, when you first try end-rhyming you don't have to worry
about line length or metrics. You can initially concentrate on the
imagery and then on finding rhymed words without worrying about a
metrical requirement.

Of course, there is virtually an infinite variety of end-rhyme patterns.
Here, Smith employs couplets in an *aa bb* pattern. He may have employed
quatrains (four-line stanzas) in the same pattern—or he may have used an
ab ab rhyme scheme. There are far too many options for us to consider
here. The great fun of writing in any kind of rhyme is to explore the sounds
and stanzaic arrangements that best enhance the poem's meaning. Feel free
to experiment with the form that appeals to you—even if you have to
make it up.

The Sonnet

Certainly a prime tool for channeling imagery, sound, and rhythm into
economic expression, the **sonnet** is the most famous type of formal poem
in English. While there are many different types of sonnets, most have
fourteen lines, rhyme, and are written in iambic pentameter. The sonnet
is often divided into two rhyming segments, the first eight lines

(the **octave**) and the last six lines (the **sestet**). Generally, the octave presents a conflict and the sestet attempts to resolve the conflict, though you have the freedom to try all kinds of arrangements.

The sonnet was invented by Italian poet Guittone of Arezzo, and it was later popularized by Petrarch, the historian and first poet laureate of Italy. The octave of the **Petrarchan sonnet** repeats its rhyme scheme (*abbabbba*), and the sestet has several possible rhyme schemes that differ from the octave (*cdcdcd* or *cdecde* or *cdedce*). Validated by Shakespeare himself, the English or **Shakespearean sonnet** usually has a separate octave and sestet, but the rhyme scheme is typically marked by three quatrains and a final couplet (*abab cdcd efef gg*). Edmund Spenser yet again rearranged the sonnet's rhyme scheme so that the **Spenserian sonnet** links octave and sestet in one stanza, thus suggesting greater continuity of argument, while closing with an independent couplet that is usually indented (*ababbcbccdcd,ee*). John Milton wrote a similar sonnet, but in the **Miltonic sonnet** the octave usually enjambs right into the sestet and the last couplet is *not* indented (*ababbcbc-cdcdee*).

Italian or Petrarchan sonnet:	*abbaabba cdcdcd*
English or Shakespearean sonnet:	*ababcdcd efefgg*
Spenserian sonnet:	*ababbcbccdcd,ee*
Miltonic sonnet:	*ababbcbc-cdcdee*

There are too many other types of sonnets to go on describing. Many poets veer from the established patterns described here, often presenting a single stanza (as in the Spenserian sonnet) or breaking up the octave and sestet into smaller stanzas. These poets may also write the sonnet in a meter other than iambic or they may begin with iambic and add or drop stresses. They may choose to write entirely in a nonmetrical rhythm. Many use the form as a foundation for blank verse, employing metrics but eschewing rhyme. Some write fifteen-line sonnets. In the beginning of the twentieth century, the British poet Gerard Manley Hopkins wrote eleven-line sonnets that he called **curtals** (*abcabc dbcdc*). Ultimately, sonnets are remarkably elastic, and you can experiment with whatever form captures your imagination.

There is no one form of the sonnet that American poets prefer. In this example, Kim Addonizio satisfies the general requirements of the form while alluding to science and music in order to riff on a classical subject for the sonnet: love.

So What

Guess what. If love is only chemistry—
phenylethylamine, the molecule
that dizzies up the brain's back room, smoky
with hot bebop, it won't be long until
a single worker's mopping up the scuffed
and littered floor, whistling tunelessly,
each endorphin cooling like a snuffed
glass candle, the air stale with memory.
So what, you say, outside, a shadow lifts
a trumpet from its case, lifts it like an ingot
and scatters a few virtuosic riffs
toward the lock-down stores. You've quit
believing that there's more, but you're still stirred
enough to stop, and wait, listening hard.

Not only does Addonizio imbue the fourteen-line frame with iambic pentameter, she mixes hard and slant rhymes in order to invest the poem with a sensual nearness. Her second-person narrator recognizes that the feeling of love is chemically charged, but her realization doesn't diminish love's desirability. Here the contemporary diction flows in a prescribed sonnet movement from uncertainty to resolution.

If you remember that the goal is to write the best poem possible, then you can choose to break from the sonnet form (or any form) as you see fit—or as your poem demands. There's no rule, for instance, requiring you to use the octave and sestet form. Nor must the poem resolve itself neatly. You may choose to hint at the resolution in the first lines or you may resort to open closure in the last. Or you may stick to the rhyme scheme and break from the metrical requirements. You may write a sonnet in seven rhyming or unrhyming couplets if you want. Or you can write a sonnet in blank verse. Your choices are virtually endless; the sonnet asks you to be imaginative in many ways.

It's a truism that all poems require imagination. The sonnet gives you a brief, comparatively fixed form, which can help the mind's eye *and* ear engage new possibilities. If you're the kind of writer who responds to the sonnet's inward challenges, the old form can help you leverage new ways of painting pictures and making poetic music with words.

The Villanelle

Some poetic forms combine both rhyme and repetition of phrases. The **villanelle** can be a lovely structure, fostering a lyrical, songlike poem. In its strictest iteration, it consists of five three-line stanzas and a last four-line stanza; thus, it totals nineteen lines. The first and last lines of the first stanza alternate at the end of every other stanza, and they repeat themselves again at the end of the last stanza. The end-sound of the second line is repeated in the second line of every stanza, but no one word is repeated. The poem is especially challenging to write because it end-rhymes two hard sounds, and two lines are used five times each. Thus the pattern is as follows:

AbAA´ ab2A ab3A´ a4bA ab5A ab6AA´

Many contemporary writers choose to veer from this arrangement, primarily in two ways: In the second lines they don't necessarily maintain the same *b* sound each time. And in order to adapt to previous or subsequent lines, they may slightly change the syntax (or word order) of the repeated lines. Nevertheless, the form maintains its sorrowful musicality because of the recurrence of lines and sounds; narrators repeat themselves, as if they are coming to terms with a fact or realization. That's why the form usually produces a poem marked by the sadness of inevitability—though sometimes the tone reflects anger or resentment about inevitability.

One of the most beautiful American villanelles ever written was published in the early 1990s by Carol Muske.

❈ Little L.A. Villanelle

I drove home that night in the rain.
The gutterless streets filled and overflowed.
After months of drought, the old refrain:

A cheap love song on the radio, off-key pain.
Through the maddening, humble gesture of the wipers,
I drove home that night in the rain.

Hollywood sign, billboard sex: a red stain
spreading over a woman's face, caught mid-scream.
After months of drought, the old refrain.

Marquees on Vine, lit up, name after name,
starring in what eager losses: he dreamed
I drove home that night in the rain.

Smoldering brush, high in the hills. Some inane
preliminary spark: then tiers of falling reflected light.
After months of drought, the old refrain.

I wanted another life, now it drives beside me
on the slick freeway, now it waves, faster, faster—
I drove home that night in the rain.
After months of drought, the old refrain.

Not only is the poem richly American in its peripatetic motion; it is a perfect expression of the kind of resignation often found in Southern California literature or film. Notice how, as the narrator drives the evening highways and surface streets, she seems to move further and further into a realization she's not sure she wants to face. As we discover in the first line of the last stanza, the woman has been intending to make a big change in her life. We can tell from the rest of the poem that the same old life is, however, the one she still has. The transformative moment is nearly heartrending: She recognizes that not only has she failed to change her life, but that any new life would add up to the same life she owns. And there it is—that alternate, similar life driving by her in the form of other people. The echoing refrain special to the villanelle form enables her to emphasize the sense of entrapment brought on by routine.

Should you wish to try the villanelle, you might give the two repeated lines a declarative quality so that the lines before and after will flow comfortably. Most important, try to approximate normal figures of speech while avoiding convoluted, difficult syntax. That way you will find that even with simple language, the refrain gives the poem a melodic and existential affect that will inevitably add emotional depth.

The Sestina

Certain formal poems don't require rhyming. Instead, they repeat lines in a prearranged order. Many poets like these forms because they avoid the restrictions of rhyme while retaining the intricate melodic advantages of songlike repetition. Despite its complexity, the **sestina** is the most popular of such forms today. Consisting of six stanzas of six lines each followed by a final three-line stanza, the form doesn't necessarily require the lines to adhere to a metrical pattern. The last words of each line of the first stanza determine the order of those same end words in the following stanzas, including the tercet. Here's the pattern of end words:

$$1-2-3-4-5-6$$
$$6-1-5-2-4-3$$
$$3-6-4-1-2-5$$
$$5-3-2-6-1-4$$
$$4-5-1-3-6-2$$
$$2-4-6-5-3-1$$
$$5-3-1$$

In the last stanza, end words 2, 4, and 6 must be used either at the beginning or in the middle of the first, second, and third lines, respectively.

As with most traditional or received forms, other contemporary poets have not always abided perfectly by the rules of the sestina. Many poets enjoy altering the forms of the end words, shrinking and expanding line length, even adding stanza breaks. In the following example, Denise Duhamel plays against expectations by having fun with the sestina form while also making fun of the culture's obsession with women's breasts. Her title plays on the midcentury advertisements in which women wore Maidenform bras and claimed that they dreamed they were doing something in new, extraordinary comfort. Much of the poem exaggerates the comic notion of the ads. Duhamel even caricatures the brand name "Maidenform," which is meant to suggest an appealingly youthful body.

❈I Dreamed I Wrote This Sestina in My Maidenform Bra

In the 30s, A-cup breasts were called nubbins,
B-cups snubbins,
C-cups droopers, and D-cups super droopers.
In the 50s, a bullet bra could make a bombshell

of most women. Pointy torpedo cups
had every Hollywood starlet hooked.

But Tinkerbell was only a 32-A, flitting past Captain Hook,
Peter Pan admiring her nubbins
as he cupped
her in his hands and snubbed
adulthood. When he dropped a bombshell—
that he wanted to be a boy forever—she drooped

in his palm, wishing for a padded bra, her eyes drooping too.
Snow White was a respectable 36-B, just enough to hook
the prince without being tawdry. Snow was a bombshell,
though, to the dwarves, little nubbins
of men she snubbed
without meaning to, filling their tiny cups

with grape juice instead of wine. A couple
of times she even mixed up their names.
                              Cinderella drooped
until her fairy godmother found her the right bra. Snubbing
her flat-chested stepsisters, Cinderella hooked
herself into one sturdy 38-C underwire and two luscious nubs
emerged through her ragged blouse. The bombshell

of the ball, she was afraid to drop a bombshell
on Prince Charming, that she'd be cupping
well water and cleaning cinders by morning, nubbins
of pollen and feathers stuck in the straw of her droopy
broom.
    Sleeping Beauty almost looked like a hooker
with those 40-D knockers which seemed to snub

the Evil Queen's saggy cleavage. When the Queen's mirror snubbed
her in favor of the younger "fairest of them all" bombshell,
Evil cast her spell and Sleeping Beauty was off the hook
(at least when it came to housework). She lazed around, her cupped
hands solemn across her waist. All the tulips drooped
towards her to whisper into the pink nubbins

of her ears: *Never snub your dreams, drink from the cup
of your bombshelled unconscious, where para-droopers
unhook nubbins of meaning as you snooze in your Maidenform Bra.*

THE POET'S NOTE CARD

Shapes of the Imagination

1. Free verse is the primary rhythmic standard in contemporary poetry.
2. Counting syllables ("syllabics") is a good way to practice line structure before trying metrics.
3. Metrics are predetermined rhythmic patterns and lengths (e.g., "iambic pentameter") that poets sometimes use as guides for their lines.
4. Many contemporary poems are marked by a "ghost pentameter," i.e., a free-verse rhythm that approximates the cadence of iambic pentameter.
5. Conventional forms (i.e., sonnets, villanelles, and sestinas) are challenging structural devices giving poets an opportunity to invent strategies that appeal to contemporary readers.

Famous for using humor to expose the absurdity of social mores, Duhamel shows us how advertising can make women ridiculously self-conscious about their breasts. In this case, the reserved lyric sound of the traditional sestina is undermined by the cartoonish sound of her own merrily idiosyncratic version. Rather than refer to actual women or men, she refers to Snow White and the dwarves, Cinderella and Prince Charming. Though the sestina doesn't usually rhyme, she rhymes the first two end words, *nubbins* and *snubbins*, but she doesn't stop playing there: The nonsense word *snubbins* is transformed into *snubbed*. *Nubbins* is transformed into *nubs*, *cups* into *couple*, and so forth. She parodies the fear of fallen breasts by calling them *droopers* and *para-droopers*, thus not only critiquing an obsession with breasts but also explaining the underlying market success of the bra itself.

Like other formal poems, sestinas are tools you can use to expand imagination. Rather than challenge your facility for rhyming normal speech, the form gives you a chance to create speech that exploits elaborate repetition, both in a serious manner and in a seriocomic manner.

Ultimately all structural devices in poetry may be viewed from two points of view: that of the reader or that of the writer. Readers will normalize themselves quickly to the forms of their era. When Frost began writing, poetry was supposed to be "poetic"-sounding. Today we are a little less tolerant of traditional artifice. We prefer poems closer to everyday speech. Frost's more natural, realistic style was a bridge from the old expression to the new. In fact, one of the founders of modern poetry, Ezra Pound, said that poetic expression should be "nothing . . . that you couldn't in some circumstance, in the stress of some emotion, actually say." This is not to say readers today disapprove of formal poems. Rather than form-led turns of phrase, we simply wish to see received forms contemporized in one way or another.

For you, the poet, forms are not straightjackets. Even the most rigid structural requirements can serve to liberate your unconscious mind. You can turn to any form in order to organize the unpredictable world around you and stimulate your imagination.

WRITING EXERCISES

1. *Syllabics poem.* Write a poem no longer than twenty-five lines in syllabics. (You may want to try writing a fourteen-line, rhymeless sonnet in syllabics too.)

2. *Poem in blank verse.* Write a poem in blank verse. Remember, blank-verse poems consist of lines that have the same number of syllables and have the same pattern of stresses. They are "metrical," but they do not rhyme.

3. *Rhyming poem without metrics.* Write a poem that rhymes in the pattern of your choice. Avoid establishing a given meter; simply feel the freedom of the cadence within the stricture of your rhyme. Try not to go much beyond twenty lines.

4. *Rhyming poem in syllabics.* Write a poem that rhymes while using the same number of syllables in each line. At first, try not to go beyond twenty lines.

5. *Rhyming poem in metrics.* Now write a poem that rhymes while also using a metrical cadence.

6. *Sonnet.* While concentrating on imagery, try writing a sonnet using the template on the following page. Experiment with ways

to sustain relatively normal diction. Consider using enjambment.
You might also try slant rhyme. Both of these techniques will help
your language remain natural.

_____ (a)
_____ (b)
_____ (b)
_____ (a)
_____ (c)
_____ (d)
_____ (d)
_____ (c)

_____ (e)
_____ (f)
_____ (e)
_____ (f)
_____ (g)
_____ (g)

7. *Sonnet without rhyme.* Try writing a sonnet that maintains the
   usual iambic and fourteen line structure but doesn't rhyme.

8. *Sonnet without metrics.* If you'd like to loosen up the sonnet form,
   write one without metrics and with or without rhyme.

9. *Villanelle.* Try writing a villanelle. You might consider writing
   about a subject that involves habit or routine, say, something
   about work or commuting. Perhaps you might write about a person
   who has to take care of a sick relative every day. Or you might
   write about a daily babysitting job or a daily job working as a
   dishwasher.

10. *Broken villanelle.* If you are attracted to the lyrical sound of the vil-
    lanelle but find that the form is a bit restrictive, skip most of the
    rhyming *except for the lines that are repeated.*

11. *New Pattern villanelle.* If you decide that the ordering of words is
    too strict, please feel free occasionally to change the pattern or
    repetition.

12. *New Form villanelle*. Or if, like Duhamel, you feel that you might gain emphasis of meaning by changing the form of the words or even the stanza structure, go ahead and break from the formal requirements where you see fit. Remember, the point is to make a good work of art, not to bear allegiance to any one form.

13. *Sestina*. Try writing a sestina. Write your first stanza and then simply use the six end words in the received order for the rest of the poem.

14. *Predetermined sestina*. Instead of writing out the first stanza, this time try coming up with the end words *before* you write the poem. Spend some time thinking about the kinds of words that can function as both verbs and nouns or both nouns and adjectives. Try to make sure the words are both interesting and reasonably easy to enjamb.

9

STANZAS, PROSE, AND THE FIELD OF THE PAGE

Organizing Words on the Page

Received forms such as sonnets, sestinas, and villanelles have been handed down over the centuries with the idea of maneuvering the poet into solving the challenges of the metrical pattern, rhyme scheme, or repetition by inventing new manners of expression. You might find it helpful to start with a traditional form, only to break from the requirements slightly—or, like Barbara Hamby, entirely. On the other hand, you may apply form to a draft that's not quite coming into focus. There are, in fact, formal poetic devices that, while not considered received forms, may enhance a draft. These less restrictive forms help to arrange the text, the shape, and occasionally the white space of the page itself. Some poets begin the poem with these forms. Others find that when a poem may not be clicking along as effectively as possible they can apply these formal arrangements to the old draft as a way to facilitate new kinds of phrasing or angles of inquiry. Sometimes it's a matter of altering a stanzaic pattern before the poem opens up for them. Other times it's a matter of inserting more blank space between lines or between words in a single line. And at still other times it's a matter of dispensing with lines altogether and trying prose itself as a new "form."

Uniform Stanzas

As you've seen, some poets write a poem that's one long stanza or column, such as the poem we saw in Chapter Four, "Little Boy" by B. H. Fairchild. Poets often write in this style in order to convey irrevocable continuity or relentlessness. Others break the column by indenting key lines as does Lorna Dee Cervantes in "Uncle's First Rabbit." The indented line is often called a **dropped line.** Indenting lines in a column gives you some of the velocity of the columnar poem while indicating important shifts in time, place, or attitude. Yet other poets write in stanzas of irregular length, much in the way Thylias Moss does in "Maudell's Moon." Each stanza in this kind of poem simply adheres to the specific rhythm and duration necessary for the speaker.

As we saw in Chapter Five, however, many poets prefer to employ **uniform stanzas,** i.e., stanzas of the same number of lines. Uniform stanzas can be a particularly helpful organizing tool, especially when the poem shifts between differing attitudes or events. In the following poem by Alan Michael Parker, a tired working mother suddenly finds herself thinking about deeply important questions in life. In fact, the questions are so unusual that she thinks a god has visited her to do the asking. Parker employs the three-line stanza (often termed the **tercet)** as a tool to organize the otherwise scattered sense of her day.

Two Questions

The lunch shift finished, she leans against a dumpster,
catches her breath, smokes a cigarette.
The god arrives: What have you brought?

Only a brush, a book, and this, she says,
holding up the cigarettes and lighter.
What is important? She thinks the answer

must be the book, but it's not a very good book.
The book? But the god is no longer there.
She looks up. That's how a god should disappear,

she thinks. In a narrowing shaft
between tall buildings the light becomes shadows,
the dumpsters become monsters,

and the fire escapes drip with moss.
A few yards down the alley, a cat scratches
into a garbage bag, the plastic smacking, a sound

like applause. What is important?
Back inside the restaurant,
she checks the setups, restocks, tips the busboys.

If she speaks to anyone, she can't remember.
How like a god not to let me remember, she thinks.
At home there's still an hour before

picking up the kids from daycare.
On the table, the brush, the book, the cigarettes.
She'll need to get groceries for dinner;

she'll bring the kids to the store.
The brush, the book, the cigarettes:
something is important.

She considers how one of the objects
speaks to vanity, one to vice, one to learning,
although the book is not a very good one.

She flicks a bit of fluff across the table.
Of course, the questions might be symbolic,
since the god's a god: What have you brought?

She sips her tea, strong tea, China Black,
kicks off her work shoes, a relief.
What have you brought? What is important?

Good questions for a god to ask,
better than her own. She writes them down
on the back of a takeout menu,

rummages around, finds magnets in a drawer,
and sticks the menu to the fridge.
She checks her watch: time to get the kids.

The uniform stanzas add a visual and organizing structure to the harried thoughts of the woman. Notice that Parker enjambs the ends of most of the stanzas so that the poem can mimic the way the woman's endlessly busy life feels. You might wonder, Does she ever find the answer to the two questions?

When your stanzas are of the same length you don't have to maintain the same rhythm in them or the same number of syllables. As we noted in Chapter Five, you may find that it's good to practice uniform stanzas in order to help organize images in a poem. Two-line stanzas, or **couplets,** often lead a poem to read a bit quicker. In some cases, three-line stanzas **(tercets)** and four-line stanzas **(quatrains)** may help to slow the poem down further, as might five-line **(quintet)** and six-line **(sextet)** stanzas. You can even use radically differing line lengths within the uniform stanza form. Or, in order to indicate complexity of thought, you might, for example, alternate between two- and four-line stanzas. The whole point is to add some kind of set structure to the poem, thereby bringing confusing or chaotic events into a semblance of order.

Aeration

Many contemporary poets practice **aeration,** arranging lines with a great deal of spacing throughout. Aerated poems usually employ indentation and some double-spacing to make the poem seem mutable, chaotic, or whimsical. Most aerated poems use the open space to indicate a kind of mental independence in which the mind may "free"-associate quickly and reflectively.

In the next poem, Jacqueline Marcus considers the way the natural beauty of Hawaii can lead us to ponder the afterlife. Some critics have said that a poet should use the page as if it were a field onto which the poet projects imaginative language. The field, after all, seems open to infinitely different possibilities. Notice how Marcus uses aeration to demonstrate the manner in which the mind might associate a place with a corresponding sensation as if mental and topical geography cohere as print on the page.

✺Hanalei Bay

I could have easily stayed all summer,
lulled by the waters,
          taking the long way out to sea

when the tides rush slowly in,
tipping the waves magenta, upshore
from the trees.
        I could wait for the rain

to diminish this spot like a last chord,
easily, and without regret,
                                but something out there in the shifting light

breaks you,
and so you row a little closer to the shore.

A small breeze unbraids the bamboo, exaggerating its brilliance.

Let it fall with the waves in a downpour,
effacing the thread of rocks,
                            and the sun's loose claim to grief,

where fishermen walk the reefs, outside of time.

Birds turn *again* and *again* like hand-written notes,
scattered against a green sky.

Maybe we're here, just once, to remember these dazzling pines,
and the hush of waters,
                        and the low blue clouds

just barely touching the sea?

Maybe there is no final enlightenment,
                            no promise of heaven —

only the moon,
a sailboat skirting the harbor, the flurry of birds

in the sure ease of the heart.

As you can see, the lines seem to float. The speaker is fascinated by the way
the lush vista inspires thoughts of the metaphysical world. In the presence
of such inexhaustible beauty, the speaker wonders if this current paradise
isn't the only paradise. The floating images provide the reader with a different kind of freedom, a temporary effortlessness in which we are satisfied
with our own current existence.

You might prefer trying to write an aerated poem on the computer
rather than in longhand. As with any poem, the computer allows you to
experiment with different line breaks and visual arrangements, and is especially helpful when you need to visualize such improvisational spacing.
While writing an aerated poem, try out different structural looks until you
feel that the form of the poem corresponds to its sense.

Visual Caesurae

In order to indicate hesitation or deep thought, some poets insert white space right in the middle of a line. Adrienne Rich and James Dickey are famous for doing so, especially in some of their longer poems. Usually called **visual caesurae,** this technique is sometimes an effective way to render a fragmented thought process. (While some pauses are rendered by commas and other visual punctuating devices, an ordinary **caesura** is a slight breath pause in an unbroken line.) In the following poem, Stuart Dischell's narrator is out late at night by himself, experiencing a desperate, lonely moment in which he feels unable to think with confidence:

Between Two Storms

It was the hour between the dog and the wolf
The sun in the far corner   the half-moon rising
I was out   walking again   the iced-over
Unreflective street brittle underheel   there was
Something I wanted to wish for but I could not
Find it among the scattered notions   I could not
Cough it up like a bone in my throat for it was
Already dissolving   a half-eaten lozenge
Bitten   bitter   broken   I complain too much
Can't keep a secret   try not to tell myself anything
Anymore   just take it in like breath   the streets
The traffic   the glances people see with
Before passing   O   a star fell in the sky
Far away   in the yellow lights of a living room
A woman was   closing out the night   leaning forward
Over the sill   pulling down the shade   not
Abruptly or slowly but evenly   decisively   as if
All patterns and reflexes of her life brought us
To this one moment   a brownstone apartment   the back
Of her hand facing the window   her palm inward
Fingers bent in an absent wave   the crease of a lifeline
Farewell   the old year was done   the first square
Of a new calendar filling in   I kept on   I had
Little else to do   I was not expected anywhere

> It was good to be   insignificant   undesired   loose
> As a leaf scuttling along the pavement   a bit out
> Of season but still here   watching the cloudy evidence
> My occupation of the cold free air

The forced breaks give each line a staggered, hesitant quality that reveals the narrator's stop-and-go thinking. The speaker can't quite figure out what he needs; he only knows that he's outside in the cold evening, unsure of himself, clearly beset by existential anxiety. Notice that Dischell doesn't place the visual caesurae in every line—and yet in some lines he makes use of it more than once. The break doesn't appear with perfect regularity; if it did, it might seem false or programmatic. After all, the individual moments of anyone's tentative thinking are not paced out in regular intervals; they're erratic. Most poets use visual caesurae sparingly, mainly because the faltering, uneven rhythm can frustrate a reader. Dischell is clearly expert at using the long pause to show us how a worried, even disturbed personality has trouble engaging the world.

When you first try visual caesurae you might use the device a few times here and there in the poem. Keep in mind that the forced break is especially good at showing a person's cognition slowing down, as if the mind is stuttering. But also keep in mind that most people don't think this way very often.

The Prose Poem

Until now all the model poems we've read are lineated; they employ lines that end before the right margin. But because prose poems eschew line breaks, they give you an appreciation of lineated poems. After all, almost by definition, lines and stanzas afford you the ability to invest individual units of expression with tension. Many lines end before the phrase or clause does. That ending makes the reader a little anxious: What comes next? The subsequent line modifies the inference of the preceding line. There's tension at the point of the line break. When writing a prose poem, the challenge is to find other ways to ratchet up the dramatic pressure of the poem.

One of the qualities of the prose poem is its apparent naturalness. After all, the prose poem has complete sentences, not line breaks, to stop its potentially endless flow; it may proceed in the manner we talk. The challenge for the prose poet is to find ways to invest the whole poem with excitement, even though you don't have the benefit of the line. There are plenty of devices to choose from. Like regular poems, prose poems are often marked by persuasive rhythm, internal rhyme, repetition, alliteration, narrative, and, of course, intense lyric moments. In the best prose poems, the imagery can be startling.

This short prose poem by Robert Hass derives great power from both surprising imagery and a startling conflict between two people.

A Story About the Body

The young composer, working that summer at an artist's colony, had watched her for a week. She was Japanese, a painter, almost sixty, and thought he was in love with her. He loved her work, and her work was like the way she moved her body, used her hands, looked at him directly when she made amused and considered answers to his questions. One night, walking back from a concert, they came to her door and she turned to him and said, "I think you would like to have me. I would like that too, but I must tell you that I have had a double mastectomy," and when he didn't understand, "I've lost both my breasts." The radiance that he had carried around in his belly and chest cavity—like music—withered very quickly, and he made himself look at her when he said, "I'm sorry. I don't think I could." He walked back to his own cabin through the pines, and in the morning he found a small blue bowl on the porch outside his door. It looked to be full of rose petals, but he found when he picked it up that the rose petals were on top; the rest of the bowl—she must have swept them from the corners of her studio—was full of dead bees.

The poem is certainly provocative, and readers may sympathize with either or both of the characters. In a way, the absence of lines reduces the usual surface tension. Hass invests the poem with an extraordinary neutrality by using measured, careful language, drawing out the brief, superficially quiet events with even pacing. The surprising imagery of the last sentence makes a small moment between people into a powerful statement about sexuality, the body, lust, and honesty. Lines aren't necessary. One well-written paragraph can be remarkably memorable.

Of course you can write a prose poem using multiple paragraphs. In fact, some prose poems employ paragraphs the way lineated poems employ stanzas. Such paragraphs serve as visual markers that grant order to chaos while also offering a kind of visual rhythm, as in this mesmerizingly weird poem by Thylias Moss. After reading the poem, we may deduce that when the speaker was a child she had an imaginary friend and that the child has now grown into an adult with a split personality. The friend has not faded away.

An Annointing

Boys have to slash their fingers to become brothers. Girls trade their Kotex, me and Molly do in the mall's public facility.

Me and Molly never remember each other's birthdays. On purpose. We don't like scores of any kind. We don't wear watches or weigh ourselves.

Me and Molly have tasted beer. We drank our shampoos. We went to the doctor together and lifted our specimen cups in a toast. We didn't drink that stuff. We just gargled.

When me and Molly get the urge, we are careful to put it back exactly as we found it. It looks untouched.

Between the two of us, me and Molly have 20/20 vision.

Me and Molly are in eighth grade for good. We like it there. We adore the view. We looked both ways and decided not to cross the street. Others who'd been to the other side didn't return. It was a trap.

Me and Molly don't double date. We don't multiply anything. We don't know our multiplication tables from a coffee table. We'll never be decent waitresses, indecent ones maybe.

Me and Molly do not believe in going ape or going bananas or going Dutch. We go as who we are. We go as what we are.

Me and Molly have wiped each other's asses with ferns. Made emergency tampons of our fingers. Me and Molly made do with what we have.

Me and Molly are in love with wiping the blackboard with each other's hair. The chalk gives me and Molly an idea of what old age is like; it is dusty and makes us sneeze. We are allergic to it.

Me and Molly, that's M and M, melt in your mouth.

*What are we doing in your mouth? Me and Molly bet you'll never guess.
Not in a million years. We plan to be around that long. Together that long.
Even if we must freeze the moment and treat the photograph like the
real thing.*

*Me and Molly don't care what people think. We're just glad that
they do.*

*Me and Molly lick the dew off the morning grasses but taste no honey till we
lick each other's tongues.*

*We wear full maternity sails. We boat upon my broken water. The
katabatic action begins, Molly down my canal binnacle first, her water
breaking in me like an anointing.*

From beginning to end of this poem, Moss uses a repetitive rhythm that
adds a tension-filled order to the surprising developments. Each paragraph delivers another idiosyncratic picture of the narrator's interior
life. Perhaps the narrator has decided that she's not going to hide the
fact that she is psychologically divided into two people; by the end of
the poem she's giving metaphoric birth to her imaginary friend. (It helps
to know that the word *katabatic* refers to a warm, *descending* breeze or
wind.) It's as if the speaker announces that she's a split personality;
in fact, she declares her right to be just who she is. The use of italics
may intend to suggest the speaker is talking to herself. The poem is
made eerie by the fact that the speaker is not at all embarrassed by her
mental illness.

Just as the columnar poem with lines can create a sensation of relentlessness, a prose poem like this can produce a similar freefalling impression:
This speaker is not returning to world of the normal. For some readers the
poem may seem to cross the boundaries of civil decorum. But reality is not
always limited to socially acceptable expression—and neither is poetry.
In this case, the speaker knows she's different, and she asserts that difference as strength.

Most prose poems don't need the degree of oddness manifest in either
Hass' or Moss' poem—though as with all poetry idiosyncrasy helps. While
lineation is not an option, there are plenty of other ways to energize the
prose poem. In fact, "An Anointing" uses italicization, puns, a memorable
voice, alliteration, and other devices. It also relies on a strong, headlong
rhythm that is enhanced by repetition; the subject "me and Molly" is
repeated throughout. The poem gets much of its power by listing.

THE POET'S NOTE CARD

Nonformal Forms

1. Uniform stanzas can often help to bring an unruly or disorganized series of images into a more cohesive unit.

2. Some poems benefit from using "open space," that is, spacing the poem so that it seems aerated by the whiteness of the page. Such arrangements often resist the weighty directness of a conventionally shaped poem, facilitating, instead, a somewhat delicate, even provisional approach.

3. Visual caesurae are blank spaces in the middle of a line. These forced breaks can render the way a person's cognition might slow down, as if the mind is stuttering, usually when that person is under great stress.

4. Deceptively challenging, prose poems require that you marshal tools other than the poetic line.

Of course, there are myriad other devices you can use. Often, what's most fun about writing prose poems is discovering all the different techniques you can employ to generate a lively interest in the reader.

WRITING EXERCISES

1. *Stanzaic poem.* Write a poem no longer than twenty lines without stanza breaks. Reset the poem with stanza breaks. Use two-, three-, four-, five-, or six-line stanzas. Which works best for you? Do the stanzas offer a helpful sense of organization, or did the single-stanza column provide a more beneficial continuity to the poem?

2. *Aerated poem.* Try writing a poem that employs much open or "white" space throughout. See if the aeration helps to suggest a free-associating or meditative frame of mind.

3. *Visual caesurae.* Write a poem about a protagonist who is suddenly in dire mental trouble. Perhaps he can't come to terms with the

death of a recent friend. Or perhaps she has just received a bad medical diagnosis. Or perhaps the protagonist has gone without sleep for too long. Use visual caesurae to help demonstrate the individual's inability to think well.

4. *Prose poem.* Write a poem in prose. Try not to exceed 250 words, and use only one paragraph. Concentrate on action verbs, imagination, and surprise.

5. *Prose poem with "stanzas."* Write a prose poem, but try not to let any one paragraph contain more than one sentence. (And no cheating with semicolons!) Decide if the poem works best as a prose poem or as a lineated poem.

10

SURREALISM

The Logic of Alogical Images

We can look at a scatter of stars in the night sky and see mythological figures. We can look at clouds passing in the day sky and see ships or trains. We can splotch paint on the sidewalk and see Uncle Jake's face. Like Ezra Pound, we can take fragmented phrases of poetry and synthesize connections. Human beings seem compelled to keep things orderly. Why? Why don't we accept disorderly arrangements as nothing more than unconnected events, random data?

It seems that evolution produced in us an ongoing facility to classify or categorize, to make sense of information whether it is connected to a larger system or actually quite arbitrary. We don't always act reasonably, but our minds have a habit of making "logical" sense of stimuli—and as we develop out of infancy and far into adulthood, we tend to guide new stimuli through the same mental pathways that have served us in the past. This redundancy can be a problem, of course, because it means we get stuck in the same old habits of thinking. Because our way of processing stimuli gives us some control over our lives, we feel threatened when we forfeit our usual manner of thinking.

But surrealist poets want us to do just that—forfeit our usual way of thinking. They want us to cognate "outside the box," i.e., in a manner that affords unanticipated options for understanding. They usually want to liberate us from our dependence on ordinary logic, from the dictates of reason. Like surrealist painters Salvador Dali, Max Ernst, and René Magritte, surrealist poets intentionally create images that cannot exist in objective reality. They favor *alogical*—not *illogical*—thinking. Usually traced back to nineteenth-century French poets, **surrealism** is a type of art that renders nonsense or dream imagery in order to make us think in a different way. Many contemporary American poets practice different surrealistic techniques, but they all have one thing in common: They understand that no good poem is entirely surreal; there must be some link to objective reality. If you want to write surrealist poetry, your poem needs to keep some connection to the real world. A surrealist poem that is nothing but surreal may seem irrelevant to everyone but you.

While all poets develop ways for breaking from their quotidian thinking, surrealist poets can seem even more removed from the strictures of everyday logic. They are adept at freeing their imaginations from the usual one-to-one similes. You may be writing about a rock and are not sure what you're going to say, but there's something about that rock that intrigues you. For one thing, it's almost perfectly round. For another, it feels a little lighter than it should. There's something about the rock that makes it seem more than, well, a dull rock. But you can't quite figure it out. You try describing it. You write "the round rock looks like a grapefruit," but not only is this simile boring—it doesn't quite capture what you sense about the rock. A surrealist poet might approach it from a different perspective. Your rock might produce grapefruit juice, cut itself into bitesize wedges, and speak a foreign language. By the time you're finished with the first draft, you intuit that the rock isn't so different from your friend Jake, whom no one seems to understand either. You want readers to be taken aback by the weirdness of a rock that tastes like a grapefruit and speaks Peruvian Spanish—yet when the poem makes the connection to your friend Jake, readers may ultimately understand what you're getting at.

Of course, you may decide not to not call the character in the poem Jake, even though your friend Jake is the guy you're really thinking of. You may want to protect Jake's identity. It doesn't matter. No matter what the name, the character is a link to objective reality, and the surrealism of your poem maneuvers readers into a different way of thinking about actual misunderstood people. By having to adjust to a Spanish-speaking rock that sections itself into grapefruit wedges, readers are forced out of their comfort zone. They come to comprehend the idiosyncrasies of personality in a new way.

Nonsense and Instinct

There are, in effect, two basic types of surrealist poems: the Dada style and the Jungian style. **Dada poets** are primarily compelled to break us out of our ordinary way of thinking. They are determined to cut loose from the chains of reason. Like their predecessors in the visual arts in the early twentieth century, some Dada poets were influenced by Freud, who pioneered the exploration of the unconscious and the hidden psychological forces that compel us to behave as we do. They occasionally employ images that may correspond to our unacknowledged impulses. Because the sex drive roils in the subconscious, phallic and vaginal images can appear frequently in these poems. But exploring the Freudian subconscious is not the first intent. Dada poets want to make us stop thinking in old ways; they want human beings to see *all* aspects of reality. They believe the first step to comprehending existence is to divert ourselves from routine paths of thought.

A Dada image is often powerful because it upsets the objects of the world in a way we understand to be impossible. Here's a poem by David St. John about a child coming to terms with the death of a relative. Notice how the opening lines immediately force us to abandon our usual way of seeing:

Iris

VIVIAN ST. JOHN (1891–1974)

There is a train inside this iris:

You think I'm crazy, & like to say boyish
& outrageous things. No, there is

A train inside this iris.

It's a child's finger bearded in black banners.
A single window like a child's nail,

A darkened porthole lit by the white, angular face

Of an old woman, or perhaps the boy inside her in the stuffy,
Hot compartment. Her hair is silver and sweeps

Back off her forehead, onto her cold & bruised shoulders.

The prairies fail along Chicago. Past the five
Lakes. Into the black woods of her New York; & as I bend

Close above the iris, I see the train

Drive deep into the damp heart of its stem, & the gravel
Of the garden path

Cracks under my feet as I walk this long corridor

Of elms, arched
Like the ceiling of a French railway pier where a boy

With pale curls holding

A fresh iris is waving goodbye to a grandmother, gazing
A long time

Into the flower, as if he were looking some great

Distance, or down an empty garden path & he believes a man
Is walking toward him, working

Dull shears in one hand, & now believe me: The train

Is gone. The old woman is dead, & the boy. The iris curls,
On its stalk, in the shade

Of those elms: Where something like the icy and bitter fragrance

In the wake of a woman who's just swept past you on her way
Home

& you remain.

The poem's opening line ("There is a train inside this iris") instantly
delivers an image that cannot occur in objective reality. Trains don't exist in
flowers. And St. John isn't satisfied with only one surprise. The train flies
out of the iris and quickly becomes "a child's finger bearded in black
banners." But soon enough, almost without transition, we're back inside the
train. The poem continues to disorient us at nearly every step.

Among other reasons, St. John maneuvers us into an alogical realm so
that we'll reconsider the concept of time. Children typically see time as
irregular, either standing still or suddenly hurtling fast as a train. Adults
eventually come to perceive time as steady and linear. St. John's dedication
implies that the poem is about a woman who has died, and thus we can
infer that the child in the poem experiences the radical vagaries of time
because of the death of that woman, perhaps the speaker's grandmother.
The stunning, continual shifts to unlikely or impossible events force us out

of our comfortable way of perceiving time and our habit of repressing or rationalizing death. The adult language and tone suggest that although the boy has grown into adulthood, he still carries with him that original disorienting sensation of time that stops and goes without prediction, especially when he thinks of the death of those he loves. The poem supplies a powerful message to the boy—and to readers: Not only do those we love die, but, like time, we will *all* stop.

St. John surely did not understand that these concerns would be paramount in the poem. When you write any poem, you try to surprise yourself. But when you're writing a poem that relies on surrealist techniques, you are intent on creating nonsense images (a train coming out of an iris) that increase the magnitude of that surprise so that readers become quizzical, perhaps even doubting its veracity. At first you may not have any idea what you're writing toward; you simply follow your intuitions. The more you write this kind of poem, the more you trust the direction of the unlikely imagery. Ironically, you come to make the poem unbelievable in order to make readers believe in something they probably haven't considered.

Like Dada poets, **Jungian poets** also want to compel readers away from the ordinary paths of cognition. But Jungian poets are not focused so intently on nonsense images. Rather, they wish to create images that correspond to human instinct. A contemporary of Freud, Carl Jung believed that human behavior was influenced by archetypal images in our unconscious mind. He contended that all human beings inherit the same subconscious images, which correspond to deep instincts. Jungian writers practice what is sometimes called **deep imagery,** in which they create surrealistic, inherently archetypal images intended to strike a buried instinct in the reader. When the image is "struck," a strong instinctual feeling is triggered. Deep-image poems began appearing in the late 1960s and became especially popular during the 1970s when poets and readers became interested in the role of the unconscious or nonrational (not to be confused with irrational) mind. Robert Bly's *Leaping Poetry* is a good source book for this mode, particularly his essay "Looking for Dragon Smoke."

A deep image intends to do more than destabilize the reader. Not only may it impossibly change the rules of the world as we know them, but it may do so in a way that strikes that buried instinct in the reader. Archetypes are diverse, but they usually suggest deep-rooted sensations such as darkness (perhaps implying the possibility of death), light (life), altitude or great height (survival), depths (again, death), phallic symbols (male sexual urge), and vaginal symbols (female sexual urge). Images of ascent or descent seem to occur frequently. The sun, the moon, stars, night sky, sea, soil, rocks, holes in the ground, mountains, trees, flowers, and caves also appear with some regularity in deep-image poems.

While most of these poems employ a series of leaping images, when you're starting out it's best to concentrate on one (or at most two) in your individual poems. In Section Five of Galway Kinnell's long poem "Little Sleep's Head Sprouting Hair in the Moonlight," the poet is urging his son to avoid devaluing the experience of loving another person, and he urges him "to hear under the laughter / the wind crying across the black stones." Later, in Section Six, the poet sees in his son's eyes what he saw once in his father's eyes.

> a tiny kite
> wobbling far up in the twilight of his last look:
>
> and the angel
> of all mortal things lets go the string.

These surreal images, set in a real context, are understood best on the subconscious, or "deep," level.

Charles Wright is one of the most practiced of Jungian poets. In this short poem, he finishes with a surrealistic image intended to strike a buried instinct that will give us the sensation of rising:

❈ Spider Crystal Ascension

> The spider, juiced crystal and Milky Way, drifts on his web
>   through the night sky
> And looks down, waiting for us to ascend . . .
>
> At dawn he is still there, invisible, short of breath, mending his
>   net.
>
> All morning we look for the white face to rise from the lake like a
>   tiny star.
> And when it does, we lie back in our watery hair and rock.

As with many of Wright's poems, the subject of mortality is close at hand. The poem is surely connected to objective reality. We can imagine the night sky we've seen all our lives, just as we can picture the Milky Way. And, looking up at that sky we might also see an actual spider that "drifts on his web." The "juiced crystal" describes the full thorax of the spider while also suggesting a strange star. The "Milky Way," which is host to uncountable numbers of stars, gives us larger context. We can intuit a relation between the strange, even mysterious knowledge of the web-building spider and the seemingly incomprehensible forces that animate the universe. Like the universe, the spider persists, constantly rebuilding. The speaker imagines that the spider "waits for us to ascend," which is to say it waits for us to die, to pass into a different realm.

In the last stanza we can see the surrealistic Jungian imagery work its mortal wonder: Where does the white face come from? Whose face is it? Our uncertainty makes us disoriented. Is it our own face? Are we waiting for ourselves to appear, reflected on the surface of the lake? Is the lake dark as the night sky? Are we asleep? While we may have understood the first three lines of the poem, the last stanza prepares us for the Jungian impact by taking us out of our normal way of thinking. Though we can't process the imagery clearly, we know it portends something of the unknown. Then, when we see that face "rise from the lake like a tiny star" we know the words intend something more than a reflection. By that time the most fearful of the strange images holds us rapt: "We lie back in our watery hair and rock." This line conveys another archetype: that of the bottomless sea, an image that conveys the notion of death or the transition to and through death. The image better suggests descent and ascent; all of us ("we") are simultaneously sinking down to the bottom of the lake and we are floating up to the sky. More important, the archetypal imagery sets off deep emotion in us. We understand the poem on the gut-level perhaps even better than we do on the intellectual level.

Contemporary surrealist poets usually write somewhere between the Dada and Jungian styles, offering up eccentric images that sometimes have deeper significance than intentionally nonsensical images. The excitement lies in letting your creative impulses take off while keeping your surreal imagery tethered to the real world.

Dream Poems

Some people mistakenly believe that a surrealist poem *must* be a dream poem. While surrealist poetry may have dreamlike qualities, **dream poems** are specifically about dreaming. Like all surreal poems, good dream poems are always connected to objective reality. What's more, the dream component may only be a small—though usually dramatic—component of the poem. Often the dream reveals something about the protagonist that he or she might not be able to articulate. After all, while few psychologists believe that all the images in a dream stand for specific psychological facets of the dreamer, most believe that the images and events in a dream are less revelatory than the feelings associated with them. Here's a poem by Denise Duhamel in which she has a fear—perhaps irrational?—that her husband will die soon.

❋Bangungot

Ever since my husband told me about *bangungot*
and taught me how to say it—
three short nasally syllables, a cross between
banana and coconut—I've been worried
he's going to get it, that he'll die in his sleep.
Some Filipinos believe a demon sits on a man's chest
or violent nightmares are the real killers.
My husband thinks it's too much
fish sauce or shrimp paste late at night,
that third helping of rice. *Bangungot*
strikes men 25–40, men who like to eat
then snooze. I try not to let my husband do this
and suggest, instead of television, a walk after dinner,
a game of cards. But sometimes I have places to go.
Sometimes I fall asleep before he does.
It's then I dream of my husband's stomach—
a pot of rice boiling over, a banana so ripe
its own skin cracks. Or I fly, just from the waist up,
a *manananggal,* a vampire that can only be killed
with salt, a vampire who kills men in their sleep.
The top of the body leans into my husband's chest
and I demand he teach me to pronounce the word
that doesn't look like it's spelled. He is confused,
asks me *Where are your legs?*
By the time I get them back,
I'm a widow in black ballerina flats.

As you can see, the poem ends on a dream. While the first two-thirds renders waking reality, the ending of the poem offers no clear interpretation. We are left to decide what the dream means. Has her husband died? Surely not. The dream is a specifically concrete, if idiosyncratic, rendition of the speaker's emotional state. We know that a man's stomach is not likely to boil over with rice, that it cannot also be a cracking banana. We know that she doesn't lose her legs and find them again. Perhaps most interestingly, we know that she cannot fly, that she's not a vampire. The vampire image may be ironically helpful: Perhaps the speaker worries that her own worrying may result in her husband's death. As readers we can feel the narrator's fear for her husband as well as her fear of fearing.

As in this poem, a dream can be a fascinating way to bring a repressed emotion into the open. Should you wish to try a dream poem, you may certainly start with a dream or two that you've actually had. Of course, you don't have to limit yourself to actual dreams. Most often, it's best simply to make dream sequences up—as long as readers find your dream sequences believable in the context of the poem.

Dreamtime and Magical Realism

In certain cultures—e.g., Australian, Indian, and Korean—there are people who believe that dream imagery reveals more than a buried emotional condition. For these and many other indigenous peoples, dreamtime is a unique sleep state during which it is possible to communicate with legendary tribal beings, some in human form, others in animal form. Some Native American tribes assert that dreamtime is a realm in which individual and collective knowledge exists. Native American poets writing in English often exploit the myths and symbols they've been raised with. The owl, fox, bear, wolf, deer, raven, coyote, and other animals appear frequently, each usually connoting a certain type of consciousness. Native American poets likewise may employ the concept of dreamtime to dramatize their subjects. Because dreamtime consists of dreaming, their poems can be deeply surrealistic. Human beings, animals, plants, even the earth . . . all may act in a way that we could never observe in "objective reality."

A member of the Muskogee Tribe, Joy Harjo often uses surrealistic devices to render Native American suffering, as in the following prose poem.

❊ Deer Dancer

Nearly everyone had left that bar in the middle of winter except the hardcore. It was the coldest night of the year, every place shut down, but not us. Of course we noticed when she came in. We were Indian ruins. She was the end of beauty. No one knew her, the stranger whose tribe we recognized, her family related to deer, if that's who she was, a people accustomed to hearing songs in pine trees, and making them hearts.

The woman inside the woman who was to dance naked in the bar of misfits blew deer magic. Henry Jack, who could not survive a sober day, thought she was Buffalo Calf Woman come back, passed out, his head by the toilet. All night he dreamed a dream he could not say. The next day he borrowed money, went home, and sent back the money I lent. Now that's a miracle. Some people see vision in a burned tortilla, some in the face of a woman.

This is the bar of broken survivors, the club of the shotgun, knife wound, of poison by culture. We who were taught not to stare drank our beer. The players gossiped down their cues. Someone put a quarter in the jukebox to relive despair. Richard's wife dove to kill her. We had to hold her back, empty her pocket of knives and diaper pins, buy her two beers to keep her still, while Richard secretly bought the beauty a drink.

How do I say it? In this language there are no words for how the real world collapses. I could say it in my own and the sacred mounds would come into focus, but I couldn't take it in this dingy envelope. So I look at the stars in this strange city, frozen to the back of the sky, the only promises that ever make sense.

My brother-in-law hung out with white people, went to law school with a perfect record, quit. Says you can keep your laws, your words. And practiced law on the street with his hands. He jimmied to the proverbial dream girl, the face of the moon, while the players racked a new game. He bragged to us, he told her magic words and thats when she broke,
  became human.

But we all heard his voice crack:

What's a girl like you doing in a place like this?

That's what I'd like to know, what are we all doing in a place like this?

You would know she could hear only what she wanted to; don't we all? Left the drink of betrayal Richard bought her, at the bar. What was she on? We all wanted some. Put a quarter in the juke. We all take risks stepping into thin air. Our ceremonies didn't predict this. Or we expected more.

I had to tell you this, for the baby inside the girl sealed up with a lick of hope and swimming into the praise of nations. This is not a rooming

house, but a dream of winter falls and the deer who portrayed the
relatives of strangers. The way back is deer breath on icy windows.

The next dance none of us predicted. She borrowed a chair for the
stairway to heaven and stood on a table of names. And danced in the
room of children without shoes.

You picked a fine time to leave me, Lucille.
With four hungry children and a crop in the field.

And then she took off her clothes. She shook loose memory, waltzed
with the empty lover we'd all become.

She was the myth slipped down through dreamtime. The promise of
feast we all knew was coming. The deer who crossed through knots of
a curse to find us. She was no slouch, and neither were we, watching.

The music ended. And so does the story. I wasn't there. But I
imagined her like this, not a stained red dress with tape on her heels
but the deer who entered our dream in white dawn, breathed mist into
pine trees, her fawn a blessing of meat, the ancestors who never left.

If you're not well-versed in Native American culture, a poem like this may
be particularly challenging to understand, though Harjo certainly intends
for all readers to access its meanings. While the magical deer dancer may
not exist in our waking reality, the surrealistic events aid the poem in
asserting her existence in dreamtime. In real time there may be a woman in
a red dress; she may be drunk; she may be pregnant; her high heels may be
taped. She is the poem's connection to the real world.

In the plot of this poem, however, the woman seems to have crossed over
from another realm to act as a kind of guiding totem for the "Indian ruins" in
the bar, most of whom are drunk and probably unemployed. Just as we're startled out of our quotidian thought patterns upon reading about her, the patrons
of the bar are startled—at least temporarily—out of their longtime depression.
The famously irresponsible Henry Jack, for example, straightens out so much
that he stops drinking, leaves the bar, and returns money he owes. Ultimately,
we understand the woman in the red dress in one of two ways, depending on
whether we employ our usual real-time way of seeing or the dreamtime way of
seeing. If Harjo doesn't use surrealism, the poem will have virtually no effect
on the reader. The dreamlike quality of the writing gives it persuasive power.

Harjo's poem is an extraordinary example of **magical realism,** a genre of
literature in which rational and supernatural views of reality coexist. Though

THE POET'S NOTE CARD

Unreal Realities

1. Surrealistic poetry often uses dreamlike images to portray the workings of the subconscious mind.

2. No good poem is entirely surreal; there must be some link to what we think of as "objective reality." A surreal poem which is nothing *but* surreal may seem irrelevant to all but the writer.

3. There are generally two types of surrealist poetry: Dada (originated primarily by French visual artists) and Jungian or "deep imagery" (founded primarily by Latin and South American writers).

4. Dada is a type of surrealism that deliberately defies reason by making use of nonsense images; Jungian poetry combines both realistic and fantastical events to create a dreamlike world.

5. In American poetry, "deep imagery" is a Jungian type of poetry that features weird or incongruous images that, in turn, are designed to strike a buried instinct (or an archetype) in the reader.

6. Some poets employ a kind of surrealism that is inherent in the concept of "dreamtime," a state in which human beings have access to ancestors and higher truths.

7. Dreamtime surrealism is much like magical realism, a genre in which the rational and the nonrational can balance each other.

primarily employed by fiction writers, magical realism is a type of surrealistic writing certainly adaptable to poetry. The form allows any writer to rectify opposing ideas. Harjo's poem depicts Native Americans stuck in an alcoholic depression while also being connected to a liberating, transcendent solution.

As you may have noticed, surrealism is a type of art that lends itself to the consideration of those things we may not like to think about: e.g., mortality, injustice, and violence. For instance, most people don't like thinking of death; they use oft-practiced mental tricks to avoid thinking deeply about dying or the deaths of others. Because surrealism shakes us out of our usual manner of engaging—or avoiding—the world, it's a tool that you may want to try when you're faced with a subject that's not necessarily off limits, just hard to face.

WRITING EXERCISES

1. *Dream poem.* Write a poem based on a dream you've actually had. (You may wish to keep a journal of your dreams.) Make sure the poem can make sense to somebody other than yourself. It must have some connection to reality.

2. *Inserted dream poem.* Write a poem set in ordinary life or what is sometimes referred to as "objective reality." Try to place the protagonist in some kind of difficulty. Now have the protagonist dream about something that may seem strange, even bizarre, but is actually related in some way to the person's troubles. After the dream, come back to "reality." Try to use images in everyday life and in the dream to transition in and out of each. What has the person learned? Render the aftermath of the dream.

3. *Dada poem.* Write a poem that employs one or more surreal images. As we know, surreal images are usually nonsensical, but they can jolt the reader's rational approach to the poem in a way that can produce unusually vivid understanding. Make sure it's linked to the real world.

4. *Deep-image poem.* Write a poem that makes use of a deep image, that is, a surreal image that employs deeply felt meaning. Try to keep the image situated in a readily accessible, objective context. It may be best to begin with a real situation.

5. *Dreamtime poem.* Imagine that another world exists parallel to your waking world. Perhaps your relatives live there; perhaps you simply project their existence in this other realm. Write a poem in which one of your ancestors crosses in and out of that realm in order to warn you about a problem. Don't make his warning too obvious. Keep the ancestor's way of communicating cryptic. Remember, no matter what the ancestor says or does, the protagonist must find a way to change. It's often best if the transformative

moment occurs (or fails to occur) in the main character of the poem. The ancestor probably shouldn't be a godlike figure who magically changes the protagonist.

6. *Magical realism poem.* Writing in the third person, imagine a character who exists perfectly well in objective reality but who can also perceive another parallel realm in which many of the physical laws of the universe do not adhere. Depict what he sees in that parallel world when something traumatic occurs, i.e., the death of a friend, a robbery, a car accident, or a house fire. How do the beings in the parallel world act differently from those in objective reality? What does he learn from them? Try to render the transformative moment with surreal imagery.

11

WRITING ABOUT SADNESS

The Elegy

One of the ironic aspects of human behavior is the fact that crying sometimes can feel good. The act of crying can be an emotional purging in which sadness is relieved. Like crying, the act of *describing* our sadness—or describing the cause of it—may also diminish pain. When we write poems about things that sadden us we also find that readers tend to experience our grief and then vicariously feel the pleasure of expiating it. **Elegies** are primarily lyric poems conveying the sad interior life. Originally written to mourn the loss of a person who has recently died, the contemporary elegy may also mourn the loss of a state of being. Since the time of Shakespeare, poets have written poems that express deep grief, and the form is still among the most popular written in English-language poetry. After all, who better than a poet can express the complex emotional turbulence of grieving? And who else is equipped to do so while not giving in to sentimentality?

Generally elegies express grief while offering some kind of consolation, though there are poets such as Larry Levis whose poems offer very little in the way of comfort. The elegy takes readers into the sweetness of grief without spilling over into excess emotion. It does not usually offer irreconcilable sadness; rather, it sometimes makes sadness a medium for passing through the big impediments to happiness. Ironically, elegies may offer readers the slightest sensation of heroism. We deeply miss the person (or state of being) that has passed. We have survived the loss. We know we will go on.

Imagery and Restraint

The paradoxical pleasure you get in writing the elegy lies in immersing yourself in your own sadness. Perhaps you're sorrowful because someone has died. Perhaps you're saddened by the passing of a beloved way of life. Either way, once you have transitioned to such a feeling you really must practice restraint; otherwise the poem will grow sloppy, i.e., sentimental. You should focus on the concrete details of the situation; let the images render the depth of emotion. It's often best to employ visually intriguing metaphors that render the sadness you feel, even when the narrator's exterior may seem poised, seamless.

The following poem by Stanley Plumly employs a nearly surrealistic series of images in order to convey the narrator's desperate desire to be once more with an old friend who has died in middle age, the day after his birthday. Because Plumly attends to the details so specifically, the poem never runs off into excess:

❦November 11, 1942–November 12, 1997

My friend's body walking toward me
down the Pullman passage of his hallway.
He's naked as if he's just risen
from a bath and forgotten what it is
he's supposed to do next. He looks cold,
candle-white, with a sort of sunburn
on his face, especially his mouth,
which is open on a vowel. And there
seems to be an almost visible vertical
line drawn through him, so that half
of him is taller, half in tow.
It must be afternoon, since the daylight

is going and the doorway behind him
disappearing. Now it's colder.
Now I realize that for the longest time
I've been waiting for him, and need
to think of something, and that
he's expecting it, the way silence
sometimes promises. Then suddenly
he's in front of me, and I can see
how damp he is, how anointed with oil,
how all the color's focused in the eyes,
how the coral of the brain shines through
the forehead. And though he doesn't say so,
because he never would, I'm sure he wants me
to hold him, say his name, make him warm.
But when I try he puts his hand inside
his heart and offers me the stone,
then the Armistice poppy, and then
the bowl of bright arterial blood.
And from where the scar is, where they
saved his life and failed, the umbilical
intestine, impurities and purities of kidneys
and the liver, the two lungs out of breath,
and breath itself, cupped till it runneth over.

It's as if the man had lifted himself magically from the embalmer's table. Even though the images of the naked man are striking, Plumly refrains from overdramatizing the speaker's longing for his old friend. The unclothed body becomes the focus of all that can go wrong with health, how the flesh is susceptible to disease. The "scar" indicates that doctors tried to save him, that he was likely sick in a hospital, perhaps with cancer.

We might ask, "Is the speaker dreaming?" Probably. Certainly the images own a surrealistic affect that render the astonishment the narrator initially feels. But the poem is both powerful and deeply poignant because the images suggest that the speaker has to face the irreversible fact of death. The virtually exact span of a lifetime—fifty-five years from birth to death—makes the friend's death that much more eerie. (Elegists often fix an exact date to the poem in order to make the person's death—and, thus, his or her life—that much more real.) Here, Plumly combats sentimentality by offering up a difficult, even grotesque series of images. Accordingly, the tone of the poem is at first one of amazement. But that incredulity ultimately gives way to elegiac resignation, as if the speaker were going through the stages of acceptance. We refuse to accept the death; then we are astonished by it; then we come to accept it.

Threnody

We enjoy experiencing good elegies, even though, like blues songs, the poems are about mortality or irrevocable loss. The Greeks used to call a song of lamentation **threnody,** which implies a deep flowing river of sorrow. That's why it's best that you make sure the poem's sound is suitable to the emotion. Rarely can a high-velocity poem express sorrow. Anxiety perhaps, but not sorrow. Most elegies are characterized by a quiet kind of verse musicality. Some elegists prefer longer lines, usually eight to twelve syllables, because the longer line requires a greater breath length, often approximating the less broken, smoother pace of people reflecting on whatever is mourned.

Here's a poem by Susan Wood. The early lines could be about the change of seasons—at least the first nine lines. Notice how the extraordinarily lush, evocative pacing seems to grow more and more meditative as the poem goes on and the lines grow slightly longer.

Campo Santo

This far south November
might just as well be summer
some days, it's that green
and hot. Leaves don't turn
here, or fall, drifting down to be raked
into bonfires of their own color.
Weeks from now we'll look up
and—suddenly it seems—find them
gone, we won't know where.
That's what I thought of, seeing you,
your son two months dead. How,
from now on, you'll look up
from whatever you're doing—planting
bulbs of pale narcissus, say, or
scattering food for the family of ducks
that floated down river to live

in the reeds behind your house—and find
yourself, surprised again, flush
against his absence.

A day like any other. Today, for instance,
sweating, we bent and stooped like gardeners,
papering his grave with flowers,
blue for iris, yellow for daisy, even
the white lily so beautiful
we plant it in the hands of the dead.
You wanted, you said, to see it from the road.

Across town, in the Mexican cemetery,
every grave is piled high like this
with paper flowers, so gaudy
and touching the hills bloom
all year long. It is not because they are poor,
you see, but because they love the dead
that much. It seems, from the road, really
to be a garden. *Campo santo,* they call it,
holy field, and even those without belief
say it is blessed by the dead who lie there,
because, surely, all of them were loved once
by someone. Some of them are still remembered.

The Mexican boys who were your son's friends
come each night to this field.
They bring offerings, cigarettes and beer, play
their loud music for him to hear. They leave
letters pressed under stones.
To them, it is holy, dying young
in this man's world. It was just beginning
for them, this world, the day they stood
in a crowd of mourners, their faces stunned
and open above the starched white shirts.
For us, it had continued.

When I drove away from your house that day
I heard the Bach concerto for two violins,
the first violin low and then another,
higher, piercing, and then both of them

together, answering what will not be
consoled. I stopped the car and wept
because I could do nothing else.
There were months we had been like strangers
to each other, distant and awkward, though
I could not say why. Now it had ended,
and I remembered a story a friend had told me,
how when he was young he had loved
a Beethoven sonata so much he had played it
every day, again and again. And then, somehow,
he didn't play it anymore—went away, maybe,
or lost the record, and in time forgot.
Driving across the Bay Bridge ten years later,
he heard it suddenly, after all
those years, on the radio and was overcome
by grief for all that he had lost.

I thought of that again this evening
when we went down to the river.
It was not yet dark, the air
gray and slick with the coming chill.
You stood on the bank and held out
your hand. I stood away from you a little,
watching, because the ducks will not come
for anyone but you. The large brown one,
the male, came to you and gravely
began to eat from your hand, as though
being careful not to hurt you.
I saw then that nothing could
comfort you. Not your friends
who love you, not this life
you will go on living.
I don't know how else to say this.
Which is the greater sorrow, to feel
you can't live without him or to find,
after all, that you can?

The image of the ducks, drawn so innocuously in the early stages, becomes
the central image of the poem, gently illustrating what they both don't
wish to say: that the child will never return. But the conversational music

of the poem seems equally effective in rendering its intent. The sentences flow with an informal ease, the way two longtime friends might speak quietly to the other. And Wood employs commas here to make sure we never move too quickly, always slowing down the cadence to match the inevitable, continuing sadness.

And yet that sadness is not simply about the death of the child. The narrator is deeply concerned about the change in her relationship with her friend. After all, the friend is permanently changed, irrevocably scarred. It's often said the worst grief anyone can experience is the death of a child. The narrator is elegizing a lost state of being: She and her friend may be able to have a good relationship again, but that relationship will never be what it once was because the friend will never be the happy person she used to be. They are no longer "strangers," but the change has come: "I saw then that nothing could / comfort you. Not your friends / who love you, not this life / you will go on living." In the past, the narrator and the friend could offer each other helpful comfort. Because of the friend's unalterable loss, the narrator will never be able to help. And thus the narrator mourns not only the loss of the child but, more immediately, the loss of the old friendship.

Wood's poem models the kind of tone that is most often associated with elegy. Centuries ago a threnodic poem would rhyme and the cadence would be dominated by a predetermined rhythm. But in contemporary poetry, an effectual threnodic sound is often measured out by a kind of subtle, free-verse pacing that you intuit as you write. As you sink into the sadness of the subject you're writing about, allow your own sense of grief to determine the poem's tone.

Expectation and Surprise

Some elegies work against our expectations. Rather than sound reflective and resigned, they can make use of shorter, punchier lines. The resulting sound can surprise readers out of their usual expectations about our methods of grieving. How would you characterize the tone of this tragicomic elegy by Ruth Stone?

Curtains

Putting up new curtains,
other windows intrude.
As though it is that first winter in Cambridge

when you and I had just moved in.
Now cold borscht alone in a bare kitchen.

What does it mean if I say this years later?

Listen, last night
I am on a crying jag
with my landlord, Mr. Tempesta.
I sneaked in two cats.
He screams NO PETS! NO PETS!
I become my Aunt Virginia,
proud but weak in the head.
I remember Anna Magnani.
I throw a few books. I shout.
He wipes his eyes and opens his hands.
OK OK keep the dirty animals
but no nails in the walls.
We cry together.
I am so nervous, he says.

I want to dig you up and say, look,
it's like the time, remember,
when I ran into our living room naked
to get rid of the fire inspector.

See what you miss by being dead?

You can tell right away that Stone's voice—her attitude—is radically different from Plumly's and Wood's. Though it's written in a quickly accessible style, the poem renders a complex sorrow, combining abject loneliness ("cold borscht alone in a bare kitchen") with angry humor ("See what you miss by being dead?").

As "Curtains" demonstrates, you don't need to remain in one unbroken sorrowful tone in your elegy. You can vary that tone to include other emotions. Clearly, grief is a complex emotional state, and the elegy is flexible enough to incorporate many different feelings. As with virtually all good poems, the key is to provide the kinds of fascinating images that will draw a reader along your journey.

The elegy is a durable genre that can help you come to terms with profound change. Strangely, we often like to write elegies because we need to expiate our sorrows. Articulating sorrow is a method of grieving. Bereavement in the form of poetry gives you a chance to reorient all of the

THE POET'S NOTE CARD

How Sadness Feels Good

1. Elegies are among the most popular genres of poems to write.
2. Elegies mourn the loss of a person or state of being.
3. Generally elegies express grief while offering some kind of consolation.
4. Elegies are primarily lyric poems, conveying the sad interior life.
5. Many elegists write in longer lines (eight to twelve syllables).
6. Most elegies are characterized by a quiet kind of verse musicality.
7. When writing an elegy, it's best to try to invest the poem with powerful feeling while employing great restraint.
8. Intense emotion, never sentimentality, is what's needed.
9. Elegies can render many different types of emotions, not just sorrow.
10. Elegies can include many forms of expression, from reverential speech to street talk.

aspects of your life after experiencing significant loss. (Some emerging poets even find the elegy an addictive form.) Ultimately, you might keep in mind that all poems—no matter how personal they are, no matter how much they help us engage life—are, before all else, works of art. The first duty of the poet is to make something beautiful. And, as you know, beauty in the elegy or any other type of poem requires alluring imagery and honest sentiment.

WRITING EXERCISES

1. *Traditional elegy.* Write an elegy about someone who has died. Remember that the traditional elegy expresses sorrow about the deceased. As with all writing, it's especially important that you avoid clichés, i.e., easy, common expressions that have lost their

effectiveness. Try to provide the reader with good honest emotion that doesn't exceed adult sentiment.

2. *Elegy about a lost state of being (third person).* Some elegies simply lament the passing of a state of life or being. These might include the loss of a friendship due to a misunderstanding, or the loss of the ability to play basketball due to a permanent injury, or the loss of eyesight due to an accident. Write an elegy in the third person that renders the interior life as the narrator mourns the loss of something other than a person.

3. *Elegy about a lost state of being (first person).* Try the above exercise, but now in the first person. Try to stay clear of the saccharine or extra sad expressions that seem to go beyond the realm of frank adult feeling.

4. *Tragicomic elegy.* Keeping in mind Ruth Stone's poem "Curtains," try writing a poem in which you remember the comic moments you shared with a person who has died. Don't let the poem's humor be simply funny. Without becoming maudlin, invest the poem with a conflict that implies a deeper point of view.

5. *Elegy for yourself.* Imagine that you've died, but—because of some mysterious process—you have also been asked to write an elegy for yourself. The elegy will be a poem distributed at your own funeral. Will you mourn your own death? What will you say about yourself? What will the conflict be?

6. *Elegy with dream.* Write an elegy about someone who has died—but in the elegy render a dream that brings that person back to life. You realize you only have a few moments to say something to the deceased. You can't afford to be sentimental. What will you say?

7. *Elegy for a friendship.* Think of a friend with whom you've had a falling out. Write a poem that mourns the loss of the friendship. Describe what went wrong without assessing blame. Then imagine what it would take to resume the friendship. If such a resumption is impossible, use imagery to describe what prevents the reconciliation.

8. *Elegy for a love relationship.* Write a poem that elegizes an old romantic relationship. While depicting the problems that led to the end of the romance, imagine what would have happened if that relationship had succeeded.

12

POETRY AND EROS

The Predicament of the Love Poem

For radically different reasons, love poems have been as popular as elegies. After all, most human beings seek out a partner to love, a complementary "other." Our hearts spill with large and small ecstasies. We want to tell the world our joy. Because we often write love poems at the very moment we're in the throes of love, they can be exhilarating to write. For the same reason, they can be difficult to write. Nothing makes us happier than love, but very little makes us less critical than love. And there's the rub. The line we wouldn't write at any other time may seem deliriously perfect today. Weeks from now, still in love perhaps but in an aesthetically objective state of mind, we find ourselves a little chagrined at the lines we've written. We may ask, "Where did that come from?" but in truth we will know.

Though usually begun with the best aesthetic intentions, love poems often start poorly for two reasons: Writers resort to clichéd language, and they abandon the need for conflict. The language of romantic intimacy isn't gooey; the kind of saccharine baby talk you may hear between young lovers in the first stages of their relationship is rarely the language of real love; it's the language of naiveté. Good love poems are sustained by a charged imagery that holds the reader's attention. And even those poems with good imagery may be absent the inner pressure that animates art.

Conflict and Tone

Some of the best love poems balance strong romantic feeling with gritty assessment. Since all good poems require effective imagery and a compelling **tension** (i.e., stress that emerges from a problem), love poems need some kind of trouble to explore. In this poem by Norman Dubie, a husband confronts several problems at once.

Radio Sky

The blue house at Mills Cross
Where the night's last firefly
Strikes its light out in a burst pod.

Under the cool stairs
You raised the chrome visor
On my aunt's old G.E.:
A faint band, green numerals
And a backlighting of amber tubes—
Each is glass, prophylactic,
With cosmic noise straight from the Swan.

Your sister, Phyllis, had been unkind. It was hot.
Our towels floating in the tub upstairs,
We lit candles
And you poured the iced tea.

Later in bed you turned on the television
To where a station had signed off;
Making the adjustments in the contrast
We watched snow, what Phyllis said
Was literally the original light of Creation.
Genesis popping like corn in a black room. Still,
Something out of nothing. Knowing

We can't have children
You watched the flecked light

Like a rash on your stomach and breasts.
Phyllis

Is a bitch was my reply.
We made love, shared strings of rhubarb
Leached with cream. We slept
In the blue snow of the television
Drifting under the familiar worn sheet.

Dubie's arresting imagery draws us into the conflict immediately. Notice that we never encounter the clichéd images of love. Not soaked in the reverential tone of some love poems, Dubie's language is sharp, detailed. It's a very hot, muggy night. Though the reference adds texture, we don't absolutely have to know that Mills Cross is the location of a famous radio telescope in Australia with which scientists were able to measure sounds emanating from the universe. It does help to know that the "old G.E." is a radio that used large, glowing tubes long before the considerably smaller transistors were available. Old radios of the type would produce a good deal of static ("cosmic noise") between stations as the dial was turned. The mysteries of astronomy offer an important existential context for the troubled couple. They can't get pregnant, and the husband's sister-in-law has been critical of their infertility. Dubie draws stunning imagery from the ordinary surroundings, in this case a radio and a television. He depicts the way a husband and wife maintain their relationship despite the disappointment and uncertainty in their lives. Their own "genesis" must be limited to a continual rebirthing of their mutual love.

When you show lovers encountering obstacles, your poem is going to be more persuasive than one in which you show them simply smiling and kissing and cooing. In many love poems a conflict arises because the impediment to happiness is often an impediment to love. As in "Radio Sky," the following poem by C. Dale Young demonstrates how lovers have to find ways to succeed at loving each other despite strong obstacles.

Exile

Clothed only by the sound of the sea,
we stood naked on our balcony, masters
of all that lay before us, the green life

of the croquet lawn dotted again
and again by the cultured hibiscus,
its blooms the ready medium

of the master pointillist (read: gardener)
who now takes lessons from no one
but the river that has nurtured gardens

far more exotic than this, and on the sides
of cliffs, no less, as if to flaunt its virtuosity.
At that hour, even the handful of glare

left over from midday had to succumb
to the sound of the sea, its tireless percussion.
Sanded, our dark skin darker,

we had climbed seventy-four steps
into the heart of the palazzo, our suite
the necessary haven, the fort

we create no matter where we live.
And so, exhausted by the sun, we stood there,
two men among shadows, the sunlight

kept at bay by leaves, the two of us staring
at coconuts bobbing in the surf, strange skulls
trying their damnedest to remind us of nothing.

Here, Young elegizes an ideal but presently impossible context for love. At first, the luxuriant, descriptive language that begins this poem renders more traditional kinds of romantic imagery. The vacationing couple is naked in their hotel suite, overlooking the sea. But as the poem proceeds, the imagery demonstrates how a shadow darkens their relationship. The speaker describes the suite as a "necessary haven, the fort / we create no matter where we live." The lovers are so threatened that they must always shore themselves within a "fort," a military image certainly not associated with the free, copious feelings of love. We soon understand why: The lovers are "two men among shadows." They may be in a foreign country, but no matter where they are, the pervasive homophobia around them is an impediment to their love. The last image in the poem is riveting: The coconuts in the surf seem like float-ing skulls that try "their damnedest to remind us of nothing." The speaker's inability to love freely is shadowed by the culture's resistance to him and his partner.

Even though the circumstances of their lives force the lovers to be secretive, the poem itself must be accessible. The love poem has a public audience; that's why you want to make sure that the poem speaks to readers who don't know anything about the people in the relationship. While this poem may be based on a specific event experienced by two men, it provides enough detail that anyone can understand its "plot": They would like to relax; they are two lovers on vacation, thinking of nothing more than the sea. The last line suggests, however, that a dangerous bigotry makes doing so impossible. Ultimately, homophobia forces a conflict in the speaker: How can he ever be comfortably in love?

Often the impediment to happiness is not derived from a force external to the relationship. Because good love relationships require intimacy, many poets write about the transition from simply being acquainted with a person to being very close. Frequently the very fact of unfamiliarity can be a roadblock. We may be made anxious by our uncertainty. Some love poems recognize a negative characteristic in either the protagonist or the partner, which adds authentic tension to the poem. In the following poem by Ai, it seems the two lovers, probably married, have not weathered the vicissitudes of time very well.

Cruelty

The hoof marks on the dead wildcat
gleam in the dark.
You are naked, as you drag it up on the porch.
That won't work either.
Drinking ice water hasn't,
nor having the bedsprings snap fingers
to help us keep rhythm.
I've never once felt anything
that might get close. Can't you see?
The thing I want most is hard,
running toward my teeth
and it bites back.

The narrator has become numb with time. If nothing else, she's desperate to feel something with her partner. For her, emotion associated with pain (i.e., biting) is better than absence of all sense. The speaker intends to shock the husband into confronting his role in their deteriorating relationship. Her anxiety results in a kind of language far removed from that associated with love.

Love poems may portray the problems that lovers must overcome in order to fall and remain in love. Or they may be about the problems that keep them apart. Either way, try to keep in mind that the imagery and the sound should be just as fresh as those in any other kind of poem. Your readers will be bored with language they've often heard. The poem can ride a traditionally romantic, even verdant sound as long as it remains contemporary, authentic, and without sentimentality. Or it can be pointed or angry or challenging. (And let's face it, sometimes writing about angry love can be as inspiring as writing about heartwarming love.) You should also try to remember that somewhere inside the protagonist there is usually a barrier to healthy love. A happy love poem overcomes the barrier, while a heartrending love poem succumbs to it. Or, as in "Radio Sky" and "Exile," a tentative middle ground may be rendered. "Cruelty" is another kind of middle ground: a fierce challenge, predicting no clear outcome.

The Language of Desire

Romantic love is an emotion almost inevitably connected to desire. Desire, in turn, is the impulse to have or acquire. In poems about desire the protagonist usually wishes to acquire a lover. Yet you should keep in mind that for many of us, desire precedes love. We find ourselves sexually attracted to a person, and if that person suits a host of other conscious or subconscious requirements (high intellect, obvious kindness, a good sense of humor), we may ultimately fall in love. While all good poems should be written from an adult perspective, there is a long tradition of writing poems about the first or early desires of our teenage years. These poems thrill us with a recollection of powerful erotic craving, while also suggesting how we develop into the people we are as adults. In the younger person can be seen the adult.

Written from both an adolescent and adult point of view, the following poem by Tess Gallagher renders the freefalling sensation of a teenage girl's earliest desire.

❀ Fresh Stain

I don't know now if it was kindness—we do
and we do. But I wanted you with me
that day in the cool raspberry vines, before

I had loved anyone, when another girl and I
saw the owner's son coming to lift away
our heaped flats of berries. His
white shirt outside his jeans so
tempting. That whiteness, that quick side-glance
in our direction. We said nothing,
but quickly gathered all the berries we could, losing
some in our mirth and trampling them
like two black ponies who only want to keep their backs
free, who only want to be shaken with
the black night-in-day murmur of hemlocks
high above. Our slim waists, our buds
of breasts and red stain of raspberries cheapening
our lips. We were sudden, we were
two blurred dancers who didn't need paradise. His shirt,
his white shirt when the pelting ended, as if
we had kissed him until his own blood
opened. So we refused every plea and
were satisfied. And you didn't touch me then, just
listened to the cool silence after. Inside,
the ripe hidden berries as we took up our wicker baskets
and lost our hands past the wrists
in the trellised vines. Just girls with the arms of
their sweaters twisted across their hips, their laughter
high in sunlight and shadow, that girl
you can almost remember as she leans into the vine,
following with pure unanswerable desire, a boy
going into the house to change his shirt.

The imagery here is dominated by color and tactility. Gallagher even uses the title "Fresh Stain" to suggest an initial ripening: Like the berries, the speaker is on the verge of being consumed by a powerful force. The poet intuits the link between earliest desire and later adult understanding. As in this case, poems about first loves or lost loves are often elegiac. They may risk excess sentimentality, but, if handled with restraint, they can be insightfully evocative.

If adolescent desire requires the kind of language reserved for describing excess, confused feeling, adult desire can sometimes require a language for more complex emotion. In this poem by Ralph Black, for instance, the narrator is acutely aware of the difference between simple lust on one hand and the richer complex of sexual arousal on the other.

❧ Slicing Ginger

> Not sex. Not sex,
> but sexual: the way
> the weather hangs
> at the edges of sight,
> pressed and warm as any
> lover to my hand, slides
> just under the soaked
> brown skin, opening
> the earth of it, opening
> the undiscovered, white-
> fleshed seam in the scarred
> and sacred earth: the
> lemon-sweet, lemon-
> sweet ringing of bodies
> through the room.
> Plumes of longing bleed
> in my hands as the small
> blade pares into the
> mole-blind, uprooted
> incantatory fruit—the
> slices hitting the
> hot oiled iron with
> a singing of fire on
> wet wood, and the tiny
> suns exploding there:
> huge and redolent and
> almost human.

Black's key metaphor transitions from a comparison to a sudden realization. Initially the poem tells us that the act of slicing ginger is "not sex" but it is "sexual," a key difference. Preparing ginger reminds the speaker of the fertile, subterranean feeling that attends sexual love. Because he's more interested in that feeling than in imagining the act of sex itself, he uses images from the natural world and from the body to evoke a sense of profound emotional depth. By the end of the poem the slices of ginger sing; they're "suns" or "wet wood" exploding on the iron with great force. In fact, the force is so great that he's surprised to recognize that it's "almost human." As in Black's poem, you might remember that human sexuality is so powerful that you can link desire to the simplest act as long as you make the context of the poem believable.

Erotic Poetry

Of course, when we speak of love and desire we may end up speaking about the **erotic.** The word *erotic* applies to words that are intended to arouse. A good erotic poem typically owns a kind of advantage that other types of poems may not, because by its very nature it is necessarily **illicit,** that is, the poem is perceived as taboo, off-limits, dangerous. And, just as illicitness can amplify the sex between cheating partners, illicitness can heighten interest in a reader. Good erotic poetry typically renders sexually titillating work in order to demonstrate some insight into our sexual impulse. But we must take care, because erotic poems run the risk of being *merely* titillating; a good erotic poem must render something more than carnal pleasure; it must be insightful *about* carnal pleasure. In an erotic poem often what is not described intrigues the reader. Restraint can be an asset.

Conversely, sometimes you might find that a more comprehensive description of a sexual act is needed in order to dramatize and validate the poem's point. Here's a poem by Dorianne Laux about a conflict a woman experiences while making love with a man.

The Lovers

She is about to come. This time,
they are sitting up, joined below the belly,
feet cupped like sleek hands praying
at the base of each other's spines.
And when something lifts within her
toward a light she's sure, once again,
she can't bear, she opens her eyes
and sees his face is turned away,
one arm behind him, hand splayed
palm down on the mattress, to brace himself

so he can lever his hips, touch
with the bright tip the innermost spot.
And she finds she can't bear it—
not his beautiful neck, stretched and corded,
not his hair fallen to one side like beach grass,
not the curved wing of his ear washed thin
with daylight, deep pink of the inner body.
What she can't bear is that she can't see his face,
not that she thinks this exactly—she is rocking
and breathing—it's more her body's thought,
opening, as it is, into its own sheer truth.
So that when her hand lifts of its own volition
and slaps him, twice on the chest,
on that pad of muscled flesh just above the nipple,
slaps him twice, fast, like a nursing child
trying to get a mother's attention,
she's startled by the sound,
though when he turns his face to hers—
which is what her body wants, his eyes
pulled open, as if she had bitten—
she does reach out and bite him, on the shoulder,
not hard, but with the power infants have
over those who have borne them, tied as they are
to the body, and so, tied to the pleasure,
the exquisite pain of this world.
And when she lifts her face he sees
where she's gone, knows she can't speak,
is traveling toward something essential,
toward the core of her need, so he simply
watches, steadily, with an animal calm
as she arches and screams, watches the face that,
if she could see it, she would never let him see.

Laux has provided so much graphic detail for at least two reasons: First, she
wants the reader to experience the sexual arousal. Second, and more important, she wants that arousal to enhance the point of the poem. She knows
that the act of sex carries with it a physical kind of knowledge: "her body's
thought, / opening, as it is, into its own sheer truth." Ultimately this
knowledge leads the speaker to realize that our usually more cognitive, con-
ditioned ways of thinking might find our aroused bodies repulsive. If we

THE POET'S NOTE CARD

Romancing the Poem

1. A good love poem must have a conflict.

2. Love poems are often marred by excess sentimentality.

3. Some of the best love poems balance strong romantic feeling with gritty assessment.

4. Love poems can be sabotaged by the pervasive clichéd language around us, especially in mass media. Find fresh ways of describing strong emotions.

5. Poems about first loves or lost loves are often "elegiac"; they may risk excess sentimentality, but, if handled with restraint, they can be insightfully evocative.

6. The love poem has a public audience; make sure that the poem is accessible to all readers.

7. Erotic poems run the risk of being merely titillating; a good erotic poem must be about something more than carnal pleasure, even if it is simply insightful about some aspect of carnal pleasure.

8. In an erotic poem often what is not described intrigues the reader. Restraint can be an asset.

9. No poem succeeds simply by telling. To a greater or lesser extent, virtually all erotic poems render their key ideas by depicting or implying sexual acts.

10. Often described as "transgressive," some poems take risks by crossing the border of decorum into a taboo manner of expression that may repel some readers entirely or persuade others to reconsider their assumptions.

knew we looked the way we do during sex, the poems is saying, we might never want our partner to see us. Laux knows that no poem succeeds simply by telling. She has to show us this idea by showing us the physical goings on.

Despite the myriad sexual images of American advertising, the puritanical American impulse still abides. All poems that mention sex have the potential to offend someone somewhere. **Transgressive** poems cross the border of a reader's sense of decorum into a potentially prohibited manner of expression. When Allen Ginsberg wrote "Howl," with its numerous and graphic depictions of sexual acts, he was counting on just that reaction; he wanted his imagery to shock people out of their habitualized way of thinking. Of course, what's transgressive for some is perfectly fine for others. You will have to determine what makes you uncomfortable—and what may make your reader uncomfortable. Since discomfort is not necessarily a bad thing, you will need to decide how much you want to risk with regard to your reader. Taking risks in creating striking imagery is necessary. Sometimes, it is necessary to shake your reader out of commonly held perceptions.

WRITING EXERCISES

1. *Love poem.* Write a love poem without any clichéd language or excess sentimentality. It may be narrative or purely descriptive. Like the relative portrait exercise, your love poem might recognize a negative characteristic in either you or, preferably, the person who is loved. Recognizing a vice or character flaw will add authentic tension to the poem.

2. *Love-under-siege-poem.* Write a poem in which familial, political, or cultural forces are aligned against two people so that sustaining their love for each other is difficult. You might render those forces with the kind of gritty imagery not typically associated with love poems. Or you might begin with a more traditionally romantic tone that eventually gives way to a grave or fearful sound.

3. *"Dangerous love" poem.* Write a love poem about someone who really doesn't seem to warrant love but who possesses some alluring intangible quality. It's your job to render that quality. The poem may be written in the first, second, or third person. For instance, imagine an older student who falls in love with a man who wears black leather, rides a motorcycle, and comes through town on irregular visits. The student knows the motorcyclist is never going to make a commitment, but . . .

4. *"First love" poem.* Write a poem about a first love. Try to render the link between those early sensations of love and the later,

mature understanding the protagonist achieves (or, perhaps, fails to achieve). Remember, like all childhood poems, this kind of poem needs to have adult application. And, like elegies, poems about first loves or lost loves are often written in a threnodic tone. You might find that sad-sounding language helps you to move your reader, but try to avoid excess sentimentality.

5. *Anti-love poem.* Write a poem that professes passionate love for someone, but try to invest it with an attitude or style of language that is *not* conducive to expressing love. In this kind of poem the narrator may be *in* love, but he or she distrusts love. The language should be deeply ambivalent.

6. *Breaking-up poem.* Write a poem that describes two people breaking up. You might consider employing an older narrator looking back on the breakup. Or you might have an omniscient narrator describe the breakup in the present tense. Use a strong visual metaphor to characterize the problem that drove them apart. Provide the texture of the event: What did their faces look like? What was the weather like? What did their voices sound like?

7. *Erotic poem.* Write a poem that employs erotic description to make a point about human nature. While focusing on whatever you feel is erotic, be sure not to lose focus of the fact that any successful poem about the erotic must ultimately be about the same thing all other good poems are about: conflict in the human heart. Remember that the erotic poem is one of the most difficult poems to write because the language of physical love is typically very clichéd. Be fresh and adult in your language.

13

THE POETRY
OF WITNESS

Restraint

It's probably happened to you: You're watching television and suddenly a news story captures your attention. Perhaps political prisoners in China are being held for years without being charged. Or maybe you recognize the profound stupidity of a foreign war depicted on the screen. Or perhaps adolescent girls are being mutilated in Malaysia.

Maybe the story is located closer to home. Maybe a new study proves that African Americans are sentenced to jail at a much higher rate than whites who commit the same crimes. Or maybe the local government has lost track of several sex offenders right in your hometown. You can feel it: Something's not right. Maybe you have relatives in China or Malaysia. Maybe you have a brother in the army. Maybe you're African American. Maybe you're the parent of a young girl.

Or maybe you have absolutely no connection to the injustice you see before you; you just can't believe how wrong it is. You actually become physically upset.

For a poet, this is a time of truth. Some poets believe they can forfeit aesthetics as long as they communicate their point of view. Sometimes called **activist** poets, they think it's more important to take an angry stand than to make sure the poem succeeds artistically. They like to ride their rage into the poem. They want to infuse their words with anger against the particular brutal inequity that enrages them. Of course, by sacrificing the aesthetic quality of a poem, they communicate less effectively. They evoke less resentment in their readers, not more. They don't want to accept the unavoidable: When writing about injustice it's best to stay off the soapbox. A political poem rarely works as a diatribe or a rant. Like so many antiwar poems in the 1960s, the poems of activist poets are usually preachy—which means they're dull.

No matter what the subject, good poets recognize that their own emotions help to facilitate the creative act. To make good poems, it's best to feel deeply and adhere to aesthetic standards. After all, it would be very hard to write a strong love poem or elegy if you didn't feel much for the subject. But as a writer, you usually want to channel your emotion within the form of the poem. All poems, including those about political topics, must be held to an aesthetic standard, not a standard based on point of view. No matter how passionate you are, you still have to find fresh ways to express yourself. You still have to attend to form and tone and imagery and cadence. Remember, the most difficult subjects to write about are politics, religion, sexual love, and sports because these are soaked in clichéd language, often betraying simplistic, preconceived ideas. That's why poets prefer to discover the poem's "idea" while in the act of writing the poem—especially when they're working on a political poem, which, broadly speaking, is a poem that explores injustice.

While good poets have objected to an infinite number of wrongs, most political poetry in the United States has been concerned with war, race, and social inequities. No matter which of these is the focus, poets find ways to critique either the fact of the injustice or the psychological effect of it—or sometimes they critique both.

War and Witness

There have always been two opposing views of war. In one, war is seen as a kind of opportunity for men—and now women—to prove their valor. In the other, war is perceived as an inhuman mechanism that turns both sides physically and emotionally grotesque. Often, people who hold this latter view still believe that war, especially as a defensive measure, may be necessary, at least in certain circumstances and under certain conditions. These people typically object to the idealized glorification of killing. The best poets find ways to make the reader witness the effects of war, no matter their ideological position. But writers do not have to have been in a war to create a poetry of witness. Poets, after all, are practiced in imagination and empathy. With a little research and a willingness to confront the agony of combat, they can make literature that serves to awaken readers.

Some poets wish to render a highly realistically mental evocation of the soldier at war. Such poems sometimes require more length than usual. In the following poem Dorothy Barresi finds a way to reproduce the horrific chaos of battle and its psychological aftermath.

Little Dreams of War

Machine gun fire was hitting the beach.
It made a sip sip sound like someone
sucking on their teeth.

We had to crouch or crawl on all fours
when moving about the beach.

The British coxswain cried out,
"We can't go in there.
We can't see the landmarks."

There was nothing to be done
about the mistake.

Clicks and counterclicks:

mortars, bazookas, two frag grenades, white phosphorous flares,
sulfa, morphine Syrettes—
"one for pain, two for eternity."

"Terry stepped on a mine. It split open his foot
like a shoe on a last.
As I walked by, I said, 'So long, Terry.' I still wonder
if he made it to the hospital."

I saw a boy on fire, the soles of his boots were on fire.

Is this the drop zone?
Is that a bug bullet or a black seed?

Planes whined
like horses about to die.

Then men dug in for the night wherever they could,
some in the sand, some at the seawall, some on the bluff slopes
others in the hedgerow on the plateau
getting drunk on stolen Calvados.

"Good evening, 82nd Airborne. Tomorrow morning
the blood from your guts will grease
the wheels of our tanks."

Men lately drawn from the ways of peace.

Talk about luck!
I saw a dead first louie on the beach.
From his musette bag
I fished a bottle of Black and White scotch
and two cartons of cigarettes wrapped in wax paper.

Our coordinates were fixed.

The pipes were dripping wet, the turbines
hissing.

"We do not feel majestic," Jenkins wrote his wife in May.
"There are too many pinpricks in this life. The eternal drill,
the being pushed around, and hobnailed boots and
sweaty socks, and now the caged existence."

I saw a man with half his face
hanging from his neck;
he was holding up his dog tags for me to read.
"The purpose is recognition," he said, crying,

then he ran up the gun emplacements
and threw a grenade
in the embrasure.

There was nothing I could do about the mistake.

"Back it up! Back it up! Put the damn thing in reverse."

Is dissolve more poetic
than a jump cut?

In Reno, Nevada, that day
the casinos closed
and only sixteen couples filed for divorce.

"Hey asshole," my commanding officer kept yelling,
"Can you shoot?
Can you handle a boat?
What do you know about radios?"

This poem is effective because it may be, as the title tells us, a series of dreams, or it may be a series of actual events from a battle. Is the speaker a poet who was once a soldier? Is he remembering the battle, or is he actually in the battle? Either way, we're placed in the fragmenting psyche of a combatant. Together, the concrete details of the poem and its open, irregular form help to convey the splintering sensations that attend the need to fight and survive simultaneously.

Barresi makes sure all the specifics are especially convincing. Key words and references indicate that the battle probably takes place during World War II on D-Day at Omaha Beach in Normandy, France. We know the British infantry and the American 82nd Airborne are participating in a battle near the sea. The soldiers take a break and drink "Calvados," a sweet brandy made in France from apples. Then out of the dark the enemy taunts the soldiers, perhaps on a bullhorn or a PA system: "Good evening, 82nd Airborne. Tomorrow morning / the blood from your guts will grease / the wheels of our tanks.'" A "coxswain" is a naval captain who steers the boat and has charge of its crew. The battle is obviously taking a hellacious physical and mental toll on the men. During the battle a dying man still charges courageously up a hill to throw a grenade into an "embrasure," an opening in a wall through which soldiers can fire their weapons. Many are dying, while others are being doctored. "Syrettes" were small hypodermic devices for administering drugs, usually painkillers such as morphine. And soldiers used "musette bags" for carrying personal supplies through the war and onto the battlefield. The narrator—who may be a poet dreaming of the battle he survived—finds a famous brand of Scotch whisky in the bag belonging to a first lieutenant ("a dead first louie").

By the end of the poem, Barresi surprises us with a brief turn out of the narration when she mentions the jump cut and the divorcing couples. These five lines provide contrast and irony. Is this the way someone might deal with war, by suddenly dissociating from the event and imagining how they would retell the story? By imagining that the lives of others were suddenly, almost mysteriously changed as well? The effect is disorienting—and then we're back in the middle of the war, and the commander is barking questions at the speaker.

Occasionally Barresi resorts to a kind of blanket abstraction, but it's never clichéd, and it's always in context. For instance, she repeats an idea: "There was nothing I could do about the mistake." As historians have long documented, there were many strategic mistakes made during the invasion at Normandy. Barresi knows that it's best to validate the use of abstraction by establishing a base of vivid images. Ultimately, the poem seems to suggest that not only is war devastation, but that the battle stays with the soldier forever, that there's no exorcising it from consciousness.

Barresi finds fresh ways to convey the terror and maiming that characterize war. When you begin to write such poems it may help to keep in mind what the poet John Ciardi used to tell his classes: "The only facts a poet needs to know are those that have to do with the subject of the poem." If you're writing about a military battle, you should understand the language that authenticates the experience, though of course you want to avoid falling into jargon that will weary the reader.

Writing About Racism

In American literature there exists a long history of poems and stories about the pain of race relations. Earlier poems in this book by Yusef Komunyakaa and Lorna Dee Cervantes dramatize racial issues. In this poem, Martín Espada demonstrates the crime as well as the depths of racism from which it arose:

Two Mexicanos Lynched in Santa Cruz, California, May 3, 1877

More than the moment
when forty *gringo* vigilantes
cheered the rope
that snapped two *Mexicanos*
into the grimacing sleep of broken necks,

more than the floating corpses,
trussed like cousins of the slaughterhouse,
dangling in the bowed mute humility
of the condemned
more than the *Virgen de Guadalupe*

who blesses the brownskinned
and the crucified,
or the guitar-plucking skeletons
they will become
on the *Día de los Muertos,*

remain the faces of the lynching party:
faded as pennies from 1877, a few stunned
in the blur of execution,
a high-collar boy smirking, some peering
from the shade of bowler hats, but all
crowding into the photograph.

Espada's poem ends with an image that makes its powerful point: The individuals who lynched the two Mexican men were so caught up in the hatred of the mob that they actually wanted to be remembered in photos. Their racism was so pure—and so collective—that they were without self-consciousness. And the criminal justice system itself was so racist that no one feared being documented at the lynching because they all knew that they'd never be prosecuted. The image of the lynchers "all / crowding into the photograph" expands out from this one grotesquely inhuman act to so many that took place in the American nineteenth and twentieth centuries: Whether you were Mexican, African, Asian, or Native American, there was a time when you were considered so insignificant that you were outside the scope of lawful protection. You were hardly a person at all.

Again, in order to be convincing, it's usually best to make sure your poem is validated by as much actual historical detail as you can manage without burdening the poem with minutiae. Not only does Espada offer the place and the date, he also employs a photo from the era, making it a kind of eckphrastic poem. When we realize the photo exists we might realize something else: The lynching is fact. Two men died this way. People—these people in this photo—actually murdered them. His poem is not a superficial rant or a diatribe. Just as photos from the Holocaust, or Darfur, or September 11th act as proof of nearly inconceivable barbarism, the photo as described in Espada's poem serves as a gut-level marker, as veracity. To further authenticate the reading experience, Espada also employs Spanish words, thus rendering the bicultural lives of the victims as well as the narrator looking back into history. As most marginalized people know, one of the difficulties of being a member of a subordinate group is that you live in two cultures at once and can rarely be comfortably at home in either. If Espada didn't use the Spanish terms, such an implication would not come through as readily.

Poems About Gender

Since the 1960s many male and female poets have been writing about the detrimental effects of a society that greatly skews gender behavior. Sometimes poets describe how a patriarchal society makes women compete with one another in an unhealthy way. In this poem, Ginger Adcock Hendrix makes use of comedy while demonstrating how an adolescent girl grows depressed about her own body and sexual status.

The Arithmetic of Girl Beauty

—Thoughts after living every day with "The Brady Bunch,"
"Scooby Doo," and "Gilligan's Island"

Marcia Sucks. This is what Jan thought, all that
Other Girl angst rolled up inside her and only
Alice the Maid to sympathize—Velma never said so,
but she hated Daphne (For the scarf. *Gimme that
scarf*, she must have been thinking.)—The day
Marianne took a coconut to the head, got all
dressed up in Ginger's other dress, the one
with the sparkles, and sang *I Wanna Be
Loved By You* as she shimmied to the edge
of the bamboo stage, I was leaning in with all of me.
Tell Him. Please tell him, Marianne.
But she never got the job done. The dress fit her,
but she didn't fit the dress.

We never said *You Be Ginger*
or *I'll Be Marianne.* We knew
the picking had been done—there were two
kinds of girls in the world. You never saw
two Beauties together, though occasionally
the Other Girls would pair up and turn their backs
on possibility. Beauties were not nice to us,
but we needed their fair proximity.
There were dark hallways to stand in
near the boys who adored them, bottles
to spin, tree houses to crouch in.

And they needed us—there had to be three
for kissing: one boy, one girl he wants to kiss,
and another one to make it look like it's kissing
he wants, and not the girl. It was a simple matter
of finite, mathematical sets of three.

When I drive my car now on open roads,
this is what I look for, what I know one day I'll see:
Velma in a scarf, hightailing it
down a dirt road behind the round wheel
of that Mystery Machine—Marianne with her hair
set free from those crimping bands—and Jan,
the secret locket wrapped around her fist
like a dull-toned brass knuckles.
I'll slow my car, pull over to the side and let them
tear past. And I know they'll be waving
right at me through a cloud of dust—majorettes
in a hazy parade.

Seriocomic poems such as this one use humor to make readers see the dark truth in a situation. We may laugh because we've watched repeat episodes of the three television shows. If we're female, we may laugh because we can relate personally to the damaging behavior. Jan, Velma, and Marianne all long to be beautiful like Marcia, Daphne, and Ginger, but as the poem says, "the picking had been done." The world around these women (and around the speaker when she was a girl) knew who would receive credit for beauty and who would not. In fact, the culture made beauty the most important quality a young woman could have; and it was the ticket to the only culturally approved job: motherhood. Of course, beauty and motherhood are good things, but no life should be limited to such narrow parameters. "The Arithmetic of Girl Beauty" renders how, in the midtwentieth century, social rules insisted that girls who were not recognized as "Beauties" would have to make do; they would never live a special, self-confident life. Of course, even the "Beauties" are locked into one way of being, maintaining their looks in order to attract a man. Beneath the narrator's comic tone is sad resignation.

Like Adcock Hendrix's poem about these divisions, many poems by women have detailed the way societal forces make females "feminine" and males "masculine." These forces seduce both sexes into believing that certain prescribed ways of behaving are critical if one is to be suitably male or female, despite that fact that these forces are narrowing and often destructive. Hendrix's poem demonstrates how most women can be emotionally disfigured by social expectations. Of course, as sociologists have explained for decades, such expectations clearly skew male behavior too.

In the following poem by Michael Ryan we can see how men suffer from male behavioral expectations.

The Ditch

In the ditch, half-ton sections of cast-iron molds
hand-greased at the seams with pale petroleum waste
and screw-clamped into five-hundred-gallon cylinders
drummed with rubber-headed sledges inside and out
to settle tight the wet concrete
that, dried and caulked, became Monarch Septic Tanks;
and, across the ditch, my high school football coach,
Don Compo, spunky pug of a man,
bronze and bald, all biceps and pecs,
raging at some "attitude" of mine
he snipped from our argument about Vietnam—
I mean *raging*, scarlet, veins bulging from his neck,
he looked like a hard-on stalking back and forth—
but I had started college, this was a summer job,
I no longer had to take his self-righteous, hectoring shit,
so I was chuckling merrily, saying he was ludicrous,
and he was calling me "College Man Ryan"
and with his steel-toed workboot kicking dirt
that clattered against the molds and puffed up between us.

It's probably not like this anymore, but every coach
in my hometown was a lunatic. Each had different quirks
we mimicked, beloved bromides whose parodies we intoned,
but they all conducted practice like bootcamp,
the same tirades and abuse, no matter the sport,
the next game the next battle in a neverending war.
Ex-paratroopers and -frogmen, at least three
finally-convicted child molesters, genuine sadists
fixated on the Commie menace and our American softness
that was personally bringing the country to the brink of collapse—

in this company, Don Compo didn't even seem crazy.
He had never touched any of us;
his violence was verbal, which we were used to,
having gotten it from our fathers
and given it back to our brothers and to one another
since we had been old enough to button our own pants.
Any minute—no guessing what might spring it—
he could be butting your face-mask and barking up your nostrils,
but generally he favored an unruffled, moralistic carping
in which, I, happy to spot phoniness,
saw pride and bitterness masquerading as teaching.
In the locker-room, I'd sit where I could roll my eyeballs
as he droned, but, across the ditch,
he wasn't lecturing, but fuming, flaring
as I had never seen in four years of football,
and it scared and thrilled me to defy him and mock him
when he couldn't make me handwash jockstraps after practice
or do pushups on my fingertips in a mud puddle.

But it was myself I was taunting. I could see my retorts
snowballing toward his threat to leap the ditch
and beat me to a puddle of piss ("you craphead,
you wiseass"), and my unspading a shovel from a dirt pile
and grasping its balance deliberately down the handle
and inviting him to try it.
Had he come I would have hit him.
There's no question about that.
For a moment, it ripped through our bewilderment
which then closed over again
like the ocean
if a cast-iron mold were dropped in.
I was fired when the boss broke the tableau.
"The rest of you," he said, "have work to do,"
and, grabbing a hammer and chisel, Don Compo,
mounted the mold between us in the ditch
and with one short punch split it down the seam.

This dramatic poem uses clashing sounds and imagery to demonstrate the way most men have been raised to aspire to violence, physical conflict, and oneupmanship. As the poem makes clear, too often males are valorized by foolish

face-to-face confrontation. Many intentionally seek out such altercations.
Though they have been disputing the Vietnam War, these two men don't have
to go to war—yet they are inexorably drawn to battling each other. It's as if
they both need the quarrel in order to feel good about themselves. The
narrator is "chuckling merrily" because he enjoys challenging his old
coach. And yet one of the moments that make this poem so effective is the
narrator's realization of how foolish he is: "it was myself I was taunting." This
self-recognition is what transforms the narrator; he recognizes his own com-
plicity in the male foolishness. In effect, he sees that he's become his old coach.

When you write poems about gender one way to get the poem started is
to picture the early events that helped to make you who you are. And it's
always helpful to begin writing without wanting to convey a big idea. You
want your reader to be moved by your imagery. Try to avoid being
excessively didactic or overdetermining.

The Question of Culpability

In an essay entitled "Poetry and Commitment," the poet Jonathan
Holden suggests that some of the best political poems are those that seem
to make the reader responsible for the injustice. When readers feel even
faintly culpable or responsible they register the injustice more deeply
(though they may resist at first). In Louis Simpson's poem about the
weapons trade and foreign policy, the speaker directly addresses the reader.

On the Lawn at the Villa

On the lawn at the villa—
That's the way to start, eh, reader?
We know where we stand—somewhere expensive—
You and I *imperturbes*, as Walt would say,
Before the diversions of wealth, you and I *engagés*.

On the lawn at the villa
Sat a manufacturer of explosives,
His wife from Paris,
And a young man named Bruno,

And myself, being American,
Willing to talk to these malefactors,

The manufacturer of explosives, and so on,
But somehow superior. By that I mean democratic.
It's complicated, being an American,
Having the money and the bad conscience, both at the same time.
Perhaps, after all, this is not the right subject for a poem.

We were all sitting there paralyzed
In the hot Tuscan afternoon,
And the bodies of the machine-gun crew were draped over the
  balcony.
So we sat there all afternoon.

From the outset, Simpson establishes a mock intimacy with the reader. In effect, he sets up a confrontational relationship; he challenges us to agree with him, but his tone is manipulative: "That's the way to start, eh, reader? / We know where we stand—somewhere expensive— / You and I *imperturbes*, as Walt would say. . . ." If *imperturbes* means "unperturbed," we can assume that the speaker imagines that he and we are sitting outside in cosmopolitan comfort at an Italian villa. We haven't asked to be *engagés* (engaged in pleasant conversation) with the narrator, but he has put us right there in the middle of the situation.

Why would he do this? For one thing, he wants to intrigue us; he wants to draw us into the action of the poem. In the highly fluid, destabilizing reality of the poem, we are not actually sitting there, but we are intimate witnesses—so intimate that the speaker makes us feel responsible for the balance of what happens. The little social group consists of a "manufacturer of explosives" and "his wife from Paris," as well as a "young man named Bruno" and the speaker, "an American," who knows these others are troublemakers. All the details enhance a growing anxiety. The speaker is not repulsed by the company he keeps. He takes too much comfort in being "superior" by virtue of his "democratic" turn of mind. And yet, ultimately, that's the center of the hypocrisy.

Without making any pronouncement, the poem forces us to confront our own conscience: If our "democratic" government ignores weapons manufacturers who profit from the indiscriminate sale of arms, how can we feel superior? How can we avoid guilt?

New poets should remember that any political poem runs the risk of offending readers who disagree with its perspective. Such a risk is doubled when you ask the reader to feel culpable for the injustice. It risks being offensive *and* it risks being overdetermined. The fun is in finding a

THE POET'S NOTE CARD

Poems Against Injustice

1. Because of preconceived ideas and/or clichéd language, the most difficult subjects to write about are politics, religion, sexual love, and sports.

2. All poems, including those about those topics, succeed best when held to an aesthetic standard, not a standard based on point of view.

3. Sometimes the best political poems are those that find a way to make the reader experience injustice. Such verse is sometimes called "the poetry of witness."

4. In order to be convincing, it's usually best to make sure your poem is validated by actual historical detail.

5. Another effective way to write the political poem is to make the reader feel culpability for the injustice.

6. Even—or especially—in political poems, it is best to discover the poem's "idea" while in the act of writing the poem.

7. Try to stay off the soapbox. A political poem rarely works as a diatribe or a rant.

8. If you are to employ abstract language in a poem, it's often best to validate the use of abstraction by establishing a base of vivid images.

way to intrigue your readers while drawing them into the web of the poem. Let the events of the poem persuade readers. Though all poems may be **didactic,** some poets can be too baldly didactic. Try to avoid lecturing; stay off the soapbox. (Coyly, as if to comfort the reader he's tested, Simpson says, "Perhaps, after all, this is not the right subject for a poem.") Jonathan Holden suggests, most importantly, that you never enter into the poem with your point of view already fixed. Discovery augments creativity. As with all poems, you might try instead to discover what you want to say while in the act of writing. Let each poem find its point of view.

WRITING EXERCISES

1. *War poem.* War poems are often difficult to write because (1) most poets have not been to war and (2) there is often an urge on the poet's part to render what's obvious: War is horrible. So if you've been in war and wish to try this topic, try to get across the experience without falling into the cliché that soldiers sometimes use. If you have not been to war, try to imagine what one small instance in the middle of a battle or a strange peaceful interlude is like.

2. *War poem with epigraph.* Begin by finding a quote from a soldier's journal or a newspaper account. Use the quote as an epigraph. Now try to render what the quote does not get across: perhaps some intriguing detail that we'd never have thought of. Make that the focus of the poem.

3. *Social injustice poem.* Choose an example of social injustice that disturbs you deeply. With great attention to detail, write a poem about the worst possible outcome of that injustice or trend as it could affect a single person. Use the third person. Try to avoid the cliché and rhetoric usually associated with the subject.

4. *Political poem.* Choose a poem about a political event or trend that bothers you. Remember that the most powerful political poems are those set in the most concrete circumstances. Some are subtly understated, offering almost no commentary. Make the events or description of your poem do the talking.

5. *Racism/sexism poem.* Write a poem about an experience you had with racism or sexism. Try not to sound as if you're giving a lecture. Rather, using the first person, simply depict the events and let them speak for themselves.

6. *Sexual orientation poem.* If you're gay or transgendered and if you're comfortable with being "out" in your poetry, consider writing a poem about the difficulties you've experienced due to your sexual orientation. Though you've certainly had to deal with many instances of bias, try to limit the imagery to one or two provocative moments.

7. *Sex-role poem.* Write a poem that renders the key experiences that helped make you the type of man or woman you are today. Have you ever been restricted from engaging in certain behavior? If you are a woman, were you discouraged from athletics, from math,

from engineering? If you are a man, were you discouraged from teaching, from nursing, even from expressing emotion? Recreate these influential moments—but remember to relate these events to adult life.

8. *Gender twist poem.* Write a poem from the vantage point of the opposite sex. Imagine a critical situation or highly charged emotion or both. Convey what the person is going through.

14

STRETCHING THE IMAGINATION

The Next Challenge

By now you're a practiced poet. You've learned the difference between generic representations and detailed pictures. You've seen the way present-day idiom contributes to the sound of a poem, and how the sound of a poem helps to bear its meaning. You've worked on making evocative metaphors and intriguing narratives. You know that the imagery of any good poem renders a conflict and, ultimately, a key moment of change. You've practiced many different forms, from open free verse to a more traditional structure. You've contemporized classic subjects, from relative portraits to childhood memories, from love poems to mourning poems to political poems.

At this point you're ready to try new tools that will open your imagination to greater possibilities of imaginative expression. The following types of poems each provides a different opportunity for you to find language that renders a state of mind you didn't know you already inhabited. Each of these poems presents a motivating challenge that can lead you to create new ways of thinking and structuring language.

Eckphrasis

An **eckphrastic** poem is inspired by a work of art, usually a painting or sculpture. In the following poem, Sandra Gilbert explores the implications of a daguerreotype in order to reconsider a disturbing historical reality. Among the earliest types of photographs, daguerreotypes were made from metal coated with chemicals and exposed for long periods to light. The process usually required that the subject be perfectly still, so often photographers sought out sleepers—or sometimes dead people. Here Gilbert enters the life of a sleeping wet nurse (a woman who, after becoming pregnant with her own child, suckled the children of wealthy families).

❀ Daguerreotype: Wet Nurse

Everything about her thick—thick wrists, thick ankles,
skin thick as felt—she dawdles
through the rich man's nursery,
stupid, staring at nothing, wearing her heavy body
idly as the heifer wears her bell.

When the silk-skinned child stirs and whimpers
in its slim mahogany stall,
she yawns, offers a nipple thick as cheese,
hot as the haystacks where she lies in dreams,
legs spread to country lovers.

Rocking and dozing, oozing juice, she says
she still remembers the other child,
the wailing one she left in the suburbs
to be weaned on tea or water.
It had, she thinks, red down

on its wobbly head: or was it brown?
She sleeps. The child sucks, gurgles,
also sleeps. Behind thick lids
we see her pupils flicker, back and forth.
A small vein pulses in her neck, while

from somewhere far inside her breast, her skull,
rises the humming of an insect self, thin, elegant,

spinning a web of bitter milk
to drown the mild
breathing of the rich man's child.

The effect of daguerreotypes could be dreamy or eerie, and Gilbert exploits the strange, almost unnatural nature of the image here by imagining what the life of the woman must be like. Most of the poet's lines suggest a great exhaustion, but soon enough we can see that the woman is tired not simply from the constant attention to the baby in her charge, but because of her own child left behind. Gilbert must use her imagination to engage the woman's existence. Gilbert knows that the woman is so poor that she can only find work nursing the children of the affluent. She's exhausted from carrying the memory of her child, even though that memory has grown vague: "It had, she thinks, red down / / on its wobbly head; or was it brown?" The image draws readers into the poverty as well as the woman's psychological method of day-to-day survival.

Gilbert's eckphrastic poem is also a sociopolitical poem. She's not just interested in the injustice (here, an insensitive social system that crushes people, especially women), but also in its psychological effects. Eckphrastic poems afford you an opportunity to consider a new subject, which is not simply the artwork but whatever you discover while examining the artwork. The eckphrastic poet finds the deeper subject while in the act of writing, not simply by sitting back and looking at the painting or photo. Gilbert didn't look at the daguerreotype and plan out exactly what she would write. She looked at it and began writing. She found her point of view while making images out of the source image. Eckphrastic poems require the empathy we discussed in Chapter Six. In order to write them well, you should try to become the subject.

The Drama of Sport

Rarely is a sports poem about sports. It may, of course, start out telling us something about the game, about the fly ball hanging up there like the moon before it decides to go over the fence or drop like a shot bird to the right fielder who makes a basket catch at the wall. It might give you all the trash talk of two NFL linemen, or the pastoral description of the green green grass covered so fluidly by the graceful cross-country runner, or the last second shot to win—or lose—the NCAA basketball championship. Sports poems use sports to get at something *else*. Poets almost always seem to use the drama of sport to suck the reader in; then they turn their attention to the heart of the matter, which is always a crisis in the human heart. Here's a "baseball" poem by David Bottoms.

Sign for My Father, Who Stressed the Bunt

On the rough diamond,
the hand-cut field below the dog lot and barn,
we rehearsed the strict technique
of bunting. I watched from the infield,
the mound, the backstop
as your left hand climbed the bat, your legs
and shoulders squared toward the pitcher.
You could drop it like a seed
down either base line. I admired your style,
but not enough to take my eyes of the bank
that served as our center-field fence.

Years passed, three leagues of organized ball,
no few lives. I could homer
into the garden behind the bank,
into the left-field lot of Carmichael Motors,
and still you stressed the same technique,
the crouch and spring, the lead arm absorbing
just enough impact. That whole tiresome pitch
about basics never changing,
and I never learned what you were laying down.

Like a hand brushed across the bill of a cap,
let this be the sign
I'm getting a grip on the sacrifice.

Bottoms paints a highly textured picture of a father teaching his son, the narrator, how to bunt. (Sometimes called a "sacrifice" because the batter usually makes an out in order to advance the runner in scoring position, a bunt is a ball struck so softly that it stays well within the infield.) The father wants the boy to learn the fundamentals of baseball, and bunting is one of the most important of these. But the boy can't stop looking at "the bank / that served as center-field fence," because he wants the glory of hitting home runs.

Even after the boy grows older and plays into his teenage years, the father keeps stressing the importance of the bunt, something that seems boring to the son. Ultimately we learn that the speaker only begins to understand the father's deeper message later on in life. In the elaborate ritual of baseball signs, "a hand brushed across the bill of a cap" may be the signal to bunt. By the end of the poem Bottoms employs the word "sacrifice" to indicate both the act of bunting and the father's willingness to give so much time to his son. An adult now, the home-run-hitting narrator finally starts to recognize that the father was modeling love by sacrificing his time to give the boy a lesson. The father knows that we need to practice all the fundamentals in life, not just the oft-celebrated acts of achievement.

When you write a sports poem, you should find something new and intriguing about the drama of the athletic contest. You might think about the old scorekeeper who possesses some mysterious past; why does the basketball game he's watching trigger something revealing in him? You might imagine what it feels like to blow a tire at 210 mph in the Indy 500; how is the driver's reaction time linked to a childhood fear? You might start with a track meet in which a sophomore is suddenly about to break the school record in the 800 meters—only to stop running twenty meters from the finish line; what took place at home that led to this extraordinary refusal? Whatever you do, try to avoid the cliché of the unsuccessful athlete who suddenly breaks into stardom unless you can bring something truly original to the tale.

The Serious Business of the Funny Poem

Everyone likes a good joke. And a lot of people like funny poems. It's often alleged that humor enables us to see what we'd otherwise avoid, especially if we're asked to look into ourselves. Will Rogers once said, "Everything is funny as long as it's happening to someone else." A funny poem may be about someone else, but privately we can often find application to our own behavior. But what aspect of behavior is actually funny? The philosopher Henri Bergson once suggested that people laugh at "inelasticity." By this he meant an inability to adapt to change or recognize inconsistencies. For instance, have you ever laughed at someone who trips on a sidewalk crack and then stumbles before regaining his balance? The attempted recovery betrays inelasticity or a rigidity of habit, an automatism that some people find hilarious. But in a richer, more deeply important manner than physical clumsiness, mental, spiritual, and emotional inelasticity are worse—and therefore even funnier.

A good comic poem usually finds a way to depict some aspect of human behavior as unwittingly rigid. Surely this is the reason so many of David Kirby's poems succeed. Kirby has always had a knack for self-deprecating humor. You're often funniest in your poem when your speaker demonstrates inelasticity, as in this poem.

⊗ Sarah Bernhardt's Leg

> Dr. Denucé took it off in 1915,
> and P. T. Barnum offered Sarah Bernhardt
> ten thousand dollars for her severed leg,
> but it was burned or buried somewhere near Dax,
> in the Landes district of France.
> Years ago I looked in the library
> for Sarah Bernhardt's leg. It was not there,
>
> but now I see it wherever I go:
> by the side of the road at night;
> among the canned goods in the supermarket;
> in the back of the classroom, the shoe still on,
> the stocking carefully tucked in at the top.
> I am afraid it will turn up on my doorstep.
> I must find Sarah Bernhardt's leg
>
> before the descendants of Barnum do
> or the dogs. Leibniz said,
> "Why is there anything at all rather than nothing?"
> I say, "Why is there Sarah Bernhardt's leg?"
> Love is an act of the will,
> according to Augustine—
> things count because we say so.

Sarah Bernhardt was probably the most famous nineteenth-century actress in the world. Beautiful, multitalented, and provocative, she performed in many operas and a few early films. She also wrote novels, painted, sculpted, and modeled for other artists; she had affairs with internationally famous people. The speaker of the poem has become inexplicably obsessed with finding Bernhardt's leg, which was amputated near the end of her life after an accident. Clearly, there's nothing funny about the amputation. The poem is funny, however, because the speaker cannot resolve his own inelastic habit of mind. He can't stop thinking about the leg of this famous person, even though he knows it hasn't existed for more than a century.

No matter what you do, ultimately a good comic poem has something serious to say. If not, it's no more than a pun or a quickly dismissed joke. Kirby's poem is about the nature of obsession. Near the end, the poem takes a clever turn toward philosophy. Here's this batty speaker who knows arcane facts about Sarah Bernhardt's leg as well as a central thesis in philosophy. But is he all that batty? The narrator unintentionally shows us how humor can help us come to terms with the inexplicable mysteries of the universe. We're all rigid in our inability to understand them.

There are a number of ways to begin writing a comic poem. You might remember something you did that made everyone around you laugh—or something a friend did. You might capture a peculiar effect of speech (see Ruth Stone's poem "Bazook" in Chapter Three). Just as Kirby does, you might exaggerate a strange behavior. You might approach an absurd idea as something to be taken quite seriously. You might actually tell a joke within the poem. You may end with a funny line. You might make fun of someone's behavior and then, after having prepared the reader for a reasonably comic journey, reverse polarities and make the poem much darker in tone. The important thing is to keep your pacing crisp and make sure the reader understands the context for the comedy.

Divinity and Uncertainty

One of the special pleasures of the religious life is feeling the harmonic oneness with God and the universe. Religious people often describe this sensation as a kind of internal buoyancy in which they float safely in the arms of a divine presence. Such a sensation can be so pleasurable that some people turn to poetry in order to describe it, because the language of poetry is so well-suited for lyrical evocation. But why is it that so much meager poetry is written about religion, just as it is about love and politics?

As we've discussed, the language of these subjects is drenched in cliché. Take the sentence "Christ saved my soul." For many religious people, especially Christians, the act of redemption is central to their lives. This one sentence might even express the single most important truth of their existence. Yet the average reader of poetry would find this particular language dull if it were in a poem. Why? First, because these words have been used uncountable times. They are just too common; when used in a poem, they commit the literary sin of being tiresome. Even in a church, ministers and priests must call up their best theatrical selves in order to inflect such language with vitality. Second, language of this sort fails to intrigue readers because, in most poems, such language appears as a matter of utter fact and fails to convey a conflict. Sometimes it's easy for the religious poet to want merely to declare divine happiness. As a result there's very little struggle on the part of the speaker, very little authenticity in the transformative moment.

Good poetry anticipates a serious, adult audience that holds many beliefs. Like all other poems, a religious or spiritual poem must depict a protagonist confronting an impediment to happiness. Often that happiness depends on a protagonist attaining some degree of certainty. Like all poems, good religious poems make the human experience convincing. The best religious or spiritual poets know that all poems, especially poems about God, need to avoid the problem termed **deus ex machina**, in which—out of nowhere—some person or thing other than the protagonist overcomes the obstacle at the heart of the conflict. (The term *deus ex machina* can be translated as "a god from a machine.") The protagonist is suddenly worry-free without having done a thing. Yet a good work of literature requires that a protagonist do one of three things: face the obstacle and overcome it, be overcome by the obstacle, or battle the obstacle to a draw. In a good poem, God simply can't step in and save the day. In this next, moving poem, Jeanne Murray Walker (who has also been the poetry editor of the journal *Christianity and Literature*) effectively wrestles with questions of faith and security.

So Far, So Good

I'm peering through my son's telescope,
trying to see whether the universe has shrunk
overnight, as the *Times* claims, much smaller
than scientists thought. I don't doubt it.
If Jack plunks down his milk glass
these days, it entirely blots out Europe.
Yesterday I had to make him uncross
his arms and stop leaning on the world.
Have a little heart, I said,
wiping spaghetti off the teal face of Hungary
on his placemat. Now as he digs into
his mashed potatoes, I pray for him,
for all kids who'll soon be cut loose
into contracting space, where I could

fax this to you in minutes, where the Concorde
swims through our miniature sky like a minnow.
What keeps us, against all odds,
in a universe we know nothing about?
Jack's made it to the age of ten. So far,
so good. But the facts! My neighbor said
potatoes, if they're dug too green,
are poison. And how green is too green?
We could keel over from green potatoes
any day, from mother love, from a truckload
of bananas that neglects to swerve. Every morning
I wake up, like a hypochondriac who's cured,
to the shock that we're safe.
Peer through the telescope. Can you see
the hocus-pocus stars out there?
And scanning across the sky, what's that?
A blue eye blinking back—God, it might be—
way out at the edge, so far,
so good.

Walker's poem is anchored in specific detail, even though it depicts her wondering about the role of God in our lives. After she begins the poem by looking through the telescope at the larger universe and then looking at her son's more prosaic food plate, she asks her central question: "What keeps us, against all odds, / in a universe we know nothing about?" For her the problem is how to live without understanding how God will keep us safe. The question owns a gravitas because at any moment her son could be subject to life's dangerous vicissitudes. The narrating mother believes in God, but she can't be absolutely sure about the nature of what it is she believes in. After all, most believers are not arrogant enough to think they can fully know the mind of another person, let alone a divine being. Her perplexity even intercedes in the lines near the end: "Look into the telescope. Can you see / the hocus-pocus stars out there?" The term *hocus-pocus* may suggest irony or uncertainty—or both. That the sentiment is manifest in a question helps to render her uncertainty. By the end of the poem the blinking stars aid somewhat: She is provisionally willing to believe that the natural world is a sign of a beneficent god. Still, for her child's sake and for her own, her metaphysical vigilance will continue: "so far, / so good."

One of the pleasures of the religious poem lies in rendering the possibility—even probability—of a divine presence in the universe. But

THE POET'S NOTE CARD

More Imaginative Paths

1. An eckphrastic poem is inspired by a work of visual art.

2. Rarely about sports, good sports poems sometimes appeal to our sense of struggle.

3. In poetry the four senses other than sight can often play an important role in achieving new imaginative awareness.

4. A good comic poem is never merely humorous; the comic component always underscores the poem's serious intent. Rather than rely on puns or punch lines, it's often best to demonstrate inelasticity in the protagonist.

5. Religious or spiritual poems need a protagonist who attempts to overcome a conflict. God simply can't step in and save the day.

we must beware of that pleasure leading the poem into sentimentality. Good religious poets remain frank, even if they are frank about confronting the impediments to happiness, especially spiritual happiness. They may believe in God, but they also know that such belief does not give them pure permanent bliss in this world.

When you write the religious poem make sure you invest it with the same kind of internal struggle you would invest in any other poem.

WRITING EXERCISES

1. *Eckphrastic poem.* Write a poem based on a work of visual art. For example, start with a painting. Try to imagine the story that the painting tells. Who is the protagonist? What is the prime conflict in the painting? What is the plot? You don't have to know what the artist was actually thinking or what she came to say about the painting. Rather, you can just use your imagination to make it up.

2. *Eckphrastic poem in the margins.* Study a Renaissance painting with many people in it. (For instance, go the The Metropolitan Museum's

web site and examine "A Hunting Scene" by Piero di Cosimo.)
Concentrate on some of the people in the margins of the painting.
What do they think about the goings on at the center of the image?
Using evocative imagery, make their point of view central.

3. *Sports poem.* Write a poem about an athletic contest. Keep your
   language fresh. Make the athlete—or at least your reader—learn
   something about being human. Ultimately, all good sports poems
   are about the human condition, not about the sport.

4. *Sports poem with distraction.* You're at a major league baseball game,
   it's the ninth inning, and the score is tied. The runner at second
   base is trying to steal third. Suddenly something outside the game
   distracts you. Write a poem about this distraction. What is it?
   Why is it more important to you than the game?

5. *Comic poem.* Write a poem that intends to make your reader
   laugh. Play against expectations. Employ surprise. Some people
   think that funny poems can't be real poems—but that's nonsense.
   The general rule is that as long as a funny poem is making a point
   about human life it has just as much claim on excellence as an
   elegy or any other type of poem.

6. *First-line punch-line poem.* Do you know a good joke? Try writing a
   poem that starts with the punch line. What happens next? Who is
   laughing—or who fails to laugh? Why? Let the joke lead you into
   other comic possibilities.

7. *Religious poem.* If you're a religious person, you might enjoy the
   challenge of writing a spiritual poem. Make your narrator a
   believer, but be sure to depict the narrator in the act of confronting an impediment to happiness. Find creative ways of using
   language that's fresh and well-textured.

8. *Church poem.* Imagine that you enter a cavernous, empty church.
   If you're a believer, use imagery to convey the way the big space is
   an impediment to feeling God's presence. If you're a doubter or a
   nonbeliever, describe how the atmosphere might lead you to want
   something you don't believe in.

15

BREAKING THE RULES, NURTURING THE WEIRD

Eccentricity and Voice

We may not like to admit it, but all of us harbor certain ideas or habits we don't want the world to know about. Take Jeremy: Fascinated by the pictures and messages inside bottle caps, he's kept his favorites in a workbench drawer for years. Or Mike: While he doesn't often smell his dog's paw pads, he enjoys the scent a lot and thinks about the smell frequently. Or Claudia: She works in an accounting office and she loves the sunglasses her boss, Anna, wears so much that every month or so she secretly uses black-ink Sharpies to draw them over large photocopies of her own face. Then there's Warren: A tough corporate lawyer past age 50, he secretly carries a 1965 baseball card of Willie Mays in his wallet—and every year or so when he looks at the card he's struck dumb; he finds he literally cannot speak. If their idiosyncrasies were public knowledge, these four individuals could be perceived as weird.

In fact, though, their habits are among the many traits that distinguish each one of them from all other people. Not only do we have different thoughts, all people—not just poets—have radically different ways of thinking and feeling. Just as our bodies might perceive the transplanted organs of another person as alien, our very consciousness would be alien to another human being. You might have seen science fiction movies in which the mind of one person "melds" with that of another. The process is usually approached with trepidation, because any two minds are so foreign to each other that mental illness or death can result. Such a dramatization helps to demonstrate the fundamental uniqueness of each human being. We may use the same language, but inside, each poet is matchless.

Good poets develop methods to mine the interior, bringing their eccentricities to the surface. Rather than cover up distinguishing traits, they nurture their own weirdness. For instance, Ginger Adcock Hendrix exploited her unusually detailed knowledge of old TV shows in her poem "The Arithmetic of Girl Beauty." If Jeremy, Mike, Claudia, and Warren were poets, they may find ways to write about their idiosyncratic habits. Not only might the events described seem intriguingly unusual, but, if they were to let their true selves do the writing, their ways of expressing themselves would also be different. While the language we're taught has necessary rules that are repeated (for example, the subject-verb-object pattern in English), most poets eventually discover their own ways of manipulating the language to correspond to their own distinguishing habits of being. Which is to say, they discover their own poetic voice.

Being Different

Poets want to depict the world as they truly perceive it, and they want to project a voice that is by definition different from all other poetic voices. Developing an authentic voice takes time. You need to read a wide spectrum of poetry, and you need to try all kinds of writing styles. Most beginners rightly imitate a variety of other poets while learning the basics, just as you've been doing. You can't become the equivalent of T. S. Eliot or Elizabeth Bishop overnight. The pressure to sound unique can make some poets strain too much. They end up sounding awkward or even phony. But many poets eventually become comfortable in their own signature style, as different as it may be from that of their poet peers.

Because they abhor being boring, they risk showing the world how they see the world. For instance, Laura Jensen has written a wonderful lyric poem about boats that are "bad." As weird as it may seem, she uses personification to make the boats human:

❧ Bad Boats

They are like women because they sway.
They are like men because they swagger.
They are like lions because they are kings here.
They walk on the sea. The drifting
logs are good: they are taking their punishment.
But the bad boats are ready to be bad,
to overturn in water, to demolish the swagger
and the sway. They are bad boats
because they cannot wind their own rope
or guide themselves neatly close to the wharf.
In their egomania they are glad
for the burden of the storm the men are shirking
when they go for their coffee and yawn.
They are bad boats and they hate their anchors.

Readers may initially think it's strange to personify boats as "bad." Some may think doing so is absurd. But the very strangeness of the perception is actually not at all strange for Jensen. Her idiosyncratic view of boats may be disorienting, but ultimately it gives readers a chance to see the world in a fresh way. We're not used to thinking of boats as human, but by doing so we may come to understand people as we never have before. By staying true to her "odd" vision, Jensen gives us a newly effective way of observing and comprehending the world: Among other things, the poem shows us how it's in our nature to resist restriction (a lesson poets should learn well). At first, we resist the poem's weirdness, but if we accept the preliminary disorientation, we can engage reality in a fresh way.

That's why in the end it's best to create language that matches your way of discerning reality. As we saw in Chapter Ten, the elegy most often describes how the speaker remembers a person who has died. Sandra McPherson has written famously imaginative elegies. Here's one about a woman who has miscarried.

❈ A Coconut for Katerina

Inside the coconut is Katerina's baby. The coconut's hair, like
  Katerina's brown hair.
Like an auctioneer Katerina holds the coconut, Katerina in her
  dark fur coat
covering winter's baby, feet in the snow. Katerina's baby is the milk
and will not be drinking it.

Ropes hanging down from the trees—are they well ropes? Ropes
  on a moss
wall. Not to ring bells but used for climbing up and down
or pulling. I mean bringing. Anchor ropes on which succulent ropy
  seaplants grow.

And floating like a bucket of oak or like a light wooden dory,
  the coconut bobs,
creaking slowly, like a piling or a telephone pole with wet wires
downed by a thunderstorm over its face.

This baby's head, this dog's head, this dangerous acorn is the grocer
of a sky-borne grocery store where the white-aproned grocer or
  doctor imprints it
with three shady fingerprints, three flat abysses the ropes will not cross.

What of it? There is enough business for tightrope walkers in
  this jungle.
The colonizers make a clearing
for a three-cornered complex of gas stations, lit with a milky
  spotlight
at night.

        And here we dedicate this coconut to Katerina. We
  put our hand
on the round stomach of Katerina. We put our five
  short ropes on the fingers of the lost
baby of Katerina and haul it in to the light of day and wash
  it with sand.

Coconut, you reverse of the eye, the brown iris in white, the
  white center
in brown sees so differently. The exposed fibrous iris,

the sphere on which memory or recognizing must have latitude
   and longitude
to be moored.

or preserved in the big sky, the sea's tug of war. The tugging of
   water
held in and not clear. Lappings and gurglings of living hollows
   half-filled,
half with room
for more empty and hopeful boats and their sails.

Even though they work well for most poets, McPherson eschews the traditional elegiac formulations involving remembrance and consolation. While
the poem is narrated in the third person, we are to understand that the events
of the poem are taking place in the mind of Katerina, the mother who has lost
her child. McPherson understands that the mind of a woman grieving the sudden loss of her child is likely to be frenetic with bizarre images. Some women
would be overwrought, their antic thoughts trying to explain and compensate
for the loss. In Katerina's grief, her thoughts seem to fly around without logic.

McPherson sticks to her own vision, refusing to give in to the need for
order. She knows the poem is quite difficult to follow at first. But she also
knows that if she abandons her way of writing, the poem will not deliver
the reality of the situation as she sees it. So she portrays Katerina's fragmenting consciousness and the many strange images (a coconut, ropes, gas
stations, tightrope walkers, a jungle) that might invade Katerina's mind.
McPherson trusts that the poem is accessible, but she knows it will take
time to figure out all of the connections and implications.

When you write you should never be willfully inaccessible. No poem
should be difficult for the sake of difficulty. Some beginning poets keep
their poems hard to follow because they are afraid that the poem will not
be "profound" enough. Others write inaccessible poems because of private
references that apply only to themselves or a few people. Neither is legiti-
mate. But if, as in "Bad Boats" and "A Coconut for Katerina," your vision
requires a way of rendering images that may initially be foreign to readers,
then you should trust in yourself—especially if you're confident that the
plot is eventually accessible and the poem is organically unified.

Associative Journeys

We know that people think in different ways. Rather than think in logical
or illogical fashion, most people think associatively, a process by which one

idea or image triggers another idea or image and so on. Each person's associative thought processes proceed in a unique manner. Just as we all have distinguishing fingerprints, poets develop distinguishing voiceprints. An **associative poem** usually moves quickly, one event leading to the next. But despite its apparently random flow, a good associative poem is organic; it may seem compassless in its journey, but it's unified by theme and tone.

When writing an associative poem, the kinds of things to which you refer and the manner in which you refer to them signify your own unique style. Here's a free-flowing associative poem by Bob Hicok who uses comedy and surrealism as well:

❀ Whither Thou Goest

> Fish can have mad cow disease and I have a problem
> with that. Purity suffers and salmon can't
> moo can't paw grass with the furious
> strokes the essential bovine
> faith that there's something in the earth
> for everyone. All along I've wanted
> the good days to be the good days and not
> good from twelve to three not
> good like drilling your teeth is good
> when it stops but good like moonlight
> on my wife's hip with the sheets
> pulled back and her hair riotous
> and misconstrued. That's one thing
> and not another. That's the best use
> of a bed and two bodies working out
> the most inclusive form of redemption
> known in the universe this side
> of black holes, which is where I want
> to be considering that on the other side
> of black holes fish with mad cow disease
> are indistinguishable from Komodo dragons
> who play power forward in the NBA. I'm not
> ashamed to admit my prayers are no longer
> unconscious but loud and practiced
> to the skin of the mirror to the muse
> of the cereal box to the road as I drive
> everywhere trying to find the last 3/8"

drill this city has because I don't
believe in god but trust that pushing
veneration through my body makes god
exist if only for a second
within the chambered nuances of breath.
In my favorite prayer I apologize for not
having shouted earlier and in public say
from the back of the subway the top
of a table in a Fort Worth bar that *whither
thou goest I will follow.* This should be said
every day and with no substitutions
for the archaic *whither* which is the tender
part of the broken wheel of the phrase. This
should be repeated like the turbulence
of blood repeats harmonically or at least
until it's understood that even
if the way things are becomes the way
they are not I'll be there when mad cows
attack when madder fish swim back
through the streams when a black hole
shows up at the door wearing a tie
and promising to suck all dirt all evil
all manner of woe from this life
and smiling in a fashion that breaks
your knees. Whither or when thou goest,
how and why you flee, in what manner
or mode you glide or thrash
there's the mercy of the bond,
there's the moment you wake or refuse
to ever sleep again, there's still
your face when the wind's so fat it curls
in the field to lick its wounds,
and my promise to be there, conspicuously mad
in my devotion.

This poem promises to be idiosyncratically funny right from the start. In fact, we can't be sure where this poem is going, though a quizzical but intense uncertainty drives it. From the title on, the poem announces its relation to the New Testament passage spoken by Jesus to Simon Peter: "Simon Peter saith unto him, Lord, whither goest thou? Jesus answered,

Whither I go, thou canst not follow now; but thou shalt follow afterwards" (John 13:36). But unlike Peter, Hicok's narrator lacks surety; he isn't a believer. He's obviously searching for something else to sustain him, but in the beginning of the poem we're not sure what. He relies on humor as he struggles to locate some kind of answer.

The wildly fast associating is funny, of course, as we travel from "mad cow disease" to "salmon" to "bovine faith." Quickly we switch from the pain of dentistry to the beauty of "moonlight / on my wife's hip" to "black holes." Some of the surrealistic moments might make us laugh too. After all, if you've watched an NBA game recently, you probably haven't noticed a komodo dragon on the court. What's more, mad cow disease doesn't infect fish. For that matter, atheists aren't likely to pray. The poem's humor is enhanced by its outrageous, often impossible imagery. Yet it doesn't remain entirely humorous. By the end, we realize the speaker is longing for an absolute certainty about life—but he can't find it. So not only does he rely on humor, he also declares a commitment to his lover, a "promise to be there, conspicuously mad / in [his] devotion."

In poetry, just as no verse is truly "free," no associating is truly "free." If, like Hicok, you want to write in this style, you might try to find a connecting theme while you're in the act of linking apparently disparate images that appeal to your own unique way of seeing.

Undermining the Rules of Grammar

Though poets usually abide by the rules of grammar, they are not, as we've already seen, strictly beholden to them. Some poets use very little punctuation in order to mimic informal talk or to speed the poem up. Some employ fragments in order to render the nature of thought. Some poets go so far as to make words up in order to convey a new reality. But the rules of grammar exist because they ensure that people will communicate; they promise consistency. Every once in a while, however, you may find that some aspect of English, say, predication (subject-verb structure), might impede communicating the full intensity of your feelings. While such an instance may be rare, you might want to break from the usual syntactical structure, just as Philip Levine does in this poem.

✳ They Feed They Lion

> Out of burlap sacks, out of bearing butter,
> Out of black bean and wet slate bread,

Out of the acids of rage, the candor of tar,
Out of creosote, gasoline, drive shafts, wooden dollies,
They Lion grow.
                Out of the gray hills
Of industrial barns, out of rain, out of bus ride,
West Virginia to Kiss My Ass, out of buried aunties,
Mothers hardening like pounded stumps, out of stumps,
Out of the bones' need to sharpen and the muscles' to stretch,
They Lion grow.
                Earth is eating trees, fence posts,
Gutted cars, earth is calling in her little ones,
"Come home, Come home!" From pig balls,
From the ferocity of pig driven to holiness,
From the furred ear and the full jowl come
The repose of the hung belly, from the purpose
They Lion grow.
                From the sweet glues of the trotters
Come the sweet kinks of the fist, from the full flower
Of the hams the thorax of caves,
From "Bow Down" come "Rise Up,"
Come they Lion from the reeds of shovels,
The grained arm that pulls the hands,
They Lion grow.
                From my five arms and all my hands,
From all my white sins forgiven, they feed,
From my car passing under the stars,
They Lion, from my children inherit,
From the oak turned to a wall, they Lion,
From they sack and they belly opened
And all that was hidden burning on the oil-stained earth
They feed they Lion and he comes.

The repeated phrase ("They Lion grow") veers from our grammatical expectations, but in doing so it conveys a sense of furious, animal anger. Levine often writes about working-class life, and we can sense the rage that can build out of exhaustion from the repetitions of blue-collar labor. The workers have had it; due to their inability to get ahead, they seethe. We can sense that roiling frustration in the images, but it's the repeated phrase that delivers the biggest visceral impact.

Should you attempt this kind of experimental writing, you'll probably want to maintain syntactical convention in the balance of the poem. Levine does just this for the first four stanzas, which employ highly rhythmic but grammatically straightforward language. Though we may at first be somewhat confounded by the strange, repeated phrase ("They Lion come"), we can grasp the import of the lines because the rest of the phrasing doesn't stray from syntax we understand. In the last stanza, though, Levine brings the fury to a crescendo by using the disjunctive structure with other verbs: "from my children inherit. . . ." and "[f]rom they sack and they belly opened. . . ." The effect is to portray a massive group of angry people, an entire segment of the population, who cannot be stopped from seeking relief from daily pain nor from seeking justice from economic inequity. The poem succeeds in great part because of its unique experiment with predication.

Enigma Poems

Though they are intentionally subverting logic, some poets write as if the grammar were perfectly fine. Despite the fact that the tone and flow of the language suggest perfectly normal communication, readers lose their way. In **enigma poems,** the grammar adheres while the sense breaks down; rational thought gives way to either confusion or alogical thought. An enigma is an unsolvable riddle. (The term *enigma poem* was coined by critic Roger Cardinal.) Enigma poems consistently upset conventional referentiality. First you understand what's being said, then you don't. But the enigmatic passage usually sounds as if it ought to mean something.

In this enigma poem by James Cushing, the world's myriad stimuli overwhelm any certainty about meaning and purpose in life. The poem's language renders the way sense fails.

❧Autumn Leaves

The end of summer suggested the way
You picture yourself coming out of the rain,
The way disaster avoids collision with bright colors across
A scrim behind a captured city. With one hand
You conduct air and light, expecting only surprise,
Humor, a main idea. The landscape turns on a distant gull.

Tonight's pianist plays every song we know, breaking them like glass
After dropping on bricktop, catching stars.
He is the smiling man painted on the burning building,
At ease in his favorite armchair. My wife
Points to leaves the size of tablecloths,
Veined as madly as cabbage, breeding from the dead and all
Their muddy history. Trees know about it, and spell us
If we get tired and need to rest. But
Sometimes we are given the grace to know
When we've moved far enough in the forest of birds
And darting insects, heavy footed, feeling for the map.

As in many of Cushing's poems, we seem very close to grasping the point, but we never quite manage to. That's because his narrator is usually unable to convey the meaning of quotidian existence. Cushing is fond of saying that a poem should mean something while remaining mysterious. We can almost understand how "the end of summer" might "suggest" an idea, but then again we can't quite pin down the exact meaning. Perhaps the syntax makes sense, but how does "disaster avoid collision with bright colors"? And what cities are "captured"? A gull may turn in the air over the landscape, but how does "the landscape [turn] on a distant gull"? And how do songs break "like glass"? The poem seems to associate quite quickly but without the kind of thematic sense underlying Hicok's poetry. Unlike Levine's poem, the usual subject-verb-object construct applies. We may acknowledge the usual syntactical conventions, but there's a touch of surrealism as well. The speaker is reasonably declarative, but what he declares is just out of reach: "Trees know about it, and spell us / If we get tired and need to rest." At first we might ask how can trees "know" anything? Then we also realize that the pronoun "it" has no antecedent; its reference is unclear.

As with surrealistic poems, some parts of the enigma poem must make enough sense for the reader not to be entirely lost. All throughout "Autumn Leaves" we can grasp key words and references. We just can't quite place them in context. The end of the poem, however, manages to provide some conventional closure: "Sometimes we are given the grace to know / When we've moved far enough in the forest of birds / And darting insects, heavy footed, feeling for the map." We may not comprehend the narrator's specific difficulty, but ultimately we're told that just as our conveyance through the poem (and life) seemed virtually directionless, we know when to accept the fact that we are directionless. We

THE POET'S NOTE CARD

The Language of Risk

1. Because all human beings harbor strange ideas and habits, what seems odd may actually be the norm. In order to find an original or true voice in their poetry, good poets find ways to mine their own interior eccentricities.

2. No poem should be difficult for the sake of difficulty. But if your vision requires a way of seeing that may initially be foreign to readers, then you should trust in the vision.

3. Associative poems advance by a kind of not-quite-free association.

4. In the first half of the twentieth century it was often said that a writer must learn all the traditional forms of poetry before experimenting with free verse. Now we know it's usually best to practice referential, image-based writing before attempting more experimental forms.

5. Some contemporary poems break the rules of grammar or logic or normal sense—yet they seem to function as viscerally effective by virtue of the surprises they give the reader.

6. Enigma poems consistently upset conventional referentiality. First you understand what's being said, and then you don't. But the enigmatic passage usually sounds as if it ought to mean something. Enigma poetry helps to suggest the metaphysical uncertainties of contemporary life.

become resigned to searching for a map that in turn may lead us to, well, we don't know.

When writing this kind of poem, you might keep in mind that the special challenge is in trying to render a mystery by employing language that leads readers into a thicket of vague assumptions and unanswerable questions. Ultimately your poem almost makes sense while rendering the way some aspects of existence don't make sense.

WRITING EXERCISES

1. *Associative poem.* Write a poem that progresses almost entirely by association. Begin with an intriguing image. What does that image call up in your mind? Try to connect the first image to that new image. Now this second image should in turn catalyze yet another image. When revising, try to sustain the flow of the associational links while also unifying the images and ideas within a theme. Unless you intend a very serious tone, don't be afraid of any comic possibilities in the poem.

2. *Surrealistic associative poem.* Earlier you may have tried writing a surrealistic poem. This time, try associating quickly while creating a few surrealistic images that by definition, cannot correspond to objective reality. Make sure, however, that the poem maintains a link to the real world.

3. *Negative poem.* Sometimes we may write too rationally; this exercise uses the model of a film negative to open up the imagination to new relationships between words. In a negative, of course, all the images are reversed in shades of light and dark. Choose a model poem you like that begins with strong, straightforward imagery. Begin writing your own poem by attempting to reverse the meaning of every word through the first ten or fifteen lines. What you will have created will probably be nonsensical, but that's a good point at which to start. Now go back through your new crazy poem and see if there is a plot or theme that can be derived from the idiosyncratic lines. Revise with an eye toward making more sense, but keep in the spirit of the less rigid writing style.

4. *Word-list poem.* Sometimes we need to break away from pat ways of writing by forcing ourselves to create in a manner that fosters unlikely combinations of words. Here is a list of twelve words: *cage, eviscerate, rogue, kernel, soar, purple, frame, implode, melodic, pigeon, crease, rent.* Write a poem that's no more than twenty lines, and—in any order—use each of these words in the poem, with no two words from the list appearing in the same line.

5. *Word-list poem 2.* In order to make for an even more challenging poem, use the same words above but in exactly the order they appear.

6. *Famous poem exercise.* Here are words chosen in order from the famous three-stanza, twelve-line poem "Piano" by D. H. Lawrence:

dusk, years, boom, pressing, song, betraying, winter, hymns, burst, black, childish, flood. Before reading Lawrence's poem, write your own three-stanza, twelve-line poem using these words in the order they appear. You may use no more than two words from the list on any one line. After you finish your poem, you may wish to read Lawrence's poem and see how different it is from yours.

7. *Random words poem.* Open up a novel and blindly place your finger on the page. Write down the word (no articles, prepositions, or statement-of-being verbs). Switching pages, make a list of twelve words (four verbs, four nouns, four adjectives). Now write a poem in which you use all of the words at least once. No two words from the list may be used on any one line.

8. *Strange-story poem.* Think of the strangest story any friend has ever told you. Write a poem that tells the story—only make it both stranger and believable. If you need to, feel free to employ surrealism at different points in the poem.

9. *Enigma poem.* Students who have had some success at writing poems that exploit alogical relations may want to try this exercise. Remember that large sections of enigma poems consistently work against the kind of thinking that we mean when we use the term *making sense.* Begin your poem by grounding it in a sensible, accessible scene. Then move in and out of passages where the language "sounds" as if it were following the ordinary rules of logic while it is, in fact, heading into impossibly convoluted assertions or phrases. After the sense sabotages itself in one passage, return to a levelheaded, easier-to-follow passage. The idea is to make sure the reader understands some of the writing and then becomes quizzically confused in other parts of the writing. (Like life. . . .) Maintain the same rhythms throughout in order to ensure that truly opaque passages sound as if they have to mean something.

THE CULTURE OF POETRY

Writing Groups

If you've ever written a poem and had no one to show it to, you probably understand why a creative writing class or a writing group can be so helpful. If you're reading this book for a class, you probably already know the benefits of the writing course. Trouble is, the class will end soon. That's another reason why almost all beginning writers benefit from having a writing group that extends indefinitely in time. Consisting of perhaps four to seven people at similar stages of development, the best writing groups meet regularly, perhaps once every two to four weeks. The group not only provides help with revision, but its regular schedule provides a writing deadline that gently compels you to produce. And sometimes when the rest of the world presses its demands upon you, the group keeps you focused. While everyone is friendly enough to respect each other's work, the best groups provide both honest praise and constructive criticism. Hannah Stein says that she needs "the sounding board of other poets' observations" because "a different eye or ear observes flaws I would not have noticed, or discovers lapses I might have half-consciously allowed myself to ignore. Other times I stick to the original thought or image regardless of the group's opinion."

Remember that in class or in the workshop most people react positively to encouraging commentary rather than blunt criticism. The ideal workshop is friendly and helpful. While the celebrated American novelist Robert Stone once said that he learned more from having his feelings hurt by a writing teacher than from anything else, many emerging writers become inhibited by piercing criticism. A good guideline is to refrain from harsh or crude comments, to err on the side of civility. Each group member's job is to help the other poets improve by providing praise and constructive criticism. Participants should try to keep in mind that everyone is trying to make poems better. When your own poem is under discussion, you might find it most helpful if you listen objectively to what is said, and then decide for yourself what to revise.

Because the emphasis is on making good art, an effective writing group focuses primarily on aesthetics, rather than on whether its members disagree with a writer's particular point of view. In class most teachers make sure that comments on a writer's political, cultural, or religious point of view are rare and bear only on the way such a point of view influences the aesthetics of the poem. Such a guideline can be helpful, at least in a new workshop, until everyone gets to know one another. The best workshops give each member a chance to have an intensely good time making and revising poems. Only *you* write the poem, but your group gives you support and encouragement.

Public Readings

Poets often benefit emotionally from giving public readings of their work. Spoken-word poems are performed more theatrically than the kinds of poems we've been discussing in this book. In fact, because **spoken-word poems** are written to be performed it's virtually impossible to separate the poem from its presentation. Rarely do professional spoken-word poets read aloud from a text; they usually perform the poem from memory. The performance usually features highly comic or dramatic pieces of some length, and the poet enhances the recitation with myriad facial expressions, physical gestures, and shifts in volume. The poems benefit from the poet's acting ability.

But poems meant primarily for the page can be read aloud with exquisite results as well. Even T. S. Eliot was famous for giving an occasional but extraordinary reading of his very challenging work. Poets such as Adrienne Rich, Philip Levine, and Frank Bidart have been especially renowned for public readings. And while there is no one way to read aloud, you might consider these suggestions:

■ *Read slowly.* When you begin to give poetry readings, your heart might beat a little faster. Even practiced readers can feel the surge when the adrenaline kicks in. That's why you may not realize you're speaking as fast as you really are. Often it's best to slow your speech down, even if it "sounds" too slow to you. Try not to rush at the end of a line—and especially at the end of the poem. If anything, the ending of a poem should be read even more slowly than the rest. If you pace yourself well throughout, your listeners will follow the plot of the poem and will appreciate the musicality of your words.

■ *Read loudly.* While certain award-winning poets such as Sandra McPherson, Bob Hicok, and Angie Estes use a quiet voice to draw the audience into the poem's magic, they're pretty rare. Most poets who read in low volume risk tiring the audience. After all, listeners don't want to struggle to hear all the words clearly. Usually the poet who projects loudly and clearly will hold the audience's attention while also sounding confident.

■ *Set the poem up.* It's good to remember that most listeners have not heard the poem you're reading. They're hearing it cold. So you might make the reception clearer for them by providing some helpful information about the poem. For instance, you can clarify the plot, or explain a term, or tell them how the poem came to be—or all three. (It's best to refrain from interpreting the poem, however.) Not only will the audience appreciate the help, but you will also give them a chance to relax while they familiarize themselves with your voice.

■ *Practice.* This suggestion may seem obvious, but it's usually a good idea to practice reading your poems aloud before reading them to an audience. You might write out introductory notes as well.

■ *Project confidence.* Ezra Pound once said that poetry is "superior amusement." As with any entertainment, the audience wants to believe the poet is worth their time. After all, your listeners could be using the time to read or write their own poems. Or they could be at the movies or watching a ball game or hanging out in a bar or a coffee shop with friends. Any audience member wants to know the poet believes in the work. That's why you should rarely if ever apologize for a poem's value. Even if you're reading a new draft of a poem, you want your listeners to believe that you believe in that poem, that you think it's art worth sharing.

■ *Enjoy your own poetry.* When Ruth Stone was teaching, she gave her classes what's probably the most important advice about reading to an audience: Enjoy your own poems. You wrote them and you like them. Sure, the audience deserves your utmost respect and effort, but the most effective way to honor the audience is to immerse yourself in the creative consciousness you experienced when you were writing your poems. To this end, let all the poetic qualities of the poem take over. Confident of their poems, poets such as Sandra Gilbert, Stanley Plumly, and many others find a balance between passion and restraint. Just as they understand the difference between sentiment and sentimentality, they recognize the difference between a heartfelt presentation and inflated theatrics. They found that balance when writing the poem, and now they let the poem guide their reading of it.

■ *Leave them wanting more.* Try not to read for too long a time. It's difficult to concentrate on poetry read aloud. A standard reading by one poet lasts forty-five minutes or so. A polished professional entertains an audience for as much as an hour. If two people are reading, each would be best to finish in thirty to thirty-five minutes.

Once you learn to read well, you may find that public readings help you to revise your own work. Many poets sense the way an audience responds to different moments in a poem. When Robert Lowell gave a West Coast reading tour in the late 1950s, audiences were familiar with much of the work of the Beat Poets, especially Alan Ginsberg, whose poem "Howl" broke away from midcentury academic restrictions. Lowell found that audiences much preferred his more accessible, less formal poems, and he began revising passages to make them easier to access. The result was his groundbreaking book *Life Studies*. Sometimes an audience can help you to recognize good lines and those that need polishing, especially in narrative poems. At other times, their feedback may give you an idea about the way individual poems sound. For instance, if you tend to trip on a word or phrase more than once, you might consider polishing the rhythm.

Reading series are usually connected to colleges, bookstores, and coffee shops. Poetry is so popular nowadays that most cities and towns have regular reading series scheduled. Local arts web sites and the community calendar sections of newspapers usually announce venues, dates, and times. If you're interested in giving a reading, go to a few readings and then ask the series director how you can get a chance to read. (Any director will know of the other series as well.) Often, there's an "open mic" time during the reading, and poets who sign up can read for four or five minutes. This brief opportunity gives you a chance to practice and get the feel of the site. If you and a few friends would like to give a reading, you might see if the local coffee shop or bookstore can accommodate you.

How to Get Published

The greatest literary high involves the act of writing itself, that moment when the pen or the keyboard is suddenly a channel into a seemingly free-flowing burst of language, when you've found an intuitive stream into fresh, true expression. As James Cushing says, "when you get into the sure surge of a poem, you're oblivious of the outside world. In a few minutes you look up, and the clock tells you six hours have passed." Very little else can match such transport.

And yet, like all human beings, writers are egocentric. They want affirmation. While giving a poetry reading to a receptive audience may be a deep delight, it's even more affirming to read your own words in print. Writing and publishing are certainly two entirely separate enterprises. Though revision can be enhanced by friends and fellow poets, writing itself is a private, interior experience. On the other hand, publishing is the method by which we communicate with the world. Why write a poem if no one will read it?

Once you've written a good number of poems and you've polished them all, how do you go about publishing them? Here are a few suggestions:

Choosing Journals

First of all, you need to decide where to send your work. Some people feel it's best to start locally. In many places there are regional journals interested in publishing local poets. Check out nearby bookstores and libraries for them. Other national journals can be found in many ways: *The Poet's Market, The International Directory of Literary Magazines and Small Presses,* and *CLMP Directory of Literary Magazines* (from the Council of Literary Magazines) are all published annually and list most of the paper and electronic journals in the country. One of your best reference resources is the online site called The Poetry Resource Page (http://www.poetryresourcepage.com). Here you will find a list of most of the magazines in the country, including many that are web-based "zines." (The site also includes links to virtually every writing conference and college-level creative writing program in the country.) Each journal is listed with its editors, address, reading dates, and helpful notes about the work it seeks. As you might imagine, *The Formalist* only publishes "formal" poems, and *The Wallace Stevens Review* only poems that make reference to the great American poet Wallace Stevens. Less obviously perhaps, *The Minnesota Review* is interested in poems with distinct sociopolitical themes, and *Image* is interested in poems with religious or spiritual themes. Most journals, however, are reasonably eclectic in their tastes.

So choose journals that are most interested in your style of poem. Before you start submitting, read the magazines in your local or university library. Though it's probably happened, it's nonetheless hard to imagine a beginning poet receiving an acceptance from *The New Yorker* or *Poetry Magazine.*

Submitting Poems by Mail

Editors want to be confident in the professionalism of their writers. Therefore, presentation counts. Here are a few standard rules:

- Choose three to five of your best poems and print them neatly. Make sure there are no typos, grammar mistakes, or spelling errors.
- While some poems may go beyond one page, never print multiple poems on any single page.
- Be consistent in your formatting. For instance, you might want to justify all your poems on the left side. Don't justify a few on the left and others near the center.
- Since editors like to shuffle poems around, print your name on every sheet, and don't staple your poems together.
- Most editors discourage using a full-size manila envelope, but a 6- by 9-inch envelope is fine.
- Of course, if you're including a cover letter, make sure it is as clean and correct as the poems. If you're just starting out and have never published poetry (or anything else for that matter), then you don't have to send a cover letter. But if you have something helpful for the editor to know, a brief cover letter is probably a good idea. While you should never "explicate" or otherwise explain your poems, you might mention where you've studied creative writing or that you've published a few poems or that you've won a contest. Remember, at best a good cover persuades the editor to read your work more carefully; the quality of the poems will determine whether they're accepted or not.

Nowadays, many magazines prefer not to send your poems back, but you should always send along a self-addressed stamped envelope for an acceptance letter or rejection note. Since editors usually return only an acceptance or rejection note, it's often best simply to affix enough postage for a one-ounce first-class letter.

Submitting Poems by Email

While most journals are still printed, more and more journals exist as web "zines." *Blackbird*, *The Mississippi Review* and *ForPoetry* are among the most popular. Some poets prefer zines because the poems are often more widely available to readers, while others prefer hardcopy journals because these are perceived as less transient. Whether availability or permanence is an issue for you, both types of journals can be very good—and there are many similarities in submissions policies. More and more journals of both types are accepting poems by email. Some want them submitted as attachments and others want them printed as text. You may enjoy spending an afternoon on-line checking out the different magazines and reading their submissions guidelines.

Keeping a Submissions Log

Always track the poems that you send out in a submissions log of some kind. Many people use index cards, with one card for each magazine and the date and names of the poems submitted. Some poets use a logbook and simply keep a record of each submission by date and journal. Most poets are more inclined to record their submissions on a computer. Whatever method you choose, keep a record of any comments you receive from editors. If they are encouraging, you want to know so that in your next cover letter you might remind them of their comments. The most important thing is to keep sending your work out—and then go back to writing. Be productive. Don't simply wait around for replies.

Simultaneous Submissions

Simultaneous submission is the term for sending the same poem to more than one magazine at a time. Years ago, when this practice was universally considered unethical, literary magazines would respond to a submission in two to six weeks. For a number of reasons, that's rarely the case today. For one thing, because computers make it easy for poets to send out so many poems so quickly, magazines receive more poems than ever. The result? Editorial offices are sometimes flooded. Furthermore, editors are usually poets themselves, and they often teach or hold down other jobs. Their time is limited.

Some journals only print one issue per year, and they wait until the end of the submission cycle before deciding what they'll accept. Some magazines are famously late, or don't reply at all. In a recent year one writer submitted poems to twenty-six magazines. While three journals returned work in four weeks or less, six took over five months. Two never returned the poems. The average return time was over four months. Generally, it's a good idea to pick up one of the directories or to go to the journal's web site and read the submissions guidelines. If the journal says "no simultaneous submissions," then don't send them. If a simultaneously submitted poem is taken, then immediately write a brief note withdrawing the poem from the other journals.

Rejection and Acceptance

Keep in mind that every single publishing poet gets rejection slips. One writing teacher tells his students to send their first submissions to *Poetry Magazine* so they can get their first rejection out of the way. You should remember that every editor has a unique aesthetic. If you sat ten poetry editors in a room with one-hundred random unpublished poems and told them they had to choose ten for their publication, no two editors would choose the same ten. In fact, most would have a wide variety of different choices. That's one reason that you should not be discouraged by rejection. "Editorial needs" might be another. For instance, a magazine may have already accepted a poem about hiking the Appalachian Trail, so your poem about hiking in Maine may be redundant to the editors, no matter how good it is.

Some editors also like to develop relationships with poets, often making suggestions about why they rejected the poems. Believe it or not, such a note is a very good sign. It means the editor wants you to keep sending poems to the journal. If you have strong, finished poems to submit, send them out to that journal right away. It may be difficult, but refrain from sending new, rough poems. Even though they may want to see more of your work, editors will quickly become discouraged by hurriedly written, unpolished submissions.

When good fortune strikes and your poem is accepted, you'll probably want to take a well-deserved moment for breathing in the invigorating air of accomplishment. You'll tell a few friends and family members. Maybe you'll treat yourself to a good dinner at your favorite restaurant that night, perhaps a glass of really fine wine. But your work on that poem isn't quite over. Most magazines will send you galleys to proof. They'll ask if you have any last changes to make. Check the copy they send to make sure everything looks good. One of the rules of proofreading is to read both copies backwards. That way the syntactical flow of the language will not carry you inadvertently past any mistakes.

Generally, poets don't want to make any last-second changes in the poem. But, if you had made one or two revisions after sending it out, now is the time to change the galleys. Then put the lovely success of your acceptance behind you until the poem appears in the journal, usually months later. Just as you want to make sure the rejection letter won't impede your writing, make sure the acceptance won't distract you from writing. The acceptance is a confirmation of your ability as a poet, but it's only a beginning.

Students benefit from publishing, but not for bluntly egoistic reasons. When you garner the recognition that comes from an acceptance and seeing your own work in print you will grow that much more confident about writing. That's why Sandra Gilbert gives her students very good advice about submitting poems: Always have envelopes ready. When a rejection comes in, she says, simply send out those poems again. That way, you're not thinking about the rejection, and you can get back to what is most fun: writing poems. Surprising yourself with your own words.

CREDITS

Addonizio, Kim, "So What," *What Is This Thing Called Love*. New York: Norton , 2004. Reprinted by permission.

Ai, "Cruelty," *Vice: New and Selected Poems*. New York: Norton, 1999. Reprinted by permission.

Baggott, Julianna, "Monica Lewinsky Thinks of BIll Clinton While Standing Naked in Front of a Hotel Mirror," *Lizzie Borden in Love: Poems in Women's Voices*. Carbondale: Southern Illinois University, 2006. Reprinted by permission.

Barker, Wendy, "Persephone's Version," *Let the Ice Speak*. Greenfield Center, N.Y.: Ithaca House, 1994. Reprinted by permission.

Barnes, Jim, "The Sawdust War," *The Sawdust War*, Champaign: University of Illinois Press, 1992. Reprinted by permission.

Barnes, Jim, "Touching the Rattlesnake," *La Plata Cantata*. Ashland, Ohio: Purdue University Press, 1989. Reprinted by permission.

Barresi, Dorothy, "Little Dreams of War," *Rouge Pulp*. Pittsburgh: University of Pittsburgh Press, 2002. Reprinted by permission.

Black, Ralph, "Slicing Ginger," *Turning Over the Earth*. Minneapolis: Milkweed Editions, 2000. Reprinted by permission.

Bottoms, David, "Sign for My Father, Who Stressed the Bunt," *Armored Hearts: Selected and New Poems*, 1995, Copper Canyon Press, Port Townsend, WA. Reprinted by permission.

Brown, Susan, "Smoke," *Buddha's Dogs*. New York: Four Way Books, 2004. Reprinted by permission.

Cervantes, Lorna Dee, "Uncle's First Rabbit," *Emplumada*. Pittsburgh: University of Pittsburgh Press, 1981. Reprinted by permission.

Coffman, Lisa, "The Pelvis," *Likely*. Kent, Ohio: Kent State University Press, 1996. Reprinted by permission.

Coleman, Wanda, "You Judge a Man by the Silence He Keeps," *African Sleep Sickness: Stories & Poems*, 1990, Black Sparrow, Boston, MA. Reprinted by permission.

Cushing, James, "Autumn Leaves," *You and the Night*, 1991, Cahuenga Press, Los Angeles, CA. Reprinted by permission.

DeFrees, Madeline, "With a Bottle of Blue Nun to All My Friends," *Blue Dusk: New and Selected Poems 1951–2001*, 2001, Copper Canyon Press, Port Townsend, WA. Reprinted by permission.

Dischell, Stuart, "Between Two Storms," *Good Hope Road*. New York: Penguin Group, 1993. Reprinted by permission.

Dubie, Norman, "Monologue of Two Moons, Nude with Crests, 1938," *The Mercy Seat: Collected and New Poems 1967–2001*, 2001, Copper Canyon Press, Port Townsend, WA. Reprinted by permission.

Dubie, Norman, "Poem," *The Mercy Seat: Collected and New Poems 1967–2001*, 2001, Copper Canyon Press, Port Townsend, WA. Reprinted by permission.

Dubie, Norman, "Radio Sky," *The Mercy Seat: Collected and New Poems 1967–2001*, 2001, Copper Canyon Press, Port Townsend, WA. Reprinted by permission.

Duhamel Denise, "Bangungot," *Queen for a Day: Selected and New Poems*. Pittsburgh: University of Pittsburgh Press, 2001. Reprinted by permission.

Duhamel, Denise, "I Dreamed I Wrote This Sestina in My Maidenform Bra," *McSweeney's Internet Tendency*. San Francisco, Calif., 94110. Reprinted by permission.

Espada, Martín, "Two Mexicanos Lynched in Santa Cruz, California, May 3, 1877," *Rebellion Is the Circle of a Lover's Hands*. Willimantic, Conn.: Curbstone Press, 1991. Reprinted by permission.

Fairchild, B. H., "Little Boy," *The Art of the Lathe*. Farmington, Me.: Alice James Books, 1998. Reprinted by permission.

Fennelly, Beth Ann, "Gong," *Tender Hooks*. New York: Norton, 2004. Reprinted by permission.

Gallagher, Tess, "Fresh Stain," *Moon Crossing Bridge*. St. Paul: Graywolf Press, 1992. Reprinted by permission.

Galvin, Brendan, "Kale Soup," *Great Blue: New and Selected Poems*. Champaign: University of Illinois Press, 1990. Reprinted by permission.

Gilbert, Sandra, "Daguerreotype: Wet Nurse," *Kissing the Bread: New and Selected Poems, 1969–1999*. New York: Norton, 2001. Reprinted by permission.

Grieve, Sarah, "*Jesus Christ* and *Holy Shit* in the Church Softball League," with permission of the author.

Hamby, Barbara, "Vex Me," *Babel*. Pittsburgh: University of Pittsburgh Press, 2004. Reprinted by permission.

Hanzlicek, C. G., "Room for Doubt," *The Cave: Selected and New Poems*. Pittsburgh: University of Pittsburgh Press, 2001. Reprinted by permission.

Harjo, Joy, "Deer Dancer," *In Mad Love and War*. Middletown, Conn.: University Press of New England, 1990. Reprinted by permission.

Hass, Robert, "A Story About the Body," *Human Wishes*. New York: Ecco Press, 1989. Reprinted by permission.

Hendrix, Ginger Adcock, "The Arithmetic of Girl Beauty," with permission of the author.

Hicok, Bob, "Whither Thou Goest," *Animal Soul*. Montpelier, Vt.: Invisible Cities Press, 2001. Reprinted by permission.

Hummer, T. R., "St. Augustine," *Walt Whitman in Hell*. Baton Rouge, La.: LSU Press, 1996. Reprinted by permission.

Jensen, Laura, "Bad Boats," *Bad Boats*. New York: Ecco Press, 1977. Reprinted by permission.

Jones, Rodney, "Going," *Kingdom of the Instant*. New York: Houghton Mifflin, 2002.10003. Reprinted by permission.

Keener, Luann. "The Blood-Tie," *Color Documentary*. Corvallis, Ore.: Calyx Books, 1994. Reprinted by permission.

Kinnell, Galway, "Little Sleep's Head Sprouting Hair in the Moonlight," *The Book of Nightmares*, 1971, Houghton Mifflin, New York. Reprinted by permission.

Kirby, David, "Sarah Bernhardt's Leg," *I Think I'm Going to Call My Wife Paraguay*. Alexandria, Va.: Orchises Press, 2004. Reprinted by permission.

Komunyakaa, Yusef, "To Have Danced with Death," *Dien Cai Dau*. Middletown, Conn.: Wesleyan University Press, 1988. Reprinted by permission.

Laux, Dorianne, "The Lovers," *What We Carry*. Rochester, N.Y.: BOA Editions. Reprinted by permission.

Levertov, Denise, "Earliest Spring," *Poems 1972–1982*, 1978, New Directions. Reprinted by permission.

Levine, Philip, "Innocence," with permission of the author.

Levine, Philip, "They Feed They Lion," *New Selected Poems*. New York: Knopf, 1991. Reprinted by permission.

Lindner, April, "First Kiss," *Skin*. Lubbock: Texas Tech University Press, 2002. Reprinted by permission.

Lowell, Robert, "Commander Lowell," *Life Studies/For the Union Dead*. New York: Farrar, Straus & Giroux, 1964. Reprinted by permission.

Lummis, Suzanne, "Gin Alley," *In Danger*. Berkeley, Calif.: Roundhouse Press, 1999. Reprinted by permission.

MacLeish, Archibald, "Eleven," *The Human Season: Selected Poems, 1926–1972*. New York: Houghton Mifflin, 1972. Reprinted by permission.

McPherson, Sandra, "A Coconut for Katerina," *The Year of Our Birth*, 1978, The Ecco Press, New York. Reprinted by permission.

Maio, Samuel, "Reflections from a Pastel-Covered Box," *The Burning of Los Angeles*. Kirksville, Mo.: Truman State University Press, 1997. Reprinted by permission.

Marcus, Jacqueline, "Hanalei Bay," *Close to the Shore*. East Lansing: Michigan State University Press, 2002. Reprinted by permission.

Matthews, William, "Bystanders," Estate of William Matthews. Used by permission.

Moss, Thylias, "An Anointing," *Small Congregations*. New York: Ecco Press, 1993. Reprinted by permission.

Moss, Thylias, "Mandell's Moon," *Small Congregations*. Orlando, Fla.: Harcourt Brace., 1975. Reprinted by permission.

Muske, Carol, "Little L.A. Villanelle," *Red Trousseau*. New York: Penguin Group, 1993. Reprinted by permission.

Neruda, Pablo, "Ode to Salt," *Neruda and Vallejo*. Boston: Beacon Press, 1971. Reprinted by permission.

Olds, Sharon, "The Moment," *The Dead and the Living*. New York: Knopf, 1984. Reprinted by permission.

Ondaatje, Michael, "Sweet Like a Crow," *The Cinnamon Peeler*. New York: Knopf, 1991. Reprinted by permission.

Parker, Alan Michael, "Two Questions," *Love Song with Motor Vehicles*. Rochester, N.Y.: BOA Editions, 2003. Reprinted by permission.

Plumly, Stanley, "November 11, 1942–November 12, 1997," *Now That My Father Lies Down Beside Me.* New York: HarperCollins, 2000. Reprinted by permission.

Pound, Ezra. "In a Station of the Metro," *Selected Poems.* New York: Norton, 1976. Reprinted by permission.

Rodriguez, Luis, "The Blast Furnace," *The Concrete River*, 1991, Curbstone Press, Connecticut. Reprinted by permission.

Rutsala, Vern, "The Super 99 Drive-In Chronicle," *The Moment's Equation.* Ashland, Ohio: Ashland Poetry Press, 2004. Reprinted by permission.

Ryan, Michael, "The Ditch," *God Hunger.* New York: Penguin Group, 1989. Reprinted by permission.

St. John, David, "Iris," *Study for the World's Body: New and Selected Poems*, 1994, Harper Perennial, New York, NY ©David St. John. Reprinted by permission.

Serpas, Martha, "First," *Cote Blanche.* Kalamazoo, Mich.: *New Issues Poetry & Prose*, 2002. Reprinted by permission.

Sexton, Anne, "Mr. Mine," *Love Poems.* New York: Houghton Mifflin, 1969. Reprinted by permission.

Simpson, Louis, "On the Lawn at the Villa," *Collected Poems.* New York: Paragon House, 1988. Reprinted by permission.

Smith, Bruce, "His Father in the Exhaust of Engines," *The Other Lover.* Chicago: University of Chicago Press, 2000. Reprinted by permission.

Stein, Hannah, "Winter in Fox-Light," *Earthlight.* Woodside, Calif.: La Questa Press, 2000. Reprinted by permission.

Stone, Ruth, "Bazook," *Second-Hand Coat*, Boston: Godine, 1987. Reprinted by permission.

Stone, Ruth, "Curtains," *Second-Hand Coat*, Boston: Godine, 1987. Reprinted by permission.

Walker, Jeanne Murray, "So Far, So Good," *Gaining Time.* Providence, R.I.: Copper Beach, 1997. Reprinted by permission.

Wood, Susan, "Camp Santo," *Camp Santo.* Baton Rouge, La.: LSU Press, 1991. Reprinted by permission.

Wright, Charles, "Ars Poetica II," *A Short History of the Shadow*, New York: Farrar, Straus & Giroux, 2002. Reprinted by permission.

Wright, Charles, "Light Journal," *Zone Journals*. New York: Farrar, Straus & Giroux, 1988. Reprinted by permission.

Wright, Charles, "Spider Crystal Ascension," *China Trace*. Middletown, Conn.: Wesleyan University Press, 1977. Reprinted by permission.

Wrigley, Robert, "Following Snakes," *Lives of the Animals*. New York: Penguin Group. Reprinted by permission.

Young, C. Dale, "Exile," *The Day Underneath the Day*, Evanston, Ill.: Northwestern University Press, 2001. Reprinted by permission.

INDEX OF CRITICAL TERMS

INDEX OF AUTHORS
AND POEM TITLES